CW00953537

PY

The management of buyer–supplier relations has come to be regarded as a key to achieving manufacturing competitiveness, particularly in sectors facing global competition based on both price and quality. This book is a theoretical and empirical exploration of the link between the type of buyer–supplier relations and corporate performance. Dr Sako examines how British and Japanese companies in the electronics industry manage their relations with buyers and suppliers: the empirical study comprises a three-way comparison of a Japanese customer company, a British customer company, and a Japanese company in Britain, and an analysis of 36 supplier companies in Britain and Japan. Variations of the companies' business practices are assessed in terms of technology, the nature of market competition, the national legal framework, financial structures, employment systems, and the mode of entrepreneurship.

The author identifies two distinct approaches in the two countries – the arm's-length contractual relation (ACR) in Britain, and the obligational contractual relation (OCR) in Japan – and argues that the trust and interdependence present in the latter can be a powerful springboard from which to achieve corporate success.

Cambridge Studies in Management

18

Prices, quality and trust
Inter–firm relations in Britain and Japan

Cambridge Studies in Management

Formerly Management and Industrial Relations series

Editors
WILLIAM BROWN, *University of Cambridge*
ANTHONY HOPWOOD, *London School of Economics*
and PAUL WILLMAN, *London Business School*

The series focuses on the human and organisational aspects of management. It covers the areas of organisation theory and behaviour, strategy and business policy, the organisational and social aspects of accounting, personnel and human resource management, industrial relations and industrial sociology.

The series aims for high standards of scholarship and seeks to publish the best among original theoretical and empirical research; innovative contributions to advancing understanding in the area; books which synthesise and/or review the best of current research, and aim to make the work published in specialist journals more widely accessible; and texts for upper-level undergraduates, for graduates and for vocational courses such as MBA programmes. Edited collections may be accepted where they maintain a high and consistent standard and are on a coherent, clearly defined, and relevant theme.

The books are intended for an international audience among specialists in universities and business schools, undergraduate and MBA students, and also for a wider readership among business practitioners and trade unionists.

Other books in the series
 1 John Child and Bruce Partridge, *Lost managers: supervisors in industry and society*
 2 Brian Chiplin and Peter Sloane, *Tackling discrimination in the workplace: an analysis of sex discrimination in Britain*
 3 Geoffrey Whittington, *Inflation accounting: an introduction to the debate*
 4 Keith Thurley and Stephen Wood (eds.), *Industrial relations and management strategy*
 5 Larry James, *Power in a trade union: the role of the district committee in the AUEW*
 6 Stephen T. Parkinson, *New product development in engineering: a comparison of the British and West German machine tool industries*
 7 David Tweedale and Geoffrey Whittington (eds.) *The debate on inflation accounting*
 8 Paul Willman and Graham Winch, *Innovation and management control: labour relations at BL Cars*
 9 Lex Donaldson, *In defence of organisation theory: a reply to the critics*
10 David Cooper and Trevor Hopper (eds.), *Debating coal closures: economic calculation in the coal dispute 1984–85*
11 Jon Clark, Ian McLoughlin, Howard Rose and Robin King, *The process of technological change: new technology and social choice in the workplace*
12 Sandra Dawson, Paul Willman, Alan Clinton and Martin Bamford, *Safety at work: the limits of self-regulation*
13 Keith Bradley and Aaron Nejad, *Managing owners: the national freight consortium in perspective*
14 David Hugh Whittaker, *Managing innovation: a study of British factories*
15 Bruce Ahlstrand, *The quest for productivity: a case study of Fawley after Flanders*
16 Chris Smith, John Child and Michael Rowlinson, *Reshaping work: the Cadbury experience*
17 Howard Gospel, *Markets, firms and the management of labour in modern Britain*
18 Mari Sako, *Prices, quality and trust: inter–firm relations in Britain and Japan*

Prices, quality and trust

Inter–firm relations in Britain and Japan

MARI SAKO

Lecturer in Industrial Relations
The London School of Economics and Political Science

CAMBRIDGE
UNIVERSITY PRESS

Published by the Press Syndicate of the University of Cambridge
The Pitt Building, Trumpington Street, Cambridge CB2 1RP
40 West 20th Street, New York, NY 10011–4211, USA
10 Stamford road, Oakleigh, Victoria 3166, Australia

First published 1992

Printed and bound in Great Britain by
Woolnough Bookbinding Ltd, Irthlingborough, Northamptonshire

A catalogue record for this book is available from the British Library

Library of Congress cataloguing in publication data

Sako, Mari.
  Prices, quality, and trust: inter–firm relations in Britain and Japan / Mari
Sako.
    p.   cm. – (Cambridge studies in management: 18)
  Includes bibliographical references and index.
  ISBN 0 521 41386–9 (hardback)
  1. Industrial procurement – Japan. 2. Industrial procurement – Great Britain.
  3. Industrial procurement – Cross-cultural studies. 4. Electronic industries –
  Japan. 5. Electronic industries – Great Britain. I. Title. II. Series.
  HD39.5.S25 1992
  338.5′22′0941 – dc20 91–40505, CIP

ISBN 0 521 41386 9 hardback

Contents

Contents

Part IV: Outcomes and implications

Figures

Tables

Tables

Acknowledgements

I am indebted to many individuals without whom this book would not have been possible.

I would first like to thank Ron Dore who was more than instrumental in starting me off on this research five years ago; ever since, his advice, insights and continuing moral support have been invaluable.

Next, my thanks go to the people in both British and Japanese industries, who gave generously of their time in answering my endless and sometimes impertinent questions. They must unfortunately remain unnamed for reasons of confidentiality.

I also benefited from discussions with, and comments from, many others, including Masahiko Aoki, Banri Asanuma, Susan Helper, Roger Hollingsworth, Masayoshi Ikeda, Takeshi Inagami, Tadao Kiyonari, Tetsu Minato, Itsutomo Mitui, Hideichiro Nakamura, Toshihiro Nishiguchi, Hiroyuki Odagiri, Hiroshi Okumura, Ray Richardson, Martin Ricketts, Hiroki Sato, Philippe Schmitter, Kuniyuki Shoya, Michael Smitka, Wolfgang Streeck, Yukio Watanabe, Hugh Whittaker, and Stephen Wood.

The research during 1986–8 was largely funded by a grant (ref. F0023 2298) from the Economic and Social Research Council, UK. A grant from the Central Research Fund of the University of London enabled a short research visit to Japan in spring 1989.

I am also grateful to CUP, and especially Patrick McCartan and John Haslam, for making publication of this book possible.

Last but not least, I want to thank Suma Chakrabarti for his good-humoured encouragement, patience, assistance in proof-reading, and even intellectual interest in my research, regardless of whether he was in London or in Washington DC.

Introduction

A decade ago, Arthur Okun, in his book *Prices and Quantities*, drew a distinction between auction and customer product markets. He focused on the latter, the 'vast nonauction area' (Okun, 1981, p. 134), which in his view prevailed in industrial economies outside of trading in financial assets and commodities. In customer markets, business firms set prices and wages to reflect long-term considerations to reduce costs, as well as short-term changes in markets. The long-term 'invisible handshake' (in Okun's words) between customers and suppliers, and between employers and employees, creates price rigidities which Okun identified as a cause of stagflation.

This book is also about the vast nonauction area in industrial economies. But its topic, buyer–supplier relations, is more narrowly microeconomic than Okun's, and its methodology very different in its reliance on a case-study-based socio-economic inquiry. This book identifies variations within customer markets in the way firms interact with each other, some by 'invisible handshake' and others by 'visible handshaking' (Aoki, 1984). Such variations have consequences not only for the way in which *prices* are determined, but also for other performance parameters, perhaps the most important of which today is *quality*.

Since Okun wrote, global competition in manufacturing has become more about coping with volatile market demands and rapid technological change. With correspondingly shorter product development cycles, workers and suppliers who had formerly received finalised work plans and design 'blue prints' are now expected to fill in more details themselves in half-formed plans subject to continuous changes. Manufacturing good quality products in small batches cost effectively also requires competent and motivated workers and suppliers who can respond quickly to solve local problems. But the willingness to give, and the capacity to elicit, flexible responses depend much on mutual *trust*. Without trust, it would be too risky to depend on others who may well

1

take advantage, by holding up delivery until prices are renegotiated, or not observing commercial secrecy. Thus, the 'vast nonauction area' has expanded in most advanced industrial economies, as manifested in the form of joint ventures, 'strategic alliances' in R&D, 'flexibly specialised' firms in industrial districts, and sub-contracting 'partnerships' between large and small firms. As a result, there is a heightened need for business firms to rely on trust to achieve competitive success. How trust can be established, where it is deficient or absent, is one major concern of this book.

The main questions addressed in this book are as follows. Why have companies come to rely on different modes of coordinating the design and manufacture of similar products? What company-specific, industry-specific, and society-wide factors affect the mode adopted? And how do alternative modes affect corporate performance? The empirical setting of the book is largely limited to the electronics industry in Britain and Japan. But the analysis and theoretical discussion are of relevance in a wider context.

As a starting point, it cannot be presumed that there is one single characteristic pattern of buyer–supplier relations in Japan and another in Britain. Two ideal types are therefore constructed to capture complex variations in buyer–supplier relations. They are best thought of as lying at the ends of a continuum. At one extreme, firms rely on an Arm's-length Contractual Relation (ACR) if they wish to retain full control over their destiny. Independence is the guiding principle here, which involves not only being unaffected by the decision of other companies, but also by one's own decisions (e.g. over sourcing and sales) made in the past. This often requires not disclosing much information (e.g. about costing and future plans) to existing and potential buyers and suppliers. The arm's length nature of contracts enables firms to engage in a hard commercial bargain to obtain competitive prices, although an excessive use of threats and bluffs may make some firms wary of too much antagonism. At the other extreme, firms enter into an Obligational Contractual Relation (OCR) if they prefer high trust cooperativeness with a commitment to trade over the long run. This commitment may come at the expense of taking on rather a lot of sometimes onerous obligations and requests (e.g. for just-in-time and ship-to-stock delivery). But the benefits of accepting mutual obligations lie in good quality and service, growing or stable orders, and other non-price aspects of trading born out of a tacit understanding over time.

This ACR–OCR framework should better accommodate a study of variations in business practices *within* Japan and Britain as well as

2

Introduction

between countries. In order to classify business practices along the ACR–OCR spectrum, the empirical part of this book focuses on a three-way comparison of a Japanese customer company, a British customer company, and a Japanese company located in Britain; and an analysis of a matched sample of 18 suppliers each in Britain and Japan in order to enquire into their relationships with their customers. The result shows a considerable variation in trading practices among companies studied. In particular, 4 out of the 18 Japanese suppliers had more ACR practices than the most OCR supplier firm found in Britain. This undoubtedly reflects the importance of individual company strategy concerning the trade-off between growth and short-term profitability, establishing mass or niche markets, and so on. But society-wide norms cannot be ignored, and the attempts to establish OCR-like practices by UK-based Japanese companies, like Toshiba Consumer Products (UK) Limited studied in this book, have encountered more difficulties in Britain where, despite a move towards Preferred Supplier Policy, the trading norm remains largely more ACR than in Japan.

The ACR–OCR framework is also useful for assessing the effects of varying business practices on the competitiveness of companies and, by extension, of national economies. This is a dominant concern of this book, and is a topic which, in the last decade, has attracted an increasing amount of attention. Many people in the past would have concluded, at least when having in mind the market economy vs planned economy contrast, that ACR conduces to efficiency by subjecting firms to the invigorating forces of the market, while cooperating firms in cosy OCR relations are shielded from market forces and thus are not as efficient. Put this way, the ACR–OCR spectrum may be matched with a competitive (= efficient) vs cooperative(= inefficient) contrast.

This book argues that this match, associating all types of ACR with efficiency and all types of OCR with inefficiency, is mistaken. Of course, this point is not novel to those who are familiar with the benefits of buyer–supplier 'partnerships'. 'Long-term close trading relationships with a selected few suppliers, based on trust' (i.e. OCR) has been replacing 'multiple sourcing from several suppliers on short-term contracts' (i.e. ACR) as a guiding principle of purchasing policy in British industry. In this respect, Japanese manufacturing firms located in Britain as well as in Japan are held to be exemplary, as they appear to have the desirable competitive outcomes and long-term supplier relationships. Though tempting, this association of efficiency and long-term relations (which is a feature of OCR) is not perfect either. Observe the following alternative interpretations on the sources of Japanese industrial competitiveness.

Introduction

The aspect of inter-firm relations in Japan which has most attracted attention is the way in which they constitute non-tariff barriers to trade. It is precisely this aspect which has resulted in accusations by the EEC and the USA that the Japanese market is closed to foreign producers due to 'unfair trade practices'. If Japanese glass producers persist in buying high-price soda ash from their traditional suppliers instead of much cheaper soda ash from the United States, some final consumer somewhere must be paying for this inefficiency. The markets lack the 'transparency' of price-competitive trading, and the opacity is discriminatory against foreigners. Here, the anti-competitive, protectionist element in the Japanese trading custom is under attack.

An alternative interpretation emphasizes a more positive aspect, namely business efficiency inherent in long-term high-trust business relationships. Thanks to the way in which disputes over the trade aspects of inter-firm relations have highlighted their role, a survey for the Japanese Fair Trade Commission (see Shimada, 1987; EPA 1990, pp. 197–201) was carried out in 1987 to clarify whether the nature of Japanese trading custom had any economic rationale. It attributed the apparent closedness of Japanese markets to the Japanese companies' preference for long-term continuous trading with most trading partners, not just within but across the *Keiretsu* and corporate groupings (*Kigyo Shudan*).[1] Long-term continuous trading appears 'non-transparent' precisely because of the major advantage of such trading practice, namely high-trust cooperative relations. In such relations, the customer company takes it for granted that its suppliers respond flexibly to unforeseen contingencies and fulfill exacting requirements in quality, delivery and price (Shimada, 1987, p. 42). Besides creating incentives to cooperate based on trust, long-term trading has its merit in saving on search and negotiation costs, and in greater openness in the exchange of information (EPA, 1990, pp. 197–8).

A corresponding diagnosis in Britain of its industrial decline is a mirror image of the Japanese explanation. It attributes the exposure to foreign competition of UK domestic markets to the lack of cooperative inter-firm relations: 'an emphasis on price competition and the absence of a supportive inter-firm culture encourages the openness to foreign competition at the upper end of the market on the basis of superior design and quality and at the lower end from low-cost products from NICs' (Hirst and Zeitlin 1989, p. 8).[2] Britain's industrial decline can be reversed, in this view, only if 'a supportive inter-firm culture' is created in regional and national economies, so as to create opportunities for firms to cooperate on innovation, training and other matters.

4

From the above, it appears that high-trust inter-firm relations, just like harmonious industrial relations, have come to be seen as responsible for the superior industrial competitiveness of Japan as compared to Britain. But high-trust cooperativeness in OCR is only necessary, but not sufficient, to achieve the desired outcome. A central question then becomes: if companies can achieve good quality by entering into OCR-type relations, how can they ensure that they also achieve competitive prices? The book identifies the relevant micro-mechanisms which induce OCR-inclined companies to achieve competitive results. They are, in Japan, the practice of cost-reduction targets, the use of value analysis (VA) or value engineering (VE) techniques, the publicised ranking of suppliers according to their performance, and lateral communication between suppliers through the suppliers' associations. These mechanisms give sufficient incentives for suppliers to remain competitive, and ensure that long-term contracting does not lead to cosy familiarity cushioning inefficient practices.

Outline of the book

This book is in four parts. Part I contains a discussion of theories and concepts employed in the book. Chapter 1 outlines the framework of Arm's-length Contractual Relations (ACR) and Obligational Contractual Relations (OCR), while chapter 2 discusses how various types of 'trust' contribute towards enhancing efficiency in inter-firm relations.

Part II presents the empirical analysis. An overview of buyer–supplier relations in Britain and Japan in chapter 3 is followed by a detailed examination of trading relationships at three customer companies in chapter 4, and at 36 supplier companies in Britain and Japan in chapter 5.

The next five chapters in Part III examine the factors influencing companies' disposition to enter into ACR- or OCR-type practices. Economic and technological factors are investigated in chapter 6. Chapter 7 focuses on differences between Britain and Japan in the legal enforceability of contracts and non-legal means of sanctions; chapter 8 on differences in the taste for short-term (rather than long-term) profit and stability of rewards through risk-sharing, which may partly reflect differences in companies' financial structure; chapter 9 on differences in prevailing forms of employment relations, and chapter 10 on opportunities for entrepreneurship.

In Part IV, chapter 11 examines the link between ACR–OCR patterns and corporate performance by focusing on how prices and quantities are determined between trading partners. Chapter 12 provides a summary of the major theoretical and empirical findings of the research, and draws some implications for policy and business practice. The book will hopefully provide a modest contribution to cross-national comparative industrial research, and to furthering our understanding of the sources of long-term industrial competitiveness.

PART I

Theory and concepts

1

A spectrum of transactional patterns: from ACR to OCR

This chapter sets out the conceptual framework to be employed throughout this book. Central to the framework are the two patterns, Arm's-length Contractual Relation (ACR) and Obligational Contractual Relation (OCR), which represent the ends of a multi-dimensional spectrum of possible trading relationships. First, the basic features of ACR and OCR are described. Second, major assumptions underlying the ACR–OCR patterns are made explicit. Third, socio-economic factors which may account for ACR–OCR variations are identified. Fourth, implications of ACR–OCR patterns for performance are examined. Lastly, the chapter discusses how the ACR–OCR framework relates to Williamson's transaction cost theory.

Defining ACR and OCR[1]

The Arm's-length Contractual Relation (ACR) involves a specific, discrete economic transaction. An explicit contract spells out before trading commences each party's tasks and duties in every conceivable eventuality, as far as human capacity for anticipation allows. If unforeseen contingencies arise, they are settled by resort to some universalistic legal or normative rules.[2] All dealings are thus conducted at arm's length, to avoid undue familiarity, with neither party controlled by the other. Consequently, seeking an alternative trading partner ('exit' in Hirschman's (1970) terms) is an easily available option when a contract comes to an end.

The Obligational Contractual Relation (OCR) also involves an economic contract covering the production and trading of goods and services. But it is embedded in more particularistic social relations between trading partners who entertain a sense of mutual trust.[3] Because of this underpinning, transactions take place without prior agreement on all the terms and conditions of trade. Even if the tasks and duties of each trading partner are negotiated, agreed and clearly spelt out in a contract before trading relationships commence, there is an incentive to deviate from them, to do more than is expected by the trading partner. Such an incentive results from expectations that the act of goodwill will lead to a similar response from the trading partner, and that in times of *force majeure* unforeseen crisis, one may call on the good nature of a trading partner to allow one to default in some way from the previously agreed terms of contract.

There are two dimensions which capture the essence of ACR and OCR relationships, namely the degree of interdependence and the time span for reciprocity. A state of interdependence between the buyer and the supplier is a situation in which the actions of one trading partner decisively affect the fortunes of, and the opportunities and constraints faced by, the other partner. ACR is characterised by a low degree of actual and perceived interdependence, while OCR is characterised by heavy interdependence. What underpins heavy mutual dependence as an acceptable, and even preferred, state of affairs is the existence of 'goodwill trust'. 'Goodwill trust' is a sure feeling that trading partners possess a moral commitment to maintaining a trading relationship. It may manifest itself in not taking unfair advantage of one's circumstances (for which shared principles of fairness exist) and in offering preferential treatment or help whenever the need arises. This diffuse kind of trust, which exists in OCR but not in ACR, is to be distinguished from more specific types of trust, namely 'contractual trust' (expectations that promises made are kept) and 'competence trust' (confidence in a trading partner's competence to carry out a specific task), both of which are necessary for the smooth working of any trading relationship, be it ACR or OCR. (See chapter 2 for a more detailed discussion of the concept of 'trust'.)

The other dimension of importance to the ACR–OCR patterns is the time span for reciprocity. In ACR, exact reciprocity is expected within each contract duration. In OCR, the principle of give-and-take is looser, so that exact reciprocity may be achieved, if ever, only over a very long time. The greater specificity and underlying calculation involved in reciprocal activities in ACR are a reflection of the reluctance of ACR traders to accept a favour which they feel they cannot return in the near future. In contrast, OCR traders feel that mutual indebtedness or obligatedness at any time is a normal state of affairs which sustains a relationship.

The basic features of the ACR and OCR patterns, as they manifest themselves in practice, are summarised in the table below (Table 1.1).

Table 1.1. *Features of ACR–OCR patterns*

ACR	OCR
(A) Transactional dependence **Buyer** seeks to maintain low dependence by trading with a large number of competing suppliers within the limits permitted by need to keep down transaction costs. **Supplier** seeks to maintain low dependence by trading with a large number of customers within limits set by scale economies and transaction costs.	For a **buyer**, avoidance of dependence is not a high priority; it prefers to give security to few suppliers, though may still dual or triple source (some from a fringe group of suppliers with whom it has ACR relation) for flexibility. For a **supplier**, avoidance of dependence is not a high priority, but it may well have several OCR customers (plus, perhaps, a fringe group of ACR customers).
(B) Ordering procedure Bidding takes place; buyer does not know which supplier will win the contract before bidding. Prices negotiated and agreed before an order is commissioned.	Bidding may or may not take place. With bidding, buyer has a good idea of which supplier gets which contract before bidding. Without bidding, there is a straight commission to supplier. Prices are settled after decision about who gets the contract.
(C) Projected length of trading For the duration of the current contract. Short-term commitment by both buyer and supplier.	Continued beyond the duration of the current contract. Mutual long-term commitment.
(D) Documents for exchange Terms and conditions of contract are written, detailed and substantive.	Contracts contain procedural rules, but substantive issues are decided case by case. Contracts may be oral rather than written.
(E) 'Contractualism' Contingencies are written out and followed strictly.	Case-by-case resolution with much appeal to the diffuse obligation of long-term relationships.
(F) 'Contractual trust' Supplier never starts production until written orders are received.	Supplier often starts production on the basis of oral communication, before written orders are received.
(G) 'Goodwill trust' Multiple sourcing by buyer, combined with supplier's low transactional dependence.	Sole sourcing by buyer, combined with supplier's transactional dependence.
(H) 'Competence trust' Thorough inspection on delivery; the principle of *caveat emptor* predominates.	Little or no inspection on delivery for most parts. (Customer may be involved in establishing supplier's quality-control systems).

11

Table 1.1. (*Cont.*)

(I) Technology transfer and training Only the transfer, training or consultancy which can be costed and claimed for in the short run occurs.	Not always fully costed, as benefits are seen as partly intangible and/or reaped in the distant future.
(J) Communication channels and intensity A narrow channel between the buyer's purchasing department and the supplier's sales department, with frequency kept to minimum necessary to conduct business.	Extensive multiple channels, between engineers, quality assurance personnel, top managers, as well as between purchasing and sales managers. Frequent contact, often extending beyond the immediate business into socialising.
(K) Risk sharing Little sharing of risk; how risk, resulting from price and demand fluctuations, is to be borne by each party is spelt out in explicit prior agreement.	Much sharing of risk, in the sense that the relative share of unforeseen loss or gain is decided case by case, by applying some principle of fairness.

This list is drawn up in order to operationalise the ACR–OCR patterns, so that each feature, (A) – (K), is empirically verifiable. However, because some features, such as contractualism and trust – (E) – (H) – are states of mind, there may be more than one behaviour pattern or outcome which reflect such a state of mind; only one, considered significant empirically, is taken up to illustrate each feature.

ACR and OCR are best thought of as lying on a continuum of various trading patterns. Thus, instead of regarding ACR–OCR as a dichotomous contrast, which is one possible interpretation, a trading relationship is said to be more OCR (or ACR) than another the greater the number of OCR (or ACR) features that relationship possesses. Each feature is also a matter of degree. Empirically, it is expected that any relationship would have mostly OCR features or mostly ACR features bunched together, rather than a mix of OCR and ACR features, in order to preserve the internal consistency among the features. For example, intense communication and uncosted technical transfer in OCR are supposedly sustainable only if the projected length of trading is long term, and if 'goodwill trust' ensures that disclosed pieces of information and technical know-how are not employed against a trading partner in an opportunistic manner. By the same token, companies with hybrid features may face potential problems. For example, the expectation of a brief period of trading combined with heavy transactional dependence can be a risky strategy to follow particularly if there is no 'goodwill trust'. In this sense, the individual features at each of the ACR–OCR extremes are self-reinforcing among themselves, suggesting a high switching cost from one mode of trading to another.

To summarise, ACR works towards spreading risks by maintaining low dependence on trading partners over whom one does not have much control. By 'settling the accounts' after each transaction so that nothing is owed to others, a company contains the risk of its fortune being affected by the actions of another company. Being taken advantage of (or being exploited or becoming the subject of opportunistic behaviour) by another company is a consequence of one's own failing for neither foreseeing nor insuring against the event. For this reason, ACR can be taxing on the human capacity for calculated foresight.

Not surprisingly, OCR appears precarious and fragile from the ACR point of view. Rather than remaining at arm's length, so that incentives for opportunistic behaviour are abundant, OCR traders intentionally lock themselves into a mutually dependent relationship. Intensified communication not only reduces uncertainty by making mutual behaviour more predictable, but also elicits commitment to the relation-ship, which in turn gives an incentive not to behave opportunistically. Nevertheless, if an OCR trader actually behaves opportunistically, this is treated as a serious breach of norm and a legitimate cause for breaking the relation.

Assumptions about the common context

It would be instructive to spell out the underlying assumptions about a common context within which either ACR or OCR pattern is likely to exist. These assumptions are made in such a way as to make the analysis of empirical observations feasible, or to 'operationalise' the concepts of ACR and OCR. In order to do so, it is necessary to avoid two interrelated types of pitfall. One concerns a dichotomous analytical framework in which one extreme of a dimension is defined as a residual of the other, so that only one is operationalised and not the other. Another is too high a level of abstraction which renders an analytical concept (an ideal type) impossible to verify or refute empirically. On the first kind of trap, we are well warned by Stinchcombe and Heimer, writing specifically of the contract/hierarchy dichotomy: 'A common danger of the ideal type method used in this literature is that one of the types, usually the most interesting one, is defined residually, by contrast with an empty ideal type into which very few empirical observations fall. This means not only that intermediate cases are misanalyzed, but that even the poles of contract and hierarchy are poorly defined (Stinchcombe and Heimer, 1985 p. 126–7).

As seen in the previous section and Table 1.1 in particular, care is taken so that both ACR and OCR are equally made up of empirically observable elements. ACR is not just a negative residual redefinition of OCR, or vice versa. In order to dissociate the ACR–OCR framework from the impression that one is a residual of the other, terms such as 'auction markets', 'spot markets', or just 'markets' are avoided. In fact, trading relations which the ACR–OCR framework purports to describe apply just as much to a relationship coordinated in markets (i.e. between two independent firms) as to that between two divisions of an enterprise. Elements listed in Table 1.1 are the empirically identifiable aspects of the coordinating mechanism, which go beyond a reference to an abstraction such as the Walrasian auctioneer or Adam Smith's invisible hand.

Turning to the other pitfall, namely too high a level of abstraction to render empirical observations impossible, what assumptions need to be made? First, there are the sort of assumptions which economists are most comfortable making. These deviate from the standard microeconomic model of perfect competition, perfect foresight and the behavioural assumption of individuals maximising utility and firms maximising profits but within familiar limits. In particular, it is assumed that imperfect competition prevails so that not all firms are price takers in all markets, and that competition takes place as much on differentiated product attributes, such as design and quality, as on price. Moreover, information is not perfect in the sense that (a) the price mechanism does not convey all the necessary information required to make decisions on trading, and (b) elements of uncertainty exist whenever individuals plan for the future.

This latter assumption of uncertainty is central to another group of assumptions which are made largely by those who have attempted to marry organisation theory with microeconomics. One relevant assumption in this category is Herbert Simon's concept of 'bounded rationality' (Simon, 1957). It focuses on limits to human knowledge and calculated action and is a significant modification of the idea of economic rationality so fundamental to conventional economic theory. It is because of bounded rationality that planning is necessarily incomplete, as not all contingencies can be foreseen and therefore covered by the contract. At the same time, because people cannot cope with too much uncertainty, they may choose to reduce the controllable element of uncertainty associated with people's behaviour, e.g. by building up mutual trust, rather than take the degree of uncertainty as exogenously given.

Another important assumption in this category is the explicit recognition that transaction costs exist in every exchange relation, be it within organisations or in markets (Williamson 1985). Transaction costs encompass a variety of things from transportation costs, the financial cost and time taken for negotiation of the terms of contract, to the cost of monitoring and enforcing them which may include, in the case of default, the cost of litigation. They do not derive so exclusively from a combination of opportunistic behaviour (self-interest seeking with guile) and asset specificity as Williamson had implied. Nor are transaction costs for a particular mode of transaction fixed and given, as they can be affected by conscious actions of agents, for example, by investing time and effort into building mutual trust between trading partners (see chapter 2 for a more detailed analysis of transaction costs).

Lastly, the ACR–OCR framework is founded on the idea of the business firm as a nexus of treaties (Aoki et al. 1990). Not surprisingly, the ACR–OCR framework is strictly at odds with the neoclassical theory which conceptualises the firm as a black box, no more than a technological relation between inputs and outputs. The ACR–OCR framework is well disposed to considering the firm as a nexus of contracts, but it places more emphasis on how incomplete contracts in product, labour and capital markets are executed by reference to social and moral norms. A consequence of this multi-disciplinary framework is that the performance of a firm is defined, not in terms of its profit-maximising or cost-minimising behaviour, but in terms of its X-efficiency enhancing capabilities in response to pressures from both within and outside the firm.

Socio-economic explanations of ACR–OCR variations

It is postulated that within each country, Britain and Japan, there is a range of actual trading patterns which lie on the ACR–OCR continuum. It may be hypothesised that because of differences in a variety of explanatory factors, the modal Japanese inter-company relationship is more OCR than the modal British one, but that there is an overlap in the two countries' ranges of trading patterns.

Why should we presume so? What factors explain variations in the pattern of buyer–supplier relationships? An appropriate causal model to answer this question depends on what is considered the domain of analysis, whether it is purely economic or multi-disciplinary involving

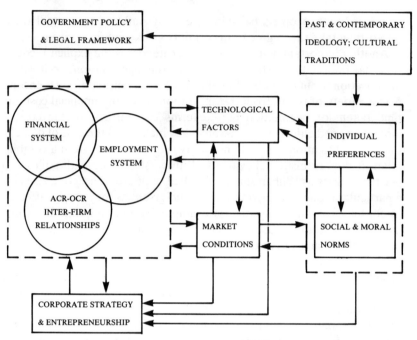

Figure 1.1 A schema of factors influencing ACR–OCR variations.

sociology, politics and history as well as economics. The more one shifts towards the latter, the larger the number of factors which become endogenous to the model and the greater the extent of multiple and two-way causation. The explanatory schema described in Figure 1.1 is a compromise between a narrowly economic predictive model and an interpretation solely in terms of specific circumstances. It is predicated on what Hodgson calls a systems view or an institutional approach (Hodgson, 1988, p. 12). It is an approach rather than a complete theory because the ACR–OCR framework cannot, for the moment, be much more than a phenomenology of patterns and mechanisms.

The ACR–OCR framework is founded on the insight of the institutional approach that no economic transaction can take place in a social vacuum. All transactions are embedded in particular social structures (Granovettor, 1985). Thus, 'the economy is a subsystem of a more encompassing society, polity and culture. It is therefore assumed that the dynamics of the economy, including the extent to which it is competitive, cannot be studied without integrating social, political and cultural factors into one's paradigm' (Etzioni, 1988, p. 5).[4]

16

A spectrum of transactional patterns from ACR to OCR

One consequence of getting into this intellectual morass rather than sticking to a parsimonious economic theory is that factors which are generally treated as exogenous in conventional economics, namely individual tastes and preferences on the one hand and technology on the other, become part of the socio-economic system to be examined. In what follows, implications of this general statement for buyer–supplier relationships will be explored with reference to Figure 1.1.

Social and moral norms

Whereas conventional economic theory treats actors' preferences and tastes as exogenously given, the present framework endogenise them by taking account of past and contemporary ideology, cultural and religious traditions, and social and moral norms. In particular, an important distinction is made between first-order preferences which may change according to whim and second-order or meta-preferences which change only after much reflection (Hirschman, 1984). Social and moral norms belong to the latter category. How specific norms come into being and change cannot be explained satisfactorily. But recognising the existence of norms signals a major departure from the utilitarian notion of action. Action is not guided solely by instrumental rationality; it is typically shaped jointly by self-interest and norms, simultaneously 'pulled' by the prospect of future rewards and 'pushed' from behind by quasi-inertial forces (Elster, 1989, p. 97). Economists are prone to regard norms which are not consistent with one's self-interest as constraints. But norms are also capable of being bases for committed action.

What norms are relevant in affecting the nature of buyer–supplier relationships? First, there are certain minimum moral norms without which no economic transactions would take place. They include norms of honesty, keeping promises and obeying laws. This is the kind of obligation imposed by society as a whole, referred to by Durkheim (1947) as the non-contractual elements in contract. Beyond these minimalist moral norms, there is a grey area in which certain 'strategic' behaviour may or may not be acceptable. For example, telling an outright lie may be unacceptable, but misrepresenting one's position by witholding relevant information may be acceptable opportunistic behaviour; if so, there is likely to be a preference for ACR to accommodate such weak forms of opportunism. By contrast, OCR is likely to emerge if opportunistic behaviour, broadly defined, is contrary to prevailing norms.

Second, Parsons' pattern variables – universalism vs particularism, specific vs diffuse, and affective-neutral vs affective – are relevant but without the usual evolutionary implications (Parsons, 1951); i.e. it is not the case that OCRs are 'traditional' relations which will eventually give way to 'modern' ACR relations with industrialisation. Thus, the ACR pattern is assumed normal and normative if people endorse a universalistic, specific and affective-neutral morality. Parties to a transaction prefer to be 'faceless': suppliers which can deliver the same goods are interchangeable for the buyer, while there is the same duty by the supplier to fulfill commitments whoever is the purchaser. If shortages of goods are foreseen, ACR traders prioritise their trading according to instrumental criteria, such as the profitability of a particular order. By contrast, OCR is associated with a particularistic, diffuse and affective morality. Under particularism, the identity of a trading partner matters. They may be prioritised not according to purely instrumental reasons but on the basis of more subtle obligations. For example, one passes on information about impending shortages only to those trading partners to whom one owes most in past trading, or with whom one has developed a high level of 'goodwill trust'. It is indeed these norms concerning reciprocity and trust of various types which dictate whether firms expect to maintain arm's length relations or enter into multi-faceted OCR relations which are difficult to break once established.

Also important to note here are the dynamics of how social norms change or break down over time. Norms may emerge and be maintained for reasons other than that they serve the collective benefit of a society. It is therefore false to assert that they change whenever they cease to serve the interest of individuals and society. However, the established norm may be undermined, and a competing norm emerge, if a critical mass of actors think it detrimental to the individual or collective good. Such a scene may be associated with changes in economic and technological conditions. For example, US and European firms have come to realise the benefits of partnerships based on less adversarial behaviour because of greater technological and market risks associated with R&D. The meta-preference has apparently changed in favour of greater cooperation, although it has not been reflected successfully in actual behaviour due to the problem of collective action or Prisoners' Dilemma, as we shall see in later empirical chapters.

Technological factors

At one level of analysis, technological factors may be treated as an exogenous set of variables influencing the ACR–OCR variations. Thus, the nation-wide range of trading patterns may be presumed to depend on the composition of various industrial sectors in a national economy. It may be hypothesised that the modal trading pattern is more OCR the greater the weight of industries producing customised goods requiring customer-specific investment. Williamson (1979) analysed the determinants of the organisational choice among markets, hierarchies and obligational contracting along this line. OCR-type relations are more likely to emerge if suppliers contribute to the product design and development process than if they do not. These propositions will be examined in chapter 6. It will become apparent that the degree of asset specificity and the extent to which suppliers contribute to design and development are not fully exogenous but influenced in part by the prior choice of ACR or OCR trading norms.

Economic factors

Related factors to be examined in chapter 6 are economic, concerning demand patterns and growth. It is posited that competition based on product differentiation rather than on price only is more likely to render buyer–supplier relations OCR. Moreover, a history of steady, rather than fluctuating, demand growth is considered more conducive to OCR as it creates a favourable condition for building mutual trust and confidence. Two-way causation is again evident as the commitment to existing relationships inherent in OCR (e.g. through an implicit guarantee of steady orders) biases demand growth towards stability.

Government policy and legal framework

Technological factors emphasise intra-sectoral similarities in ACR–OCR variations between countries. Thus, buyer–supplier relations in the automobile industry face similar technological conditions whether firms are located in the USA, Japan, or Europe. By the same token, differences between industries within a country may be large, *ceteris paribus*. In reality, however, inter-sectoral differences may be subject to a centripetal force due to the existence of national-specific institutions. In particular, government policy and the legal framework generated by it encourage or discourage businesses to enter into ACR- or OCR-type relationships with a varying degree of efficacy. This will be investigated in chapter 7.

Prices, quality and trust

Corporate strategy and entrepreneurship

Even within the same industrial sector, ACR–OCR variations may exist for a number of reasons, including differences between firms in size, human asset specificity, managerial competence, and the nature of entrepreneurship. The reason why a particular company is pursuing ACR- or OCR-type relationships with trading partners may sometimes be best understood by enquiring explicitly into its corporate strategy. Such strategy concerns the trade-off between growth and short-term profitability, about establishing market niches, about the planning time horizon affecting the requisite level of investment into physical and human capital, and about sources of finance for such investment. The choice in corporate strategy is in part affected by how a particular firm has been set up and therefore can be traced back to the nature of entrepreneurship (see chapter 10).

Financial and employment links

Viewed in this way, a business firm's choice between ACR and OCR may be affected by opportunities and constraints it faces due to the nature of contractual relations along two other dimensions. These are namely internal contracts between management and employees, and external contracts between the firm and its banks and other financiers. Aoki argued that a nexus of employment and financial contracts is more effective if those contracts are uniformly J-type or A-type (Aoki, 1989, pp. 357–9). J-type contracts, like OCR, are characterised by a greater degree of incompleteness, a diffuse allocation of residual rights of control, and greater continuity and sharing of information and knowledge enabling decentralised decision-making. J-type employment contracts require J-type financial contracts in order to preserve the continuity of the tacit knowledge base internal to the firm. By contrast, more centralised decision-making with clearer task allocation in A-type employment contracts facilitates greater inter-firm labour mobility, while well-developed security markets under A-type financial contracting provide an efficient mechanism for risk diversification.

It will be argued in chapter 8 apropos of financial contracts that ACR buyer–supplier relations are more compatible with A-type contracts and OCR with J-type contracts. For instance, OCR-type buyer–supplier relations would be difficult to maintain if they are subject to changes in the ownership of firms as in A-type financial contracting. Similarly, chapter 9 contends that OCR requires J-type employment contracts for good performance while ACR is well supported by A-type contracts.

20

Here, the continuity of employment in J-type contracts helps establish trust relations between companies, while the decentralised decision-making contributes to multi-channelled communication and flexible responses which characterise OCR relations. The central focus of empirical investigation is on the degree of importance of the consistency among the three contractual relationships between buyers and suppliers, between management and workers, and between the firm and its shareholders or banks, if ACR or OCR patterns are to result in good performance.

Implications of ACR–OCR for performance

Implications of ACR–OCR patterns for overall performance of individual firms are ambiguous because there are trade-offs among various components of performance.

One measure of good performance is the minimisation of costs in order to produce a fixed level of output. Total costs may be classified into production costs and transaction costs, the former being the cost of labour, materials and capital, while the latter refer to costs involved in trading with buyers and suppliers, such as costs incurred while negotiating prices, drawing up contracts, monitoring quality, and building up trust. We may assume that any firm, as a buyer or a supplier, is interested in minimising the sum of production and transaction costs over a self-defined time period.

Whether a firm has ACR- or OCR-type relations has different implications for the composition and level of costs. As we have seen in the preceding discussion, OCR traders prefer to share risk over a long time horizon with a few trading partners, in the hope that the benefits which result from building up trust outweigh the costs involved in not being able to freely switch trading partners as prices dictate. Because of this latter reason, OCR buyer firms may pay material and component prices which are temporarily higher than the best the market offers.

By contrast, ACR traders pursue a strategy of risk-spreading by trading with many buyers and suppliers. ACR firms can obtain the best (i.e. lowest) prices for materials and components that the market offers by playing one supplier off against another. Their capacity to do so depends on the relative bargaining power of buyers *vis-à-vis* suppliers. Buyers can command strong bargaining power (a) if the number of potential suppliers is large so that the threat to switch trading partners is credible, and/or (b) if there is excess capacity in the suppliers' industry, so that suppliers have an incentive to buy-in orders to cover marginal costs at low prices. We can state as a proposition that in a situation of excess supplier capacity, material prices paid by ACR firms are likely to be lower than those faced by OCR firms. Conversely, in a situation of tight supplier capacity, OCR suppliers tend not to adjust prices upwards as much as ACR suppliers.

Moreover, regardless of capacity utilisation, there are grounds for believing that OCR may achieve a lower total production cost than ACR. This is likely to occur if normative values governing OCR elicit greater work effort, and hence higher X-efficiency, thus reducing unit labour cost (or increasing labour productivity). It is plausible that in times of crisis, a buyer's appeal to 'goodwill trust' (similar to the exercise of 'voice' rather than 'exit' in Hirschman's words (1970)) may give greater incentives for suppliers to reduce costs than impersonal market forces. This, however, is a matter for empirical examination (see chapter 11).

Turning to transaction costs, a distinction ought to be made between the current cost component and the investment cost component. Current transaction costs are linked to negotiating with and monitoring of existing trading partners, which are higher for ACR firms (with a greater number of trading partners and a higher level of expected opportunism from them) than for OCR firms. However, the investment component of transaction costs, which is associated with activities to build up trust and confidence with each trading partner, is greater for OCR than for ACR firms. Thus, overall, it is not clearcut whether ACR firms economise on transaction costs better than do OCR firms. What is clear is that if we concentrate on the current component of transaction costs, ACR firms are willing to trade off an increase in transaction costs in order to obtain lower materials costs through bargaining, while OCR firms typically face low current transaction costs (due to past investment in 'trust') but temporarily high material and component costs.

Markets, hierarchies and networks

The preceding exposition relies much on insights provided by a number of theoretical perspectives which address the question of how firms come to decide over their organisational forms. In particular, this section clarifies how OCR relates to various hybrid modes of coordinating production, some conceptualised as being intermediate between markets and hierarchies.

Networks, strategic alliances and other intermediate forms of organisation have become a fashionable topic. Anecdotal and survey evidence of phenomena classifiable as such intermediate modes of inter-firm relations abounds. For example, the number of joint ventures and other forms of strategic alliances has increased (e.g. Contractor and Lorange, 1988). Large corporations have de-integrated in the 1980s in order to achieve leaner production and closer supplier management (Womack et al. 1990). As an alternative to mass production with large firms, the Italian industrial districts have received attention for their innovation through cooperation among small firms (Pyke et al. (eds.) 1990). In a similar vein, the entire Japanese economy has been conceptualised as a network of long-term relationships between customers and suppliers, between large firms within horizontal corporate groupings, between employers and employees, between banks and their clients, and even between government and industry (Aoki 1988; Dore 1983; Gerlach 1989; Imai and Itami 1984; Okimoto 1986).

Perhaps to reflect the empirical diffusion of intermediate modes of coordinating production, this area of study has suffered from excessive neologism recently. This is not helpful in clarifying how one coined concept relates to another. For instance, intermediate forms are variously labelled 'quasi-integration' (Blois, 1972), 'quasi-vertical integration' (Monteverde and Teece, 1982), 'quasi-firm' (Eccles, 1981), 'quasi-disintegration' and 'visible handshaking' (Aoki, 1984) the latter being a slight twisting of Okun's phrase 'invisible handshake' (Okun, 1981), 'invisible link' (Yoshino and Lifson, 1986), 'relational contracting' (Dore, 1983), 'relational contract' (Macneil, 1985), 'intermediate organisation' (Imai and Itami, 1984) or *Chukan shoshiki* (Imai, Itami and Koike, 1985; Okimoto, 1986), 'network forms of organisation' (Powell, 1990), 'dynamic network' (Miles and Snow 1986), 'industrial networks' (Johanson and Mattson, 1987), 'strategic networks' (Jarillo 1988), and 'flexible specialisation' (Piore and Sabel, 1984).

What is intermediate about these forms of coordinating production? As the prefix 'quasi' signifies, the mechanism is not quite complete integration into a single firm, but not quite exchange between two separate firms in markets either. Firms may form links or bonds of a long term, 'relational' nature, through which they become interdependent for business (Blois 1972; Johanson and Mattson 1987). There may be interlocking directorate and inter-firm shareholding (see Aoki, 1984 and Okimoto, 1986 for Japan; Richardson, 1972 for Britain). The buyer may own tools used by the supplier (Monteverde and Teece, 1982). There may also be intensive technology transfer or sharing of technical and managerial knowledge between firms (Blois, 1972). These characteristics all make the exchange of products just one aspect of multi-faceted relations between legally independent entities.

As is evident, the references mentioned above vary in their theoretical focus and contextual settings. To start with, early writers tend not to put forth an alternative theory. Instead, they give rich illustrations from casual observations of firms such as Marks and Spencer and Rolls-Royce (Blois, 1972) to show that the neoclassical fiction of firms as 'islands of planned co-ordination in a sea of market relations' (Richardson, 1972, p. 883) is highly misleading.

There has been more theorising about these intermediate modes of coordinating production in the last decade or so. The theories reviewed below are (a) transaction cost economics, (b) relational contract theory, (c) a sociological approach to networks, and (d) networks as management strategy.

Transaction cost economics originally focused on the relative cost efficiencies of market versus hierarchy (Williamson 1975). In this framework, each firm organises its productive activities either within or across the boundaries of the firm, whichever minimises the sum of production and transaction costs. The major source of transaction costs is said to be opportunism ('self-interesting seeking with guile') which firms can exploit most in a bilateral monopoly situation created by undertaking customer-specific investment. Opportunistic behaviour is assumed to be better attenuated in hierarchy than in market, because coordination within hierarchy is mainly through administrative fiat by a centralised authority, while coordination in the market is, just as in the neoclassical model, through the price mechanism albeit with more friction in haggling.

Given this conception of market and hierarchy, obligational or relational contracting as an intermediate 'governance structure' (Williamson 1979) was considered difficult to organise, as it depends on having (a) a medium degree of asset specificity generating an intermediate amount of opportunism, (b) a moderate degree of bounded rationality, and (c) an intermediate frequency of transaction. Williamson wrote later: 'Whereas I was earlier of the view that transactions of the middle kind were very difficult to organise and hence were unstable . . . I am now persuaded that transactions in the middle range are much more common' (Williamson, 1985, p. 83). 'Transactions in the middle range' are now considered common because it is possible to create incentives for independent trading partners not to behave opportunistically. Such incentives are created through the buyer's ownership of specialised tools used by its supplier (Monteverde and Teece 1982) and through making credible commitments in the form of inter-firm shareholding or reciprocal trading among other things.

24

Relational or obligational contracting is also characterised by Williamson as trading of an ongoing administrative kind in which transactions are regulated in 'a minisociety with a vast array of norms beyond those centered on the exchange and its immediate processes' (Macneil as quoted by Williamson, 1979, p. 238). Williamson, however, does not discuss what these norms might be. Instead, he concentrates on the specification of the conditions which made relational contracting a 'rational' (i.e. transaction cost minimising) governance structure and universally to be expected. The ACR–OCR framework digs deeper into the nature of incentives involved in trading by making explicit the prevailing norms, particularly those concerning opportunistic behaviour and trust, which remain unelaborated for relational contracting. The study of opportunism under ACR is no different from that of Williamson's; opportunistic behaviour is not unexpected, and it is the various ways in which one can suppress it, by law or administrative fiat or the reputation effect, which are of interest. As one moves towards the OCR end, however, an OCR-maintaining moral norm does not merely attenuate opportunism as in the case of relational contracting; opportunistic behaviour evokes condemnation, and the opprobrium attached most likely leads to breaking the trading relation.

The second relevant theory, which does recognise the importance of norms, is on relational contracts (Macaulay (1963) and Macneil (1985)). Both Macaulay and Macneil criticised mainstream legal scholars for concentrating on a legal fiction of discrete contracts which are entered into voluntarily by autonomous individuals. In reality, in their view, relational contracts of a recurrent kind, in which dependence and coercion prevail, are empirically more common. Moreover, all contracts are embedded in social relations which are shaped by prevailing norms and values in society. This brand of legal theory has been freely assimilated into the transaction cost economics approach, although Macneil himself states: 'I believe that the transaction costs approach is far too unrelational a starting point in analyzing relational contract' (Macneil 1985, footnote 45, p. 496). There is no attempt to fit relational contracts in between market and hierarchy, because Macneil's main contention is about the pervasiveness of coercion and dependence in nominally free contractual relationships, be they in markets or within organisations.

A related, third approach which takes account of the normative basis of exchange is social network analysis (Wellman 1983), which used to be applied to anthropological and sociological studies of communities, but has also been extended to study commercial relations between individuals and firms (e.g. Powell 1985; Eccles and Crane 1988). A central proposition of this approach is that every economic action is embedded in social relations, some based on mutual trust and obligation (Granovettor 1985). Once this view is endorsed, networks, as a description of formal and informal links between individuals and firms, are everywhere. All markets, including even the securities market which Okun thought typified an 'auction market', are embedded in social structures, in which the identity of traders matters, for example in who passes on information to whom.

Lastly, in organisation theory and management, networking has come to be regarded as a competitive strategy. Jarillo (1988), Johanson and Mattson (1987), and Miles and Snow (1984) all regard networks as a mode of organisation that can be created by managers and entrepreneurs to position their firms in a favourable environment. In this framework, the competitive advantage of a firm lies in its capacity to gain access to, and exploit, valued external resources and expertise through the network.

In order to clarify how the various theories of intermediate forms relate to each other, the rest of this section will address the following questions. Where does each writer stand in relation to: (a) why intermediate coordination mechanisms exist at all; in particular, what is the relative importance accorded to technical and economic conditions as opposed to value preferences in explaining their existence; and (b) whether intermediate forms are a source of superior or inferior performance.

To the first question, economists, not surprisingly, tend to give undue weight to technical conditions as dictating whether intermediate coordination mechanisms will be chosen or not. Monteverde and Teece (1982) follow Williamson's footsteps in making the possibility of post-contractual opportunism due to asset specificity the crucial determinant in the existence of 'quasi-vertical integration' (i.e. the buyer's ownership of specialised tools used by the supplier). Just like Williamson, they make a universalistic assumption about opportunistic behaviour. As mentioned above, Williamson singled out three exogenous factors – namely trading frequency, asset specificity and bounded rationality – as determining organisational forms. The ACR–OCR framework identifies more than three, but the three factors may also be treated as endogenous, while social norms – especially concerning 'goodwill trust' – are rendered exogenous in contemporaneous analysis. In particular, a preference for high trust in OCR leads to a higher frequency of trading (and communication), which may in turn reduce the extent of behavioural uncertainty and bounded rationality. It may also increase the degree of asset specificity as firms are willing to make transaction specific investments with long-term payback periods and to transfer difficult-to-codify know-how to each other.

At the other extreme, Macneil (1983, 1985), a legal theorist, has very little to say about technological conditions, and deals exclusively with the importance of behavioural norms which dictate the existence of 'relational contracts' or 'relational exchange'. Yoshino and Lifson (1986) also attribute to the Japanese a preference for high trust and exchange of obligations in order to explain the existence of an 'administrative network' between a general trading company and its affiliates, customers and suppliers. Their network is a formal institutional one, as opposed to a more informal personal network emphasised by Granovettor (1973; 1985) and by Okimoto (1986; pp. 41–2) who wrote on personal relationships among MITI officials and business leaders.

In between, there are writers who give equal weight to technical conditions and value preferences or norms. Thus, Lundvall (1988) notes that the process of technical innovation with uncertain future gains necessitates interaction either in 'organized markets' or in vertically integrated firms, but that the existence of mutual trust and mutually respected codes of behaviour renders 'organized markets' a more likely institutional outcome than vertical integration. Dore (1983), while recognising that increased capital lumpiness of new technology has led to vertical disintegration by making greater inter-firm specialisation more efficient, attributes the prevalence of 'relational contracting' in Japan relative to Britain to the Japanese preference for moralised trading relationships of mutual goodwill.

There is also variation with respect to the second question of efficiency of intermediate forms relative to market or hierarchy. First, there are economists with a transaction cost orientation, who tend to interpret all existing institutions as having evolved in an efficient way to solve problems. Then intermediate modes, where they exist, are always efficient. Thus, because of their functionalist orientation, the explanation about why a particular trading pattern exists and the efficiency implication of an existing trading pattern are one and the same thing (Dugger 1983; Granovettor, 1990).

Second, the sociological approach to networks refutes an old school of economic development and modernisation, associated with Parsons, that the embeddedness of economic action in non-economic relations is a barrier to economic development (Granovettor 1990). It might have been thought that impersonalising commercial relations by separating the economic sphere from the social sphere would enhance efficiency. But far from it, the network sociologists argue that personalised relationships with identity found in commercial and industrial transactions are not some hangover from traditional times, but a valuable foundation upon which efficient exchanges may be carried out. This is so particularly when transactions involve difficult-to-codify knowledge or difficult-to-appropriate benefits, for instance, in R&D (Powell 1990).

Third, the 'networks as strategy' school mentions increased efficiency derived from networks, which enable firms to cope flexibly in a complex environment (Miles and Snow 1986). Establishing networks is regarded as an investment for future access to other firms' internal assets (Johanson and Mattson 1987). Jarillo (1988) also focuses on investment, but is more explicit in discussing the possibility of reducing transaction costs in networks via a conscious decision on the part of entrepreneurs to invest in building mutual trust.

Lastly, some writers recognise a set of performance indicators, and that the degree to which trade-offs exist among them may be attenuated by intermediate modes of coordination. For example, Imai and Itami (1984) regard intermediate forms as combining the best of both markets and organisations, maximising both the flexibility more characteristic of market-mediated transactions and the control more effective within the firm. This consideration is related to one aspect of what Piore and Sabel's concept of 'flexible specialisation' attempts to convey, namely achieving a judicious balance between competition and cooperation in such a way as to encourage dynamic efficiency through innovation. Dore (1983) identifies different types of efficiency, and regards one type, X-efficiency, outweighing another, namely allocative inefficiency in relational contracting. Lastly, Okun (1981), the only writer with a macro-economic concern, sees 'customer markets' as generating price rigidity and a restriction of output which constitute a deviation from the social optimum.

To summarise, the general thrust of the arguments by the authors reviewed above is that a tight hierarchical control as implied by complete integration into a firm is not necessary whenever there exist other effective controls, overt or more surreptitious, including inter-firm shareholding, the buyer's ownership of specialised tools, communitarian institutions or value preferences for high trust and obligation. OCR is more closely related to the intermediate modes of transaction which focus on trust and obligation than to those which focus on tangible technological or financial links. This reasoning provides a theoretical ground for expecting a lower degree of vertical integration with

OCR-type than with ACR-type transactions, *ceteris paribus*. As Arrow pointed out, a society with a high level of trust requires less vertical integration than one with low trust (Arrow, as quoted by Williamson 1985, pp. 9, 405–6). The next chapter examines whether high-trust relations are indeed always conducive to good performance, and if so how trust can be created in new and existing trading relationships.

2

Trust and organisational efficiency

The possibility was raised in the last chapter that intermediate forms of coordination are often associated with superior performance, by combining the best of both worlds, of markets in giving flexibility and of hierarchies in giving maximum control. This chapter has two broad tasks to achieve. The first is to clarify what is meant by good or bad performance, in order to enable us to make an empirical link between ACR–OCR trading patterns on the one hand and corporate performance or industrial competitiveness on the other. The concept of performance to be discussed evolves around a particular notion of the firm as an organisation with a varying degree of capability in enhancing X-efficiency. Transaction costs are incurred in part to invest in such capability.

The second task in the chapter is to examine the concept of trust which is considered central to our understanding of how coordinating mechanisms differ under ACR and OCR. A typology of trust is developed, by making a distinction among three types of trust, namely 'contractual trust', 'competence trust' and 'goodwill trust'. Mutual trust between trading partners is seen to entail both efficient outcomes (due to freer information disclosure and commitment) and inefficient outcomes (due to greater non-pecuniary switching costs).

Allocative efficiency, X-efficiency, and transactional efficiency

The notion of good performance to be discussed in this section will be called 'organisational efficiency' for lack of a better label. It takes account of both production costs emphasised by neoclassical analysis, and transaction costs stressed by the comparative institutional approach. It also builds on fusing the notions of X-efficiency and transaction costs.

A familiar starting point is a strictly neoclassical framework, in which

30

the firm is regarded as a black box. The production function defines the technological relationship between inputs and output and the extent of economies of scale. It is assumed that technological efficiency is achieved always. The only source of inefficiency then is of an allocative nature, either due to distortions in input ratios or due to price and quantity distortions caused by the firm's monopoly power. This framework continues to be useful when the issues are ones of efficient resource allocation and of 'make or buy' decisions according to relative production costs of firms with different technology and scale.

Dissatisfaction with the neoclassical theory originated from at least two standpoints. One – X-efficiency theory – is with respect to the assumption that all firms produce on the production possibilities frontier, and the other – transaction cost theory – with respect to the assumption of perfect information, foresight and certainty rendering transactions costless.

X-efficiency theory

Leibenstein noted that some firms were more capable than others in approaching the frontier of efficient production techniques (Leibenstein 1966; see also Frantz 1988). For instance, in a comparison of two identically designed Ford plants, the German plant was found to be producing 50 per cent more automobiles than its UK counterpart with 22 per cent less labour (Leibenstein, 1987c, p. 935). The outer boundary of a firm's production possibility surface is then best treated as the maximum attainable in an ideal situation. The gap between the actual productivity and the maximum attainable is X-inefficiency which Leibenstein claims is empirically of greater significance than allocative inefficiency.

X-inefficiency exists primarily because inputs often do not have a fixed specification and therefore cannot be transformed into predetermined outputs. This may be due to: (1) individual motivational efficiency, which occurs because labour contracts are incomplete (a point recognised and thoroughly discussed by Baldamus who also singled out effort as a central concept in understanding efficiency (Baldamus, 1961)); (2) intra-plant motivational efficiency, which is attributable to the fact that there is always an experimental trial and error (including learning-by-doing) element in utilising a particular production technique; (3) external motivational efficiency, which exists because 'interdependence and uncertainty lead competing firms to cooperate tacitly with each other in some respects, and to imitate each other with respect to technique, to some degree' (Leibenstein, 1966 p. 409); and (4) nonmarket input efficiency, which concerns the ability to purchase or have access to factors such as managerial knowledge, financial capital, and trustworthiness when there are no markets for them (Leibenstein, 1966, p. 407; 1976, p. 44).

Leibenstein focuses on the first type of X-inefficiency resulting from the incomplete nature of labour contracts. Human inputs cannot be purchased outright, so that even if a detailed specification of job tasks is made in a labour contract, the actual labour input depends on the motivation to exert effort on the part of individual workers. How much effort people actually exert depends in part on individual habit.[1] It also depends on organisational factors such as the reward system and the nature of managerial authority. For example, an individual may well perform at a significantly higher effort level with less supervision, as monitoring breeds distrust and may shift effort from not easily observable (e.g. quality of workmanship) to observable aspects of work (e.g. quantity of output) (Leibenstein, 1987a, pp. 99–100). Quality is more directly affected by motivational factors than physical quantity of output, and is therefore an important indicator of X-efficiency (Leibenstein, 1984, p. 352).

There is no reason why the level of effort chosen by individuals in a firm should result in working practices most productive for the firm; hence the possibility of X-inefficiency. Moreover, increasing X-efficiency may not be easily achieved because of inertia to maintain the existing work routine. Inertial behaviour has a basic psychological foundation in comfort felt due to familiarity of habit and to predictability of other people's behaviour. Whether a firm becomes more X-efficient or not depends on the strength of this inertia and the pressure applied to it. The pressure may take the form of a sudden external shock such as a rise in the oil price, or a gradual change which reaches a critical point such as overseas competition.

Leibenstein's major contribution lies in pointing out, particularly to economists, that intra-firm efficiency is much affected by motivational factors. Similar motivational factors at work in inter-firm relations, however, only receive a brief mention, in the form of 'external motivational efficiency' and non-market input efficiency. This conceptual gap can be filled by extending the concept of X-efficiency to inter-firm relations which incur transaction costs. Leibenstein and Williamson have been relatively reluctant to draw on each other's theoretical contributions, because X-efficiency is largely about what happens inside the firm, whereas transaction cost theory starts with the neoclassical 'in the beginning there were markets' parable (de Alessi, 1983). However, it is argued here that much insight can be gained by explicitly recognising that enhancing X-efficiency often involves incurring transaction costs of both the pecuniary and non-pecuniary kinds.

Transaction cost theory

According to Coase (1937), transaction costs are the main reason for the existence of the firm. Its size is determined by equating at the margin the costs incurred in the price system and the costs of coordination within the firm. More recently, Arrow, as quoted by Williamson (1985, p. 18), defined transaction costs as the 'costs of running the economic system' being equivalent to frictions in running the system. But what exactly are to be included in transaction costs? Niehans in the New Palgrave (1987) provides one answer:

> Transaction costs, like production costs, are a catch-all term for a heterogeneous assortment of inputs. The parties to a contract have to find each other, they have to communicate and to exchange information. The goods must be described, inspected, weighed and measured. Contracts are drawn up, lawyers may be consulted, title is transferred and records have to be kept. In some cases, compliance needs to be enforced through legal action and breach of contract may lead to litigation. (Niehans, 1987, p. 676)

Williamson would agree with the above, but would contend that a combination of bounded rationality and opportunism is the core cause of why transaction costs are incurred.

In the context of bilateral buyer–supplier relationships, the focus of the present study, a thorough list of transaction costs to be borne by either or both of the trading partners may look as follows.

   (a) Search costs associated with finding new trading partners. These include the cost of advertising in trade journals and displaying at or simply attending trade exhibitions.
   (b) Costs of drafting and negotiating agreements once trading partners are identified. These include costs payable to lawyers and the time spent by purchasing or marketing personnel in negotiating terms on price, quality, delivery and confidentiality. These costs are affected by the amount of paperwork necessary, which in turn depends on the extent to which oral contacts, rather than written communication, are sufficient.

33

(c) Costs associated with managing the product flow from the supplier to the buyer company. These consist of the cost of (i) holding inventories – raw materials, work-in-progress or final goods, (ii) transportation between the supplier factory and the buyer factory, (iii) monitoring delivery and rescheduling of production if delivery is not on time, and (iv) monitoring quality by inspection on delivery.

(d) Costs to service on-going trading relationships, mainly associated with inducing compliance or mutual observation of contractual terms (to attenuate opportunism). These might range from informal methods of building up the level of confidence and trust through frequent communication to formal methods of enforcement through law which may occasionally result in litigation.

(e) Costs of adjustment associated with changing business or technological conditions, which include costs involved in changing product design, in renegotiating prices and contractual terms, and in switching or not switching trading partners. These costs include emotional costs in shifting out of inertia (as pointed out by Leibenstein) as well as costs which can be imputed to time spent by engineers, sales or purchasing personnel. The relevant cost for the decision on whether or not to switch trading partners is the opportunity cost of maintaining existing trading relations.

As shown above, transaction costs encompass virtually everything besides production costs in its strictly technical sense, i.e. direct production costs attributable to factors of production. Moreover, some parts of overhead costs, including indirect labour costs payable to the salesforce, the purchasing department, or the accounts and invoicing departments, are part of transaction costs.

How can transactional efficiency be attained? One approach, taken by Williamson, is to treat the magnitude of transaction costs due to a universal propensity towards opportunism as given, and to choose an organisational form ('governance structure') which economises on them most. An alternative approach, adopted in this study, is to assume that transaction costs can be affected by the conscious action of trading partners over time. In particular, current transaction costs can be lowered by past investments into generating trust, establishing trading norms and institutions. The components (a)–(e) of transaction costs above therefore conflate elements of capital investment (TC_I) and current cost (TC_c). Arrow (1974) has been sensitive to this investment aspect of transactions. He views the cost of acquiring and processing information as involving a large irreversible capital element, due to the time and effort spent on learning the codes (e.g. unwritten rules) and channels for transmitting information (Arrow, 1974, pp. 39–43). A similar process is at work every time a new transaction commences between a customer and a supplier. The willingness to make the investment in the trading relationship depends in part on the future appropriability of returns from such investment. Because of expectations of long-term trading, OCR is endowed with better mechanisms to appropriate benefits over time than ACR. Thus, we would expect TC_I under OCR at the start of a relationship to be greater than under ACR, but a stream of benefits from past investments to lower TC_c more under OCR than under ACR

A synthesis: organisational efficiency

As discussed above, both X-efficiency and transactional efficiency address similar issues despite differences in their focus on effort and on opportunism respectively. Indeed, the two concepts of efficiency share a common tradition which differs from neoclassical economic theory in recognising that; (a) the micro-micro analysis – examining what happens within a business firm rather than treating it as a black box – is worth exploring; that (b) uncertainty and bounded rationality are realistic assumptions which shed light on individual and firm behaviour; and that (c) not all behaviour is maximising because habits, conventions, moral imperatives and norms which partially economise on bounded rationality do not depend on careful calculation.

As noted before, both X-efficiency and transactional efficiency are difficult to quantify and measure empirically, partly because they tend to be catch-all concepts, and partly because they involve unquantifiable and difficult-to-impute concepts such as effort and opportunism. Williamson wrote: 'The difficulty [of quantifying], however, is mitigated by the fact that transaction costs are always assessed in a comparative institutional way, in which one mode of contracting is compared with another. Accordingly it is the difference between, rather than the absolute magnitude of, transaction costs that matters' (Williamson 1985, pp. 21–2). Empirical studies reported in chapters 4 and 5 involve such ordinal judgments as to the relative magnitude of transaction costs incurred in ACR-type or OCR-type relationships. Moreover, chapter 11 focuses on different incentive structures which suppliers and customers face to enhance their 'organisational efficiency.'

To summarise, sources of 'organisational efficiency' are either intra-firm or inter-firm. The former may be classified further into intraplant and trade-induced elements. First, the *intraplant* element is the familiar part of X-efficiency due to incomplete labour contracts which are resolved by different firm-specific norms. For example, even with identical job descriptions, one firm may have a norm among its workers to check up and help each other out to ensure good quality performance within a work group, while another may have workers caring about their own work but not others'. Second, the *trade-induced* element of intra-firm X-efficiency may be attributed to the incompleteness of buyer–supplier contracts. For instance, a supplier may learn to produce at low costs and high quality for an important customer by paying extra attention to his production line. Third, *inter-firm* X-efficiency is about the efficiency of a pair of trading partners put together (what Aoki calls 'relational quasi-rent' (Aoki, 1988)). For example, inter-firm X-efficiency may increase over time in a trade relationship as tacit understanding emerges over the product specification and quality requirements, in price negotiation and in planning future production.

The overall 'organisational efficiency' may be achieved over time with various costs incurred along the way. The relevant costs here are not only the costs of production inputs, which are accounted for in Leibenstein's discussion of X-efficiency, but also transaction costs. The magnitude of transaction costs depends in part on how much current costs (in searching, haggling, monitoring, switching) are deemed worthwhile incurring in order to obtain low input prices. Transaction costs are also incurred for investment in building up trading norms and institutions (e.g. the suppliers' association in Japan). The assessment of 'organisational efficiency', then depends much on what past investments have been made to establish current practices. The irreversibility of such investments renders the decision over shifting along the ACR–OCR spectrum not as smooth at the margin, but subject more to high switching costs.

The Role of Trust in Buyer–Supplier Relationships

We now turn to the examination of how moral and social norms affect organisational efficiency. In particular, we focus on the concept of trust which is central to the ACR–OCR framework, and to some intermediate modes of coordination reviewed in chapter 1. Two questions are posed and discussed in this section. First, trust in buyer–supplier relations seems to bring about X-efficiency enhancing and transaction cost reducing outcomes, whereas the expectations of opportunistic behaviour have the opposite effect. Is this always the case? Second, if trust is desirable, how can it be created and sustained in business relations? Is trust a cultural predisposition in certain societies, or can it be developed intentionally? In order to help answer these questions, we begin by identifying three types of trust relevant in buyer–supplier relations, and by relating them to varying conceptualisations of trust ranging from a social norm to an organisational asset.

Three types of trust

For economists, but for the existence of imperfect information, bounded rationality, risk and uncertainty, trust would have no function to fulfill in economic transactions. This is because trust between trading partners has a role in increasing the predictability of mutual behaviour through the honouring of commitments made, while it facilitates dealing with unforeseen contingencies in a mutually acceptable manner. Thus trust economises on the costs of transaction, monitoring and insurance. None of these would have to be incurred if there were perfect information and foresight.[2] Trust is a state of mind, an expectation held by one trading partner about another, that the other behaves or responds in a predictable and mutually acceptable manner. Predictability in behaviour exists, however, for different reasons, and this allows us to distinguish between three types of trust.

First, mutual trust may exist such that each adheres to specific written or oral agreements. For want of a better label, this type of trust may be called *contractual trust* predicated on both trading partners upholding a universalistic ethical standard, namely that of keeping promises.[3] Any business transaction relies on 'contractual trust' for its successful execution. In particular, suppliers normally agree to produce and deliver ordered goods on the basis of written (or in some cases orally communicated) orders, in the expectation that they will be paid for work done within an agreed period of time after delivery. A payment period may be agreed bilaterally or may be the industry norm if it exists. Suppliers may also be entrusted, with or without a written agreement, to keep commecial secrets. Thus, promises to be kept may not always be with reference to bilaterally agreed rules but with respect to rules more generally applicable to business as a whole. Reliance on oral agreements rather than written ones is deemed to reflect more 'contractual trust'.

A second type of trust concerns the expectation of a trading partner performing its role competently. Technical and managerial competence is at issue here and this type of trust may therefore be labelled *competence trust.* In buyer–supplier relations, as in other relations, a buyer may either entrust a supplier to carry out a task which the buyer itself has the ability to carry out, or it may entrust a specialist to carry out tasks whose technicalities are outside of his capability (just as a patient trusts a doctor).[4] In either case, it has been conventional for the buyer to inspect components on delivery in order to ascertain whether they meet the stipulated quality standards or not; here the principle of *caveat emptor* applies. Increasingly, however, quality assurance by suppliers has enabled some buyers to do away with inspection on delivery, asking suppliers to practice so-called ship-to-stock delivery straight onto the buyer's assembly line. 'Competence trust' is deemed to be higher in the latter case than in the former.

The ability to distinguish between 'contractual trust' and 'competence trust' is important in buyer–supplier relations as the following scenarios illustrate. First, a supplier may fail to deliver on time. This failure may well be due to misplaced 'contractual trust', the supplier having taken on the work with the full knowledge that the capacity to complete the order on time was lacking; alternatively, it may be an unanticipated machine breakdown which the supplier has brought about due to the lack of expertise in production control. If the buyer has the relevant information to distinguish between the possible situations (which it may not), it may respond differently. The buyer may, for instance, stop trading if the cause was attributed to lack of 'contractual trust' on the grounds that it is morally unacceptable, whereas it may decide to give the supplier another chance if the cause is lack of competence which is believed to be rectifiable in the short run. Second, a buyer may cancel a substantial part of a large order at the last minute. The supplier may interpret this to be due either to the buyer's managerial incompetence in not being able to forecast demand accurately, or to pure opportunism (lack of 'contractual trust') on the buyer's part to extract a low price for a large volume which it never intended to 'call off' in full.

A third type of trust is of a more diffuse kind and refers to mutual expectations of open commitment to each other. Commitment may be defined as the willingness to do more than is formally expected. A commitment to accede to a request from a trading partner or to any observed opportunity that would improve performance is said to be open; a commitment to be responsive to a certain category of requests, but none outside of the category, is said to be limited (following the definition by Leibenstein, 1987, pp. 166–7). This trust in open commitment is labelled *goodwill trust*. The key to understanding this type of trust is that there are no explicit promises which are expected to be fulfilled, as in the case of 'contractual trust', nor fixed professional standards to be reached, as in the case of 'competence trust'. Instead, someone who is worthy of 'goodwill trust' is dependable and can be endowed with high discretion, as he can be trusted to take initiatives while refraining from unfair advantage taking.[5] In this sense, trusting behaviour consists of actions which increase one's vulnerability to another whose behaviour is not necessarily under one's control (Gambetta, 1988)

What distinguishes 'goodwill trust' from 'contractual trust' is the expectation in the former case that trading partners are committed to take initiatives (or exercise discretion) to exploit new opportunities over and above what was explicitly promised. Such 'partial gift exchange' (Akerlof, 1982) is necessary to maintain 'goodwill trust', while it suffices merely to fulfil explicit promises to sustain 'contractual trust'.

Both 'goodwill trust' and 'contractual trust' imply the absence of opportunistic behaviour; the suspicion that a trading partner may be cheating or taking advantage amounts to distrust. However, what constitutes opportunism differs according to the type of trust. For instance, withholding a vital piece of technological information which may determine the commercial success or failure of a risky project is acting opportunistically according to the 'goodwill trust' criterion, but not so according to the 'contractual trust' standard if the trading partner is not contracted to supply such information.[6]

In all cases, the verification of whether a trading partner is worthy of trust is a matter of relying partly on its reputation before entering into new relationships and partly on discovery through experience to see if the original expectation is fulfilled (Lorenz, 1988). Reputation is relied upon more often for trust of the contractual and competence types than of the goodwill sort. Because 'contractual trust' and 'competence trust' are predicated on universalistic standards, it is possible to screen for competent and promise-keeping companies by collecting information on general market reputation as well as carrying out factory audits. By contrast, 'goodwill trust' is more contextual and therefore verifiable only in particularistic settings; a buyer and a supplier have to start trading and see if they entertain shared principles of fairness and convergent mutual expectations about informal obligations.

The three types of trust identified above exist more or less in all buyer–supplier relationships. However, the extent to which each actor may wish to rely upon any of them differs from relationship to relationship. As briefly mentioned in chapter 1, both ACR and OCR rely on 'contractual trust' and 'competence trust' to make transactions run smoothly. The central difference between ACR and OCR is in 'goodwill trust' which exists only in OCR relations. In the face of uncertainty, ACR relies least on 'goodwill trust' by making contractual terms as explicit as human capacity allows, while OCR relies heavily on it for contract execution by leaving contracts incomplete. Bounded rationality may give rise to unanticipated events with which ACR traders deal by referring to universalistic normative values. By contrast, OCR traders deal with both anticipated and unanticipated contingencies by reference ultimately to particularistic affect (emotion) which may be a source of moral commitment to persevere in adverse situations.

Relation to the broader economic theory literature

Economists have known that the concept of trust is rather important in understanding industrial development and competitiveness. Exactly a century ago, J. S. Mill wrote that 'the advantage to mankind of being able to trust one another penetrates into every crevice and cranny of human life' (Mill, 1891, p. 68). More recently, Arrow asserted that: 'virtually every commercial transaction has within itself an element of trust, certainly any transaction conducted over a period of time. It can be plausibly argued that much of the economic backwardness in the world can be explained by the lack of mutual confidence' (Arrow, 1975, p. 24). Even Williamson refers, in his discussion on markets and hierarchies, to Arrow's insight that a society with a higher level of trust requires less vertical integration than one with low trust (Williamson, 1985, pp. 9, 405–6). But the concept of trust is thus far unhappily married into economics because it can be treated as residing sometimes outside, and other times within, the discourse of economic analysis.

In the existing literature, trust has been conceptualised in multiple ways, as a given preference, as a scarce resource, as an inexhaustible resource, as a capital asset, or as a commodity for which there is no market.

(i) Trust may be regarded as a *preference* (revealed through behaviour) or a *meta-preference* (based on a belief in certain values) (Hirschman, 1984) to be treated as fixed and given. Trust is a meta-preference, rather than a mere preference, which contains an affective element in the sense that there is a motivational force, a commitment to the content of the normative value (Etzioni, 1988, p. 105). Trust, particularly of the goodwill type, as a cultural predisposition is given to this interpretation. For example, Japanese buyer–supplier relationships are said to be based on high trust because businesses prefer such 'moralized trading relationships of mutual goodwill' (Dore, 1983, p. 463). In reality, social norms do not stand still. Indeed, it is possible to trace changes over time in norms underlying sub-contracting relations from short-term adversarial trading in pre-war Japan to the present obligational contracting norm. Explaining why norms shift is strictly outside the arena of economic analysis.

(ii) Trust may alternatively be treated as a *scarce resource*, but with a different degree of scarcity or abundance from country to country. Thus, in a country such as Britain which is endowed with less trust than in Japan, so the argument goes, successful businesses come to operate with a rule of thumb to economise on scarce resources, namely to rely on an institutional environment and pattern of motivation where as small a burden as possible would be placed on trust. In this discourse, the supply ('the initial endowment') of trust is assumed to be fixed and therefore ultimately depletable. The empirical question here is therefore on what institutional checks are available to control for the abundance of opportunistic behaviour (Williamson, 1985).

(iii) By contrast, trust may be regarded as a *renewable resource* or an augmentable skill (Hirschman, 1984; Gambetta, 1988). The idea here is that trust multiplies with use; it has to be lubricated continually to flourish, while it atrophies with non-use. This aspect explains why trust relations are biased towards long-term continuous trading. It also has a peculiar implication for transaction costs, in particular that a rather large amount of resources has to be expended in order to maintain trust through frequent communication and informal sharing. Just as workers within a firm engage in 'learning by doing' (Arrow 1962) to improve on their capability, buyer and supplier companies engage in 'learning by interacting' to enhance trust.

(iv) Such trust or confidence-building activities may be bilateral and specific to a particular relationship. It is in this sense that trust is predicated on the existence of a *relation-specific skill* or asset (Asanuma, 1989) which may generate 'relational quasi rent' (Aoki, 1988). Trust in this conception is an intangible capital asset owned jointly by two parties to a relationship. What is peculiar about trust, as compared to other capital assets, again giving a bias towards long-term trading, is that it may be acquired only slowly but can generally be destroyed very quickly (as distrust breeds distrust). It becomes worthwhile investing in such a capital asset as long as mutual expectations of long-term trading exist between a buyer and a supplier so that benefits from such investment can be fully appropriated.

(v) Trust in bilateral relationships may also be predicated on universalistic reputation building (Kreps, 1990; also Wintrobe and Breton, 1986, pp. 531–2). Kreps conceptualises trust as present in repeated games, in which a contract calls *ex ante* for one party to decide *ex post* how to deal with unforeseen contingencies, with the other party agreeing *ex ante* to abide by the first party's dictates. The second party's unilateral trust is honoured only because the first party vested with decision-making authority has the incentive not to abuse the trust for fear of damaged reputation and consequent loss of future trading opportunities. This presumes that the 'reputation effect' is effective in imposing sanctions on those who are short-run opportunists. An efficient way of signalling in markets that one is worthy of trust is to build a reputation for applying a consistent set of behavioural principles even if they may not be in one's self-interest in the short run. Unilateral trust which results from such reputation building may be regarded as an intangible capital asset belonging to the party with decision-making authority, like the firm *vis-à-vis* its workers. Workers' unilateral trust towards the firm is, however, fundamentally different from bilateral trust, particularly of the goodwill type. In the former, there is no managerial trust towards employees as exemplified by their being given discretion.

(vi) Lastly, trust may be treated as an *input* for which no markets exist. According to this perspective, trust cannot be readily bought or sold because the instrumental exchange orientation destroys the very basis of trust (of the goodwill sort in particular). But it is the non-instrumental aspect of trust which in part motivates people to perform above minimum prescribed levels of effort, accounting for what Leibenstein called X-efficiency (Leibenstein 1966, p. 407).

To summarise, the concept of trust remains an uneasy mix between (a) a capital asset in which people invest for self-interest and (b) a social norm. All three types of trust are composites, but 'competence trust' may be more readily approximated to the capital asset conceptualisation and 'goodwill trust' to the social norm conceptualisation.

Trust and organisational efficiency

How trust is created and sustained

Each type of trust can be created and sustained in different ways with some interaction effects. In fact, to the extent that it is sometimes difficult to verify which type of trust (or lack of it) is responsible for a particular behaviour, and to the extent that one type of trust is predicated on another, three types of trust interact in a mutually reinforcing fashion.

First, 'competence trust', as a pre-requisite for the viability of any repeated transactions, may be attained either by 'purchasing' existing competences in the marketplace or investing in creating competences. The latter may involve the customer company transferring its proprietary technology to its suppliers, or the customer and the supplier working closely to develop jointly new products or processes. The supplier company may therefore rely on internal expertise, on bringing in experts from other organisations (including competitors), or on its customer(s) to develop into a company worthy of 'competence trust'. The customer company's choice between purchasing and investment is in part affected by whether competent suppliers are readily available in the market and in part by the preferred degree of asset specificity. The option to invest, however, would only be taken up if returns from such investment are made appropriable through the creation of 'goodwill trust' relations. It will be argued later in Part III that at least since the Second World War, Japanese companies have been obliged to create competences in their suppliers by their own investments.

Next, 'contractual trust' rests on the moral norm of honesty and keeping promises which is inculcated in people through socialisation and education. This is the minimal amount of trust embodied in ethical codes – the pre-contractual base of contracts (Durkheim, 1947) – which must exist for any civil society to function. An effective threat of litigation in the event of reneging on contracts may act as a constraint on some people and companies. However, total reliance on legal sanctions, which implies zero contractual trust, would probably mean that no written or oral contracts would be exchanged. Thus, companies may exchange a confidentiality agreement before trading commences but, ultimately, the buyer has to rely on the moral integrity of the supplier in keeping its promise not to divulge commercial secrets. 'Contractual trust' therefore comes into existence because at least some actors endorse honesty and keeping promises as a moral value and let that be known through their consistently honest and promise-keeping behaviour.

Beyond the pre-contractual foundations of contracts, there are social bonds and personal networks which make one distinguish between kin,

43

friends, acquaintances and strangers. It is often asserted that people are likely to trust those they know more than they do strangers. Knowledge about other people may be through direct contact (as friends for instance), or through assumed familiarity of people from the same social class, region, country, race or sex.

Shared normative values, which may be assumed of a group of people with similar attributes, are necessary but not sufficient to create 'goodwill trust'. A particular kind of normative standard, concerning the openness of commitment and reciprocity in exchange, must be present for 'goodwill trust' to develop. People entertaining 'goodwill trust' must therefore feel comfortable enough with the norm of open commitment to use their initiative in responding to unforeseen opportunities without expecting anything in return immediately. Here, the orientation of the relationship is in maintaining an imbalance of obligations fulfilled and favours returned at any point in time, so that mutual indebtedness sustains a relationship over time. The books are kept open, rather than accounts settled at intervals. The willingness to be in someone's debt is an important signal of 'goodwill trust'; and rushing to repay a favour just received would be considered rude because it amounts to a gentle hint of one's wish to end the relationship (Ouchi, 1981, p. 87). Of course, some people's normative values are such that open commitment and a permanent state of indebtedness are onerous as they undermine autonomy and independence. People with such values would distrust anyone's attempt to cultivate 'goodwill trust'.

A relationship of indebtedness may be established between equals, e.g. friends, or between unequals, e.g. between a patron and a client (Eisenstadt and Roniger 1984). Either way, such a relationship is typified by gift exchange, as excellently portrayed by Marcel Mauss (1966). His analysis shows that gift-giving is neither purely voluntary, spontaneous nor disinterested, as the interest lies in putting people under obligation and in winning followers (Mauss, 1966, p. 73). Similar mechanisms are said to be operating in other seemingly more commercial settings, for example, in employment relations (viz. Akerlof's (1982) partial gift exchange). Some customer–supplier relationships in manufacturing also involve much unbalanced exchange of 'gifts', which may be in the form of an informal exchange of technical information over time (von Hippel, 1987) or uncosted technology transfer by the customer to the supplier in the expectation of a very open commitment by the supplier to respond flexibly to the customer's demands. If expected reciprocal responses are obtained even after a long time, companies' and individuals' self-interests are fulfilled. Purely altruistic acts are rare if not non-existent in business.

Besides the norm of reciprocity, there must be specific norms concerning power and authority, autonomy and dependence, and fairness for 'goodwill trust' to thrive. Just as in the case of labour–management relations, there is what may be called a power inequality threshold which differs from country to country. This is the threshold beyond which one party is so powerful over the other that the weaker partner feels it is being coerced to the point of questioning the legitimacy of the stronger partner's power (Fox 1985). Such excessive power inequality has serious implications for contract compliance. In this connection, Dore wrote, in his discussion on cultural differences between countries in authority relations, that 'there are differences in the degree to which any element of organisational subordination to the will of others is seen as irksome and a derogation of one's manhood' (Dore, 1985a p. 202). Such suspicion of authority biases relationships towards ACR which minimises the scope for exercising discretionary power. Moreover, trading partners may go through the motion of negotiation and bargaining because the unilateral imposition of conditions is considered counter to the spirit of individual autonomy.

Where dependence prevails over autonomy, and if the social norm of benevolence exists in authority relations, highly power-unequal relationships are rendered acceptable. Benevolence of the stronger towards the weaker partner amounts to the latter receiving protection and favours in return for loyalty in dependent relationships. Thus, the weaker partner can rely on abstinence from exploitative or opportunistic behaviour on the part of the stronger partner. It is for this reason that OCR trading partners are more willing to accept power-unequal relations than ACR partners. The stronger OCR partner has the power to dictate the terms and conditions in which trading takes place, thus saving much on transaction costs, but in turn it restrains the exercise of 'naked power' in certain directions considered unfair or unjust. For instance, it may be well within the customer's power to squeeze low prices from its supplier to the point of the supplier going bankrupt. But it may choose to temper its bargaining power even if the availability of alternative suppliers renders the loss of the current supplier not a short-run business concern. The reason for such action is due to benevolence related to a particular norm of fairness, although it may also be due to externally imposed sanctions such as damage to reputation which has long-term financial implications.

An important question is whether 'goodwill trust' in business can be created by intent or not. Opinions vary on this issue. At one extreme is the view that trust cannot be induced at will, that it is a by-product of familiarity and friendship, or of moral and religious values which prescribe honesty and mutual love (Gambetta, 1988, p. 230). Moreover, one can come to trust friends and acquaintances, but cannot intentionally cultivate friendship for the purpose of creating 'goodwill trust'. This is because instrumentality behind manifestations of friendship is likely to undermine personal bonds, involving a psychologically deeper tie than that based on cost-benefit calculations of investment. This view leads to the proposition that only those business relations which are based on strong personal networks can rely on 'goodwill trust'.

At the other extreme, the most instrumentalist position is taken by repeated game theorists, who identify the mutual expectation of repeated trading over the long run as the only incentive for cooperation (Axelrod 1984, Kreps 1990, Telser 1987). The longer the time horizon over which repeated transactions are expected to occur, the less it pays to behave opportunistically due to retaliation inherent in a 'tit for tat' strategy, and the more advantageous it becomes to risk betrayal subsequently by taking the first move to cooperate (Axelrod 1984). Cooperation, in this game theoretic approach, has little to do with 'goodwill trust' however, because it results from continuous calculation of self-interest rather than a mutual deviation from such strict cost-benefit analysis. Cooperation, Axelrod-style, is likely to promote trust in the sense of expectations in the absence of opportunistic behaviour. But the absence stems not from internalised moral commitment but from the fear of external sanctions. Where mutual distrust is prevalent, moreover, it may be difficult to create an expectation of long-term trading.

Are we to conclude that 'goodwill trust' can only be found but never created? It appears that greater optimism is warranted at least in the business field. Evidence exists, for instance, that trust and distrust are not as black and white, that relations between those who are 'neither friends nor strangers' can facilitate the creation of 'goodwill trust'. A case in point is the French sub-contractors, studied by Lorenz (1988), who created trusting relations through the practice of partnership. For instance, customer firms offer guarantees on the level of orders and prices in exchange for improved performance on quality and delivery. Frequent personal contacts between partners, facilitated by geographical proximity, allow for much exchange of information and the giving of mutual assurances. No partner is expected to give blind loyalty to another, and every partner is judged by one's consistency of behaviour over time. This business practice has bred trust, particularly in the sense of mutual expectations of neither partner behaving opportunistically. Similarly, Smitka (1989) argues that a 'governance by trust' was created intentionally by actors in developing the sub-contracting system in the Japanese automobile industry. A related notion is 'studied trust' by which Sabel (1990) refers to the possibility of creating trusting personal and business relations in previously mistrusting environments. Trust emerges if actors successfully engage in a process of 'reinterpreting their collective past, and especially their conflicts, in such a way that trusting cooperation comes to be seem a natural feature, at once accidental and ineluctable, of their common heritage' (Sabel 1990, p. 4). The contention here is that every community has in its history past models of trusting cooperation, be they in family businesses or craft trade, which can be evoked to invent their own traditions.

In comparing trust relations in British and Japanese customer–supplier relationships, Part III will examine how each type of trust came into being. The exposition will be in terms of company strategies in the light of historical circumstances, some country-specific normative values and market and economic conditions. Singling out any one factor would give a partial picture. For instance, the assertion that at all times the Japanese have been more trusting of each other than the British makes as little sense as the statement that they have always been more harmonious by nature. It will be argued that Japanese companies intentionally created 'competence trust' through technology transfer, requiring frequent and intense communication both bilaterally and through the sub-contractors' association. A byproduct of this was 'goodwill trust', propped up also by the traditional ideas of give-and-take and common destiny, giving much flexibility to the relationship. Moreover, trust of all types was enhanced in post-war Japanese business by a favourable economic climate of rapid growth which made it easier for companies at least to honour 'contractual trust'.

Implications of trust for organisational efficiency

Transactional efficiency is enhanced whenever conditions exist which promote information flows, increase effort exertion, and reduce the need to incur transaction costs associated with curbing opportunistic behaviour. All types of trust go a long way towards creating the right conditions. First, because 'contractual trust' and 'goodwill trust' encourage the disclosure of truthful information which might otherwise be withheld or distorted for self-advantage seeking, they may improve allocative efficiency. Second, monitoring costs are low because 'competence trust' enables doing away with quality inspection on delivery; so are costs of enforcement as 'contractual trust' ensures that promises are fulfilled without resorting to threats or the actual use of external sanctions. Third, open commitment in 'goodwill trust' promises a potentially high degree of effort exertion not only in routine tasks but in dynamic responses to new situations; the resulting flexibility supported by close communication enables making savings in inventory-holding. Fourth, once trading commences, costs of quantity and price nego-tiations are low because of mutual open disclosure of information concerning future business plans and costs.

Despite these beneficial aspects, trust may be detrimental to achieving total organisational efficiency, particularly in the short run, due to the high set-up costs involved. Large costs must be incurred for investment into various types of trust to obtain open-ended and difficult-to-appropriate benefits. The initial search cost to identify suppliers worthy of entering into long-term trading may also be quite high. At the same time, 'goodwill trust' can be created only through frequent and intense communication, which sometimes extends beyond that required by immediate business. Only if such investment costs are expanded can current transaction costs be lowered under OCR. At the same time, at the company level, labour turnover makes trust building through such mechanism expensive. But if a longer term perspective is taken, so that the fruit of such investment may be reaped, the lack of trust is even more costly in current transaction costs. Thus, in the transaction cost economics framework, the objective function of the firm becomes not to minimise the sum of short-run production and transaction costs, but to maximise benefits in relation to investment costs over a prescribed time period.

Trust is also a necessary but not a sufficient factor in achieving total organisational efficiency. Particularistic open commitment created by 'goodwill trust' is a powerful springboard from which to unleash effort but at the same time is prone to closing off access by outsiders to personal networks. The openness of commitment becomes operational only in the face of external pressures for competition and change, which is greater the more open access is for outsiders. The beneficial effect of trust in creating constant and reliable expectations, which are a necessary basis for flexible responses, may thus turn into excessive rigidity. Thus, much rests on how the competitive forces become translated into effective pressure (in Leibenstein's (1976) term) or 'voice' (Hirschman's (1970) word) for change and improvement. We will return to this issue in chapter 11.

PART II

Case studies and survey

3

Setting the scene

The empirical analysis in this study is focused on three customer companies and 36 supplier companies in the electronics industry in Britain and Japan. Before zooming in on these specific cases, this chapter provides an aerial view of buyer–supplier relationships in the two countries. The first section provides some definitions to enable explicit international comparisons, and discusses some country-specific notions concerning buyer–supplier relationships. The second section surveys official and other statistics on buyer–supplier and sub-contracting structures, noting differences between sectors as well as between Britain and Japan. Against this broad background, the last section describes the nature of the companies chosen for detailed investigation.

Definitions and metaphors

As the purpose of this study is to make explicit comparisons between Britain and Japan, it would be wise to (a) provide universal definitions and (b) clarify country-specific peculiarities. This should help to avoid any misunderstandings over terminology, and to confront the potential problem in international comparisons that one may be comparing apples and pears.

Definitions

Inter-firm relations may be classified into relationships between competitors and between a buyer firm and a supplier firm. In the latter case, a *buyer–supplier relation* is established whenever there is an exchange of goods or services which are produced by one party and which are of value to the other. Goods and services bought and sold may be standardised or customised.

As a sub-set of buyer–supplier relations, a *customer–supplier relation*

51

is defined as one involving the exchange of goods and services which are customised to a degree. Customisation is defined here with reference to customer-specific design, and does not necessarily imply that dedicated equipment is required for production at the supplier (cf. Williamson's (1985) asset specificity). Moreover, the question of who specifies the design is immaterial to the definition of what constitutes a customer–supplier relationship. The customer may provide drawings unilaterally (the 'detailed specification' approach); or it may approach a supplier with a rough idea of its requirements, upon which the supplier provides a drawing to be approved by the customer (the 'black box' approach). In the automobile industry, one can identify a spectrum of customised parts, ranging from those manufactured by suppliers according to drawings supplied by the assembler to those produced by suppliers whose drawings are approved by the assembler (Asanuma, 1989). The latter type of suppliers are providing expertise in design and development as well as manufacturing, while the former type concentrates on manufacturing only.

The final category, which is a sub-set of customer–supplier relationships, is a *sub-contracting relationship*. It is defined as a relationship in which a sub-contractor processes or assembles materials provided by the customer. Thus, what distinguishes sub-contractors from suppliers in general is that the former are not responsible for procuring part or all of the materials they require for productive activities. Electronic assembly houses which receive 'free-issued' materials from customers, and CMT (cut, make and trim) workshops which receive fabrics from their customers in garment-making are examples of sub-contractors. Further distinctions may be made (a) between sub-contractors which supply both labour and machinery, and those which supply labour only, and (b) between sub-contractors located at the customer's site and those at a separate site.

The empirical investigation in this book is about identifying a variety of coordinating mechanisms for customer–supplier and sub-contracting relations as defined above.

Metaphors

Next, some country-specific peculiarities in the usage of the term 'sub-contracting' and 'customer–supplier relations' will be clarified below. This task is particularly important as there are clearly some differences in what British and Japanese businessmen understand by sub-contracting and customer–supplier relations. The major sources of discrepancy between the two countries, as argued below, are (i) the

British tendency to regard outsourcing – resorting to suppliers and sub-contractors – as a supplementary and irregular overflow activity, and (ii) the Japanese tendency to link the discussion on sub-contracting inseparably with the dualistic economic structure.

Japan

Industrial dualism is in the forefront of the minds of most Japanese policy-makers, businessmen and scholars who engage in discourse on inter-firm relations. A conventional account may begin by making a distinction between 'horizontal' relations among large firms and 'vertical' relations between large and small firms. The former may be (a) relations between competitors, such as between Toyota and Nissan; or (b) relations between members of the same industrial groupings (*gurupu*), such as between Mitsubishi Electric and Mitsubishi Bank; or (c) relations between large buyers and suppliers, such as between Toshiba and Matsushita supplying each other with different types of electronic components.[1]

The latter, relations between large and small firms, may involve either buyer–supplier, customer–supplier or sub-contracting relationships. Smaller suppliers and sub-contractors are referred to in Japan as *shitauke* firms (translated most commonly as 'sub-contractors'), which are characterised by dependence on a small number of customers, and not unusually on a single customer company.[2] They are typically organised into overlapping pyramidal structures of primary, secondary, and tertiary suppliers with firm size diminishing as one goes down the hierarchy. This hierarchy headed by a large manufacturing company, such as Toyota, is known as a vertical *keiretsu*.[3]

Traditionally, an essential feature of the *shitauke* relationship in Japan, and the one which has been the prime object of scholarly inquiry amongst Japanese Marxist economists, is said to be the exploitative nature of the relationship between the customer firm and the *shitauke* firm. Marxist scholars write in terms of monopoly capital exploiting smaller *shitauke* firms, squeezing their profits by extracting low prices and treating them as buffers in business fluctuations. Low profits in turn hinder small firms from investing in modern technology, thus perpetuating the dualistic structure in the economy. Although devoid of Marxist terminology, Japanese policy-makers, until recently, had largely concurred with this analysis of the *shitauke* 'problem', and thought it necessary to curb the market power of large monopolistic firms and to provide various subsidies to help 'modernize' the small-firm sector.[4]

Such policy concern led to the formulation of the Basic Law Relating

53

to Small and Medium Enterprises (enacted in 1963) which provides a legal definition of industrial *shitauke* firms. They are defined as small or medium enterprises (abbreviated henceforth as SMEs, defined as those employing less than 300 or capitalised at less than 100 million yen) which receive a manufacturing or repairing contract from large enterprises. An SME qualifies as a *shitauke* firm even if only part of its business is in receiving such a contract. Based on this legal definition, the Small and Medium Enterprise Agency conducts a survey (*Kogyo Jittai Kihon Chosa*) every five years. The surveys have shown that just over half of manufacturing SMEs are *shitauke* firms. Particularly high proportions of *shitauke* firms are to be found in textiles (84.9 per cent), clothing (86.5 per cent), electrical engineering (85.3 per cent), and transport equipment (87.7 per cent) (the percentages are for 1981). Moreover, the overall use of *shitauke* firms by customer firms has increased during the 1971–81 period although the figures for individual sectors are more volatile. In fact, the proportion of manufacturing *shitauke* firms has increased from 53.2 per cent in 1966 to 58.7 per cent in 1971 to 60.7 per cent in 1976 to 65.5 per cent in 1981 (Aoki 1985, p. 26), but fell to 56.6 per cent in 1987 (EAP 1990, p. 506).

This legal definition is deficient in a number of ways, even for the purpose which the Japanese policy on SMEs has set out to achieve. First, it draws an arbitrary line between large firms and SMEs, so that customer–supplier and sub-contracting relationships among large firms and among SMEs are not part of the legal definition of *shitauke* trading. Secondly, *shitauke* firms may supply standardised or customised parts as long as they are SMEs, so that they may be engaged in buyer–supplier relations of any sort. In short, the *shitauke* definition is both too narrow (because firm size is used as the defining characteristic) and too broad (as nothing else besides firm size, such as the degree of customisation of products exchanged, is made explicit). Lastly, it is not appropriate to assume that SMEs in all *shitauke* relations suffer from factors associated with the small-firm sector in the theory of dualism, such as limited access to modern technology, managerial expertise, skilled labour and capital markets.

For this last reason, and because an increasing proportion of sub-contractors are thought to be becoming technologically stronger (as attested by various surveys by the Small and Medium Enterprise Agency), the term *shitauke* is considered by some to be less and less appropriate in Japan today. For example, H. Nakamura (1985) prefers to label the majority of *shitauke* firms, particularly in engineering, as 'specialist processing firms' (*senmon kako kigyo*), and to call more independent firms which have grown out of the *shitauke* status as

54

'mid-sized firms' (*chuken kigyo*). Nakamura's need to make such a point reflects how much the discussion is entrenched in the language of modernisation. His indignation has been directed at those who refer to all SMEs as *shitauke* firms, which are considered technologically backward and stagnant. Far from being a sector holding back modernisation, in his view, the SME sector has been the engine of entrepreneurship, innovativeness and independence. A belated endorsement of such a view appears to have come from Japanese policy-makers who, in the light of the international acclaim accorded to the Toyota production system, now regard *shitauke* relationships as not a problem but a virtue underlying Japanese competitiveness (SMEA, 1986, p. 64; see also EPA 1990).

Prior to such a change in tone among policy-makers, large company businessmen tended to shun the use of the term *shitauke* for its pejorative connotation. Instead, they have come to refer to SME suppliers as *kyoryoku gaisha* (cooperating company) since the late 1950s (Sato, 1980) in order to highlight the mutually cooperative atmosphere of firms working towards a common goal. In this context, Japanese businesses have been comfortable with the image of paternalism in which the buyer company, referred to as a patron or parent, nurtures its *shitauke* firm as a child, e.g. by transferring technology and offering financial help. Such a parent–child metaphor has been acceptable as long as it is based on unequal yet mutual dependence and obligatedness over time rather than unilateral exploitation. But, more recently, the language used in industry appears to be changing from that of paternalism towards that of equal partners (SMEA, 1989, p. 101). This transformation may be attributed to the fact that buyer companies are said no longer to wish to carry the full burden of looking after their suppliers, and therefore encourage suppliers to diversify their customer base and to acquire technology of their own accord.

To summarise, the discourse in Japan on buyer–supplier relationships has been coloured by a concern for dualism and modernisation, and has tended to focus on relations between large and small firms. The legal definition of *shitauke* creates a clear operational framework for government policy, which in turn affects the way the purchasing departments of large companies classify their suppliers into large component makers and SME suppliers. The legal definition, however, remains deficient for our present purpose, which is not to make firm size the sole concern in our empirical investigation.

Britain

Matters are quite different in Britain. In comparison with Japan, there is no legal definition of sub-contracting; nor is there much recognition of

55

the fact that the survival of small firms in many cases depends on forging healthy trading relationships with large firms. This has not been a matter of concern until recently, as Britain does not have a large small-firm sector, nor does it have a pronounced dualistic structure in the economy.

Buyer companies in Britain often use the terms 'suppliers', 'sub-contractors' and 'vendors' interchangeably. An electronic assembly house may therefore be known as a sub-contractor by some companies but as a vendor or a supplier by others. However, the term 'sub-contracting' has its traditional use when there exists a prime contractor, in most cases in government procurement contracts and in construction projects. For example, prime contractors to the Ministry of Defence may commission part of the contract to sub-contractors. Similarly, a main contractor in a construction project typically resorts to sub-contracting on either a labour-only or a 'supply and fix' (in which a sub-contractor supplies the necessary materials as well as labour) basis. The steel industry also has had contractors who in turn sub-contract to smaller firms.

In areas outside defence contracting, construction and steel, the term 'sub-contractors' is often encountered in garment making, in particular to refer to companies which undertake CMT (cut, make and trim) operations on cloth provided by their customer company. CMT sub-contractors may be workshops with company status or self-employed individuals more commonly known as outworkers or homeworkers, whose low wages and bad working conditions conjure up the image of exploitation (Rainnie, 1984).

Lastly, the term 'sub-contractors' rather than 'suppliers' tends to be used in Britain for operations which are regarded either (a) as a temporary overspill due to internal capacity constraints, or (b) as peripheral non-core activities. Examples of the latter include such activities as cleaning and catering. Thus, 'sub-contracting', in its most recent usage of the term, focuses on the cost reduction brought about by the numerical flexibility it entails (Atkinson and Meager 1986).

At the same time that 'sub-contractors' are regarded as agents to be hired and fired at will, there are moves within British manufacturing towards the buyer company developing longer-term closer relationships with a selected few suppliers.[5] There is a recognition that in order to emulate the Japanese example of consistently high quality, buyer companies must turn their traditionally adversarial relationships (in which a hard bargain is struck) into more cooperative partnerships (in which buyers and core suppliers perceive common goals).[6] The child-rearing metaphor has not quite entered the British scene, although recently some

British suppliers refer to seeing through a buyer's product development project from beginning to end as taking a trading partner 'from cradle to grave'. An alternative metaphor of longer standing for British business is that of lovers and marriages. As a supplier is wont to say 'I've been trying to get into bed with X for some time now': the supplier is likened here to a seductive lover attempting to hook someone. If successful, marriage ensues, but the possibility of stormy exits and divorce are not ruled out; neither are one-night stands from time to time.

In sum, both Britain and Japan have their own sets of imagery about buyer–supplier relationships, which are interesting in themselves. But they also reflect the types of behaviour which are considered acceptable or unacceptable by trading partners, and the kinds of future expectations one may entertain of the other, as we shall see in the later chapters.

Statistical evidence on buyer–supplier relations

Having defined buyer–supplier, customer–supplier, and sub-contracting relations, this section examines the incidence of each type of inter-firm relationships at aggregated levels. There is an inevitable bias towards examining industrial structures only, but such analysis is deemed worthwhile in order to provide an overall background on buyer–supplier relations in Britain and Japan. The evidence in this section is confined to the manufacturing sector because the readily available official statistics address that sector only. In 1987, manufacturing output accounted for 29 per cent of GDP in Japan and 23 per cent of GDP in Britain.

Evidence on buyer–supplier relations

One indicator of the extent of buyer–supplier relations is the ratio of bought-in material costs to total sales. This is just the reverse of a commonly used measure of vertical integration, namely the ratio of value-added to sales. The BSO's Census of Production and MITI's Industrial Statistics (*Kogyo Tokei Hyo*) provide reasonably comparable monetary figures for calculating the ratios. Because both countries' census data take establishments as the unit of analysis, the evidence presented below concentrates on the extent of vertical disintegration of plants, not of enterprises.

For manufacturing as a whole, the ratio of bought-in material costs to total sales has been greater in Japan (at 65.9 per cent in 1985) than in Britain (at 58.1 per cent). The inter-country difference is also evident in the ratio of bought-in material costs to total input costs, at 83.5 per cent in Japan compared to 76.0 per cent in Britain in 1985.[7] Over time, the ratios of bought-in materials to sales have declined in both countries in the 1960s until the early 1970s, from 64.2 per cent in 1958 to 58.2 per cent in 1973 in Britain, and from 71.0 per cent in 1958 to 63.3 per cent in 1973 in Japan. Since the early 1970s, however, there has been a very slight tendency for the ratio of bought-in materials to increase, up to 59.7 per cent in 1978 in Britain and up to 67.4 per cent in 1981 in Japan. But no clear trend towards vertical disintegration is evident at this aggregated level.

The ratio of bought-in material costs to total sales also differs according to firm size. It is greater the larger the firm size in Japan except in very large firms (see Figure 3.1). This pattern is less pronounced in Britain. The Japanese aggregate pattern is accentuated in certain sectors, particularly in the engineering and transport-equipment sectors. In the mechanical engineering and electrical and electronic engineering sectors, the inverted U shape curve, indicating the tendency for less in-house production with greater firm size but increased in-house production beyond a certain size, is also observable in both Japan and Britain. The shape of the British and Japanese curves in the transport equipment sector is also very similar, with a tendency for greater vertical disintegration beyond a certain firm size. In all sectors, the extent of bought-in materials is greater for all firm sizes in Japan than in Britain.

Evidence on sub-contracting

Next, the statistics on sub-contracting are compared. The Japanese data on the cost of sub-contracting is more of an uncontaminated indicator as it includes the cost of work done on materials supplied by the establishment only. The British item in the census, 'cost of industrial services received', overstates the amount of sub-contracting (as defined earlier), because it unfortunately contains other work done besides sub-contract manufacturing, such as repair and maintenance of machinery and plant, which cannot be disaggregated (because the census asks surveyed firms to give the data in this composite form).

Ignoring the above difficulty, the ratio of the cost of sub-contracting to total sales for the manufacturing sector as a whole was over twice as high in Japan, at 6.39 per cent, as in Britain, at 2.88 per cent, in 1984. This pattern of Japanese firms relying more heavily on sub-contracting than British firms applies to all major sectors in which sub-contracting is commonly deemed to take place (see Table 3.1). The Japanese–British differences are remarkable particularly in the apparel and textile

Setting the scene

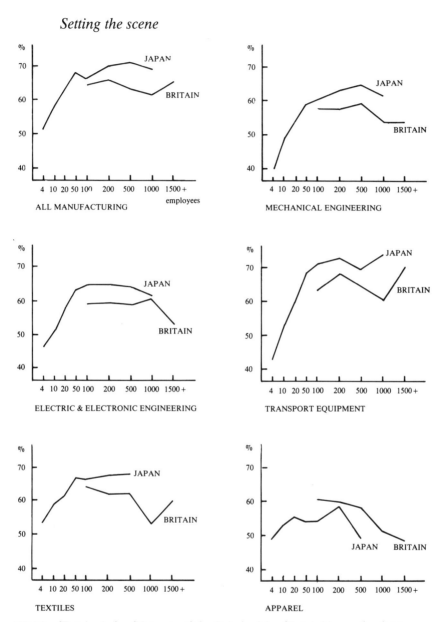

NB M = (Total sales) – (Net output) for Britain; M = (Total shipment) – (Value added) for Japan; S = Total sales or total shipment.
Sources: BSO *Census of Production* PA1002; MITI *Kogyo Tokei Hyo* (Industrial Statistics).

Figure 3.1 Extent of bought-in materials 1983.

Table 3.1. *Sub-contracting in manufacturing, by sector 1984*

	Japan	Britain
Sector	SJ/TS	SB/TS
Textiles	12.93	3.28
Apparel	20.97	3.45
Mechanical engineering	12.59	4.70
Electrical and electronic engineering	8.97	2.65
Transport equipment	5.91	1.72
All manufacturing	6.39	2.88

SJ = Cost of work done on materials supplied by the establishment; SB = Cost of industrial services received; TS = Total sales
Sources: MITI *Kogyo Tokei Hyo* (Industrial Statistics); BSO *Report on the Census of Production* Summary Tables.

industries, followed by the electrical and electronic engineering and transport-equipment industries.

Over time, the extent of sub-contracting has increased in Japan, from 4.05 per cent in 1976 to 6.57 per cent in 1986. Although there has been a marginal increase in sub-contracting in Britain also, from 2.61 per cent in 1976 to 3.01 per cent in 1985, it would be very tenuous to infer the British time trend from the 'cost of industrial services received' because of the composite nature of the measure. An alternative source for gauging the time trend in British sub-contracting is a set of surveys conducted to see if manpower flexibility has increased, in accordance with the 'flexible firm' approach, to meet uncertain and fluctuating demands (Atkinson and Meager 1986; CBI 1985 and 1989; Manpower Limited 1985; Marginson et al. 1988; Rajan and Pearson 1986). In these surveys, estimates of the proportion of firms which had increased, or intended to increase, contracting out in the 1980s varied from 23 per cent to 85 per cent. Unfortunately, however, the surveys focus mainly on sub-contracting in service activities such as catering, cleaning, security, transport and maintenance, and therefore do not give a clear indication of whether sub-contracting in component processing and assembly has also increased.

To summarise, official statistics and other survey evidence in Britain and Japan indicate that more vertical disintegration and sub-contracting exist in all industrial sectors in Japan than in Britain. Over time, the use of sub-contracting in the manufacturing sector appears to have increased in Japan, while less reliable evidence of increased manpower flexibility

60

exists in Britain for recent years. Useful though it is to examine the nationwide or industry-wide extent of buyer–supplier relations, it is not thereby possible to gauge the variations which exist in the mode of trading relationships. It is to this 'qualitative' rather than purely quantitative aspect of buyer–supplier relations to which we turn in the next two chapters.

Three customer companies and thirty-six suppliers

In order to obtain a balanced picture, both customer and supplier firms were visited, just as one might document management and labour sides of an event separately. Moreover, the promise of anonymity is believed to have enhanced the overall accuracy and balance in interviewees' accounts of bad as well as good experience. Since each company trades with more than one company, only some relationships were fully examined as two-sided stories, while one-sided stories, though suffering from possible bias, are reported where they impart some information of interest.

The three case studies to be described in chapter 4 are largely one-sided stories from the customer company's viewpoint, supplemented by some two-sided stories. The first case is a Japanese company in Japan, which we will refer to as 'JJ Electric'. The second case is a British company in Britain, referred to as 'GB Electronics'. The third is a Japanese company located in Britain, Toshiba Consumer Products (UK) Limited, TCP for short, from which permission was granted to disclose the company name after all interviews were complete. There is no parent-subsidiary connection between JJ Electric and TCP. JJ Electric and GB Electronics were chosen so as to match their size and product range as closely as possible. The two-way comparison enables the examination of differences in company strategy concerning make-or-buy decisions and procurement philosophy which is applied to manufacture similar products. The addition of TCP for a three-way comparison provides an opportunity to assess the limits to transferring 'Japanese-style' procurement practices in Britain.

The three companies belong to the electronics industry. The present study looked only at this sector partly to make a one-person research project manageable, and partly to focus on an industry with much use of suppliers and sub-contractors, which was perhaps less well researched and documented than the automobile industry. The electronics industry is similar to the car industry in its openness to global competition, but is messier to study due to a much broader product range.

Prices, quality and trust

The sample of thirty-six suppliers and sub-contractors to be analysed in chapter 5 belong to one of the two narrowly defined industrial sectors which served a range of final goods sectors including the consumer, telecommunication, data processing and defence segments of the electronics industry. These sectors are namely electronic assembly and the manufacture of bare printed circuit boards (PCBs). They were selected because of the customised nature of components exchanged, which renders the smooth coordination of production between companies their central concern.

Each of the sample suppliers and sub-contractors was visited at least once for a semi-structured interview during 1986–9, and was asked to fill in a questionnaire on business ethics (see Appendix) registered in 1989. The most likely respondents were sales managers and managing directors. No claim can be made to having a statistically representative sample. But in order to discover as diverse a range of different customer–supplier relationship patterns as possible in each sector in each country, the following steps were taken when selecting companies for interviews. First, various sources were used to contact potential companies for study. They included trade association membership lists, newspaper articles, trade journal advertisements, academic researchers carrying out research in similar fields, NEDO and its relevant little Neddies in Britain, and the National Sub-contracting Firms Promotion Association (*Shitauke kigyo shinko kyokai*) and its local offices in Japan. Second, attempts were made to select from the largest to the smallest sized firms. Although there is no literature which addresses the issue of how firm size affects the nature of trading relationships, it was conjectured that it influenced a company's relationship with other firms via its internal organisation structure and the resources it could command.

The suppliers and sub-contractors will be identified in terms of their size, country of location and sector (see Table 3.2). Size is taken to be the total of both regular and non-regular, full-time and part-time, workers employed in the relevant division of the company, excluding on-site sub-contractors' employees. In the table, J refers to a Japanese company and B to a British one. The number following the letter is the number of workers at the factory engaged in the relevant sector of study at the time of the interview. The letters in brackets which follow the country and size codes identify the sector: PCB refers to the printed circuit board manufacturing sector and EA to the electronic assembly sector. The figures in brackets in the second column are the total number of employees of the company as a whole, some companies being multi-

Table 3.2. *The suppliers and sub-contractors in the sample*

Company	Employees	Established	Company	Employees	Established
B38(PCB)	38	1976	J17(PCB)	17	1980
*B50(PCB)	50	1979	J65(PCB)	110	1970
B107(PCB)	107	1967	*J120(PCB)	120(285)	1947
B118(PCB)	118	1983	J140(PCB)	140(237)	1961
*B120(PCB)	120	1966	+J150(PCB)	150	1945
*B203(PCB)	203	1974	J220(PCB)	220	1958
B222(PCB)	222(350)	1965	J480(PCB)	480	1958
*B300(PCB)	300	1961	J650(PCB)	650	1948
B410(PCB)	410	1969	J700(PCB)	700(1400)	1945
B500(PCB)	500	1985	J1210(PCB)	1210	1961
B10(EA)	10	1985	J30(EA)	30(630)	1951
B15(EA)	15	1979	J71(EA)	71	1970
B90(EA)	90	1974	J160(EA)	160	1978
B205(EA)	205	1967	J170(EA)	170	1976
*B230(EA)	230	1974	*J240(EA)	240	1980
B350(EA)	350	1981	+J250(EA)	250	1968
B750(EA)	750	1984	J265(EA)	265	1964
*B1100(EA)	1100	1977	+J360(EA)	360	1974

N.B. $^+$ = shareholding by major customer company
* = part of a group

establishment or multi-divisional. The date in the third column refers to the founding date of the company with direct lineage.

All sample British companies are private limited companies with the exception of B410(PCB) and B203(PCB) which are publicly quoted. In the Japanese sample, excepting J1210(PCB) which became recently quoted on the Tokyo Stock Exchange, all others are private limited companies of the *kabushiki gaisha* type. Most are independent companies except for the following. J250(EA) and J360(EA) are wholly owned subsidiaries of their major customers, while J150(PCB) is partially owned by its major customer company. B500(PCB) used to be a wholly owned subsidiary of GB Electronics but was sold off in 1986, while B38(PCB) became a wholly owned subsidiary of a larger PLC in 1989. B50(PCB), B120(PCB), B300(PCB), B230(EA), and B110(EA) belong to their respective group with a holding company; in fact, B300(PCB) and B230(EA) are part of the same electronics-related group which consists of twenty-six companies. J120(PCB) and J240(EA) are part of a loose grouping of thirty-six competing firms all engaged in either

PCB design, manufacturing or assembly but without a holding company as such (see chapter 10 for more details).

In the PCB industry sample, most companies specialise in the manufacture of PCBs, but some are also engaged in other activities: e.g. assembly work in the case of B222(PCB), J140(PCB), and J650(PCB); plating for watches at J700(PCB); name plates at J150(PCB); and metal assembly, welding and painting at J120(PCB). The fact that many more of the Japanese PCB manufacturers are engaged in other activities compared to the British sample is a reflection of their older founding dates and the legacy of their original line of business before they decided to diversify into the growing area of PCBs in the 1960s.

Although PCBs may become part of a diverse range of products, the process of manufacturing PCBs is similar in all companies with slight variations according to the type of boards. By contrast, electronic assembly involves some considerable variations in components being assembled. The core of the electronic assembly companies' business is the manual and/or automatic insertion of electronic components onto PCBs (the exceptions to this being B90(EA) and B350(EA) whose main business was in wiring harness assembly). But many were also engaged in unit assembly of other larger components (such as metal and plastic casings) or even in final goods assembly.

4

The three customer companies

This chapter gives an overview of the customer-supplier and sub-contracting relationships from the perspective of three customer companies, namely JJ Electric in Japan, GB Electronics in Britain, and Toshiba Consumer Products (UK) Limited (TCP). All three companies have survived in a changing market and technological environment by adapting strategies in various areas including supplier relations. Some attempts are made to trace changes over time, but the description remains largely a snap-shot at a point in time, *circa* late 1980s. Is JJ Electric characterised by more long-term obligational (OCR) supplier relations than GB Electronics? Is TCP's practice closer to that of JJ Electric or GB Electronics? Is JJ Electric becoming more arm's length (ACR) in its dealings with suppliers in order to cope with uncertain demand and currency fluctuations? At the same time, is GB Electronics becoming more OCR in order to survive in global competition? Answers to these questions will unravel in the course of this chapter.

JJ Electric

Background[1]

JJ Electric is a company of considerable size, but by no means the largest in the electrical and electronics industry in Japan. The company employs around 38,000 regular workers and had a total sales turnover of just over 2000 billion yen (approximately £9 billion at £1 = ¥230) in the 1986/7 financial year. Like several of its competitors, JJ Electric has a diversified product range, which includes computers, telecommunications equipment, industrial electronic equipment, electronic components, and consumer goods.[2]

Despite such diversification in the post-war period, a good 50 per cent of the company's business in the mid-1960s was for the publicly owned

65

telephone monopoly, Denden Kosha, which tended to give priority to the maintenance of high quality over the achievement of lower costs. With the liberalisation of the Japanese telecommunications market since 1987, JJ Electric has had to accept lower profit margins for orders from recently privatised NTT, which constitutes around 12 per cent of its total sales. Recently, the company's product strategy has been focused on the integration of telecommunication and data processing based on a common digital technology.

Organisation structure

The current organisation structure of JJ Electric can best be understood in a historical perspective. The company headquarters is located in central Tokyo near the factory site where the company was originally founded at the turn of the century. This ex-factory site is now one of the six 'divisional sites' (*jigyojo*), most of which were built in the neighbouring prefectures of Kanagawa and Chiba during the expansion period of the 1960s. Until recently they had undertaken much manufacturing themselves. The HQ and the six divisional sites constitute the core body (*hontai*) of JJ Electric company.

In the 1980s, the pressure to expand production came into acute conflict with space shortages aggravated by high land prices. Consequently, a major part of JJ Electric's production has been shifted to its subsidiaries, while the divisional sites retain the administrative (including purchasing) and product-development functions. There are twenty-three such subsidiary factories all over Japan, most of which were newly built by JJ Electric. They tend to be located away from big cities, in north-east and west Japan, where land prices and labour costs are relatively low. The subsidiaries, for the moment, undertake production only, while design and development, the selection of suppliers, and price negotiations continue to be largely the responsibility of divisional sites. But JJ Electric has begun to give the production subsidiaries greater autonomy in decisions over product development and the choice of their own suppliers and sub-contractors. In so doing, JJ Electric intends to encourage the twenty-three subsidiaries to bid for work from the divisional sites.

Organisation of purchasing

In 1986/7, JJ Electric spent just over £4 billion (¥1000 billion at £ = ¥230) on materials and components, which accounted for around 65 per cent of the total production cost. JJ Electric coordinates the spending of this sum through a central purchasing department at the HQ, which directly oversees the purchasing departments at the six divisional sites. One merit of centralisation in purchasing is that divisional sites and subsidiaries benefit from low prices which come with bulk buying of integrated circuits (ICs) and raw materials. There are no fewer than 50 suppliers of ICs to JJ Electric (including an in-house supply which satisfies 50 per cent of JJ Electric's total needs). Multiple sourcing from five to six suppliers is normal practice for standard memory chips.

The procurement of other components is decentralised to the level of divisional sites. The divisional purchasing department is responsible for carrying out vendor appraisals for new suppliers, while the HQ formally approves each appraisal. For every new product model, the prototype and the first production batches are manufactured at the divisional site. After that stage, suppliers deliver direct to the subsidiary factory where mass production takes place. As the subsidiary companies increasingly undertake product development work, more direct links are expected to grow between subsidiary factories and suppliers.

Suppliers and sub-contractors

There are 1500 regular material and component suppliers to JJ Electric proper (i.e. the HQ and the six divisional sites). Another 1500 provisional suppliers receive one-off orders no more frequently than once or twice a year. The central purchasing department estimates that a total of 7000 to 8000 suppliers exist if supplies to the subsidiary factories are also taken into account. As it is beyond the scope of the present study to examine relationships involving all these suppliers, we focus on three sites, namely Site A (a divisional site), Site B (another divisional site), and Site C (a subsidiary factory). At times, the analysis may focus further on particular sections at these sites.

Site A
Site A, established in 1982, manages the telephone exchanges and terminals activity group. It employs around 3000 workers, most of whose job functions are in product design and development, prototype production, purchasing, and production control. The actual production of private exchanges (PBXs) and terminals (key telephones and telephones) is undertaken by subsidiary factories (including Site C which makes PBXs).

Site A's terminals section relies on 80 component suppliers to procure most (95 per cent in 1987) of the 150 component types ('part numbers') which make up a telephone. The rest of the components are procured directly by the subsidiary factory which manufactures telephones. There is a plan to increase this direct local sourcing by the subsidiary from 5 per cent in 1987 to 70 per cent of total components by spring 1988 in order to shorten leadtime from ordering to delivery. The competition JJ Electric faces in this market is stiff, particularly as its monthly production of 100,000 telephones and 2000 key telephone systems is relatively low, giving JJ Electric a domestic market share of 10 per cent or less in key telephones and a mere 2–3 per cent for simple telephones. Even after privatisation, NTT holds a 60 per cent market share in simple telephone handsets, which are procured from a pool of 300 or so Japanese manufacturers, many of which are medium-sized.

At Site A as a whole, there are around thirty assembly sub-contractors which the site has had ever since the production of exchanges first began at JJ Electric's oldest factory. Among these *kyoryoku kojo* ('cooperating factories'), five undertake final assembly of telephones for the JJ Electric terminals section, of which one supplies exclusively for JJ Electric; 60 per cent of JJ Electric's telephones are produced in-house at a subsidiary factory, while the rest are assembled either at the five sub-contractors or are commissioned on an OEM basis to other companies.

Site B
Established in 1964, Site B is the second largest divisional site in terms of workers numbering over 6000, and consists of three activity groups: the production technology development group, the wireless group, and the data-processing group. The data-processing group at the site is divided into five sections, among which the Second OA (office automation) Section handles the production planning of office and personal computers, word processors and office terminals. There are around 120 companies supplying components for the section, some directly to the three subsidiary factories (including Site C) assembling the final products.

Site B's OA Section also makes use of two final assembly subcontractors both of which have been trading with JJ Electric for over thirty years. One subcontractor employs 600; its founder used to be a JJ Electric employee, who left to set up his own company in 1947/8. This company remains 100 per cent dependent on JJ Electric for its business. The other company, employing 300, is also more or less totally dependent on JJ Electric, although it has a small embryonic own-brand business.

The reasons behind JJ Electric resorting to final assembly sub-contractors have changed over time. In the early 1960s, the company attempted to do as much work in-house as possible to control quality. But the pressure of rapid growth in production made it impossible to keep up with recruiting good quality labour at the same rate; hence the need to identify sub-contractors who had the potential for being successful recipients of technical guidance. To an extent, the same growth pressure is still present in the 1980s in certain sections of JJ Electric, for instance in telecommunications where output has been growing at 15 per cent per annum, or in the Second OA Section whose sales doubled between 1985 and 1986 due to the popularity of its 16-bit personal computers.

What is novel in the 1980s, however, is that more and more product development is carried out jointly by JJ Electric and its final assembly sub-contractors. Despite JJ Electric's capacity to attract the best among new science and engineering graduates, it cannot recruit a sufficient number of technologists of a uniformly high calibre, particularly into product development – regarded as a second best to basic R&D. This, as well as risk-sharing considerations, led to sub-contracting out some of the product development work. To achieve this end, JJ Electric is in the process of educating sub-contractors not only in production technology as in the past, but also in product development so that in the future they will be able to undertake more advanced development tasks.

From the sub-contractors' viewpoint, securing orders is no longer just a matter of offering cheap and good quality labour, assembling goods to the customer's specification and delivering them on time. Sub-contractors which remain specialised in manufacturing are destined to receive orders for older models with tapering batch sizes and declining profit margins. To avoid this fate, they must aspire to participate in product development so that they can win orders for new models.

Site C
Site C, a subsidiary factory, is under pressures similar to those which the assembly sub-contractors face. In order to obtain a headstart in the bidding process against the other subsidiary factories, Site C has engaged in own product development which already accounts for over 60 per cent of its total output. One reason for this favourable record lies in its history. Site C was originally a joint venture company between a local metalworking company and JJ Electric, established in 1944 to produce magnets and later coils for crossbar switches. By the time JJ Electric took over the site as its 100 per cent subsidiary in 1982, there was already a competent team of technologists who were engaged in product develop-

ment. Unlike other subsidiaries, which were created and nurtured in the lap of one JJ Electric activity group, Site C developed a strategy for self-help with no section taking care of it.

In fact, Site C, which employs around 1000 workers, deals with 11 different sections of various activity groups, most of which are based at Sites A and B. At any time thirteen different product types are manufactured at Site C, ranging from portable computers, facsimile machines and PBXs. Because each divisional site assigns its own favourite long-standing suppliers to Site C, there are in total 420 suppliers trading with the site. Local control over procurement is progressing as Site C pays out 70 per cent of its total purchasing expenditure directly to the suppliers. However, only 12 per cent of the suppliers are located near Site C in northern Japan, while the rest are in the Tokyo metropolitan area where local expertise in mechanical and electrical engineering is more readily available. Site C plans to increase the number of local suppliers by engaging in technical guidance for local suppliers.

Technological *reberu appu* (levelling up) of small and medium-sized firms has been declared in the White Paper on Small and Medium Enterprises (SMEs) over the years to be a major objective of Japanese policy. For some, the consequent closing up of the technological gap between large and small companies also implies independence. What does a company like JJ Electric intend for its SME suppliers and sub-contractors?

Transactional dependence

JJ Electric, in fact, is not overly concerned with the high transactional dependence of some of its suppliers and sub-contractors. A major reason for this is its diverse product range which enables some sub-contractors, which are close to 100 per cent dependent on JJ Electric as a whole, to benefit from the same risk-spreading effect as if they traded with JJ Electric and some of its competitors. A reduction in orders from one divisional site may be accompanied by an increase in orders from another, sometimes by chance because of differential product growth. But, more often than not, it happens because the purchasing departments of different divisions talk to each other out of a concern for making the overall order level from JJ Electric to a particular supplier as smooth as possible. One instance of this occurred when a divisional site asked the production manager at Site B's Second OA Section if he would make use of a PCB supplier (J650(PCB)) which would soon be left with some spare

70

capacity as orders from that site had to be reduced. Today, although the value of orders from Site B far exceeds that from the other site, J650(PCB) still belongs to the other site's suppliers' association and not Site B's. Old allegiance seems to die hard.

In reality, JJ Electric's 600 SME *shitauke* suppliers (out of the total of 1500 suppliers) were said to be on average 60 per cent dependent on JJ Electric's business. However, the degree of dependence varied significantly from supplier to supplier, and from component to component. At Site A, for example, the Terminal Section used four plastic injection moulding suppliers; 60 per cent of the total sectional need was satisfied by an SME supplier which was 30–50 per cent dependent on that section. The others were 30 per cent dependent, 5–10 per cent dependent and lastly less than 1 per cent dependent in the case of a large supplier which belonged to the same corporate grouping (*kigyo shudan*) as JJ Electric.

There were four suppliers of PCBs for the respective section at Sites A, B and C, of which one at all the sites was an internal source of supply, namely one of the twenty-three subsidiary factories. Of the Second OA Section's total PCB requirement, 55 per cent was said to be satisfied internally, while 35 per cent was supplied by J650(PCB) (which is 85 per cent dependent on JJ Electric). The rest (10 per cent) were sourced from two suppliers making prototype PCBs, J120(PCB) and J700(PCB), 55 per cent and 15 per cent dependent on JJ Electric as a whole.

JJ Electric no longer likes exclusive supply from suppliers and sub-contractors as it wishes to be morally less obligated to look after them in the downturn. An exception to this general rule was the case of some final assembly sub-contractors which were trusted not to disclose confidential technical and commercial information by virtue of their guarantee of exclusive supply. Site C's purchasing manager said that he would think twice before putting out some assembly tasks had his four main sub-contractors been taking orders from JJ Electric's direct competitors.

Procedure for placing orders

One major reason why all the PCBs are not sourced in-house is to ensure the presence of market stimulus. The procedure for allocating orders is neither complete open bidding nor straight commission. As a general rule, price quotations for new part numbers are sought from a handful of suppliers, two or three at Site A and four or five at Site C. Typically, a particular design drawing is shown to at least two suppliers. This is considered necessary in order for JJ Electric to appear even-handed and fair in the eyes of suppliers. What determines who gets an order is not just the price but also quality which tends to be taken for granted, and delivery which depends on how busy a supplier is. The production control manager has a very good idea of which suppliers are overloaded and which ones have spare capacity. The same supplier receives repeat orders in most cases where agreed price reductions were deemed satisfactory.

Another mode of ensuring that 'market forces' are at play, namely multiple or dual sourcing (i.e. splitting a part number to more than one supplier), is rarely exercised in the Terminals Section. This is because sufficient competitive pressure is exerted at the time of price negotiation and because of the short lifetime of a model (usually one a year) which makes multiple sourcing costly to manage. The Second OA Section, by contrast, resorts to dual sourcing commonly for large batches. Two PCB vendors typically receive orders for a part number split into varying ratios of 50:50, 40:60 or 30:70, where one of the suppliers is likely to be the in-house source.

Projected length of trading

With suppliers and sub-contractors which JJ Electric regards as satisfactory, the working assumption in trading is that the relationship will continue without any break. Thus, when JJ Electric says that some of its suppliers and sub-contractors have been trading with it for the last twenty or thirty years, it means that there has rarely been a single six-month period in the past when they did not receive any orders at all. In this connection, JJ Electric's concern to smooth out the level of orders to SME suppliers was noted earlier.[3] Even in dire situations of low demand, sub-contractors are said to ask JJ Electric not to make the order value nil. They wish to continue trading even if it means 1 per cent of what JJ Electric requires. With no orders, a sub-contractor cannot even come in through JJ Electric's main gate. But with just a tiny amount of business, there is always a chance for it to collect snippets of information on future trends and to appeal for an increase in future order quantity.

Given the norm of long-term continuous trading, a mere cyclical fluctuation in demand is not a good reason to sever the trading link, but consistently bad supplier performance is. Even with suppliers which had long ceased to be desirable, JJ Electric undertakes to continue giving out gradually declining orders, before trading finally comes to an end. Site C had one such sub-contractor in mechanical processing, which could not keep up with ever-demanding technological standards despite receiving much technical guidance from the site. The purchasing manager interviewed lamented not being able to make a clean, though drastic, break with unwanted sub-contractors (JJ Electric has apparently earned a reputation for being too caring), but quickly retracted his opinion:

> We have a lot to lose if a sub-contractor goes bankrupt because we didn't look after it. It's probably OK to cut the relationship immediately if the sub-contractor proves incompetent. But then we lose our social honour (*meiyo*). We also suffer from having to develop a replacement sub-contractor, from having to recover our assets from the sub-contractor, etc. It's all very costly.

Thus, JJ Electric's behaviour may be explained by a combination of a sense of social responsibility to look after weaker partners, a fear of damaging company reputation, and a motive to recover sunk costs. In order to ease the pain of adjustment for unwanted suppliers, JJ Electric may also introduce them to other sources of business and help them secure new bank loans.

At the same time, JJ Electric's managers are on a constant lookout for new potential suppliers. From time to time, whenever the existing suppliers' prices are thought to be not low enough, a spot contract to an unknown new supplier is placed as a trial. One aluminium die-casting supplier who received its first order in this fashion from Site A is currently the number one supplier of die-casting parts. The other two old die-casting suppliers still trade with JJ Electric but on a much reduced scale. According to the Site A manager, it is dangerous to have too stable a supplier base. But, at the same time, JJ Electric has to be attentive to a sense of orderliness in a community of suppliers in which no one should step out of his station overnight. Given a ranking for each component type, only gradually can a number one supplier be deposed from its position or a new entrant emerge as number one when his effort and capability becomes widely recognised by the others.[4]

Contracts and contractualism

Two types of standard 'basic contracts' (*Kihon keiyakusho*) are in use at all divisional sites. They have been drawn up by the central purchasing department, and are signed by all suppliers and sub-contractors to JJ Electric. One type is for large suppliers and the other for SME suppliers and sub-contractors for whom extra clauses exist stipulating conditions concerning the leasing of equipment and jigs and the supply of raw materials. JJ Electric, as a large company, is legally required to exchange such a contract only with SME suppliers and sub-contractors (see chapter 8).

The basic contract document concentrates mainly on procedural rules which govern the trading relationship. For instance, clause 6 states that if defects are discovered, the supplier must repair or deliver replacement parts immediately, but does not specify within how many days 'immediately' is (cf. a GB Electronics' contract specifies within five working days). The relative lack of substantive rules in such contracts makes it possible for the original contract, valid for a year, to be automatically renewed every year unless either party objects. Thus, contract signing as such takes place only at the very beginning of a trading relationship.

Clause 4 on delivery illustrates that the spirit in which JJ Electric's basic contract is drawn is not that of *caveat emptor* with sanctions. It stipulates only that the Seller notifies and obtains approval from the Buyer if it wishes to deliver before the deadline or if it is in danger of delivering late. Evidently, JJ Electric values good communication to plan production accordingly more than a sole reliance on financial 'penalty' as a sanction against late delivery.

Another clause which reveals the 'non-contractual' nature of JJ Electric's basic contract is as follows: 'Any issues which are not stipulated in either this contract or individual contracts, and any ambiguities in, and amendments to, this contract, shall be dealt with and resolved by discussion between the Buyer and the Seller' (clause 24). A similar clause is included in most other Japanese contracts governing customer–supplier relations, and underpins trading partners' mutual intent to practice 'adaptive sequential decision-making', to resolve problems bilaterally. That a compromise or conciliation can be reached in most circumstances is a fundamental assumption made here.

Quality inspection on delivery and technology transfer

Every time a new supplier is chosen, a vendor appraisal is conducted by each activity group's product quality assurance department. A company passing the inspection is given a seal of approval by the HQ. Separate audits are carried out by different activity groups on the same supplier, although one section may trust the judgment of another within the same group.

A new supplier is asked to supply samples, based on which technical guidance is worked out. It tends to be on specific aspects of production and quality control. Production starts initially in small batches. The first 2 or 3 lots are checked 100 per cent. Then sample checks are made for the next six months after which checks are reduced to an occasional three-monthly inspection. This shift from inspection to no inspection is a serious matter for suppliers, as the financial burden can be heavy when defects are discovered after assembly. For example, a PCB supplier must bear the cost of replacing not only defective PCBs, but also all non-replaceable flat components already inserted and the rework labour cost. Defects were said to occur occasionally, particularly towards the beginning of a trading relationship.

Communication with suppliers

Just like many of its competitors, JJ Electric has suppliers' associations (*kyoryoku kai*) which exist for the purpose of technology improvements among groups of suppliers and to create a sense of community among them. The HQ organises a central association with 134 members as of 1989, which is subdivided into 13 technical groups. The criteria for becoming a member are that (a) the supplier has been trading with JJ Electric for over 3 years; (b) it is dependent on JJ Electric for 25 per cent or more of its business; and (c) it has an annual value of orders exceeding ¥ 120m. Site C, being a subsidiary which has a growing number of its own direct suppliers, decided to found its own association with 43 members in 1983.

The origin of the suppliers' association organised at the HQ may be traced back to 1957 when an association was founded at the main production factory at the time, Site T. This was followed by the formation of a similar association at Site M in 1959. The following year, the two associations were merged to establish the association which exists today, although its activities were largely left to the divisional sites. It was only in the early 1980s that the central purchasing department took greater control, for example, by setting a uniform theme, such as how to shorten leadtime, for the monthly group discussion. The association also holds a New Year conference which the 134 suppliers' top managers attend to listen to JJ Electric's chairman talk about future management strategy.

Independently of the above association activities, each activity group of JJ Electric holds a meeting (*kondankai*) twice a year to disclose its future business plan, which is considered confidential. Only suppliers and sub-contractors heavily dependent on JJ Electric are invited to these meetings, numbering 100, for instance, for the data-processing group. This is the forum through which suppliers and sub-contractors gain advance information necessary to adapt to changing business circumstances.

On a more operational level, suppliers' and sub-contractors' salesmen are in touch with divisional sites' purchasing departments on a more or less daily basis, just as in the case of other large Japanese companies. At a higher level of organisation, presidents and managing directors of suppliers make regular visits to the sites once a month or once every two months, as though to remind themselves of the importance of the company–to–company (and not just the buyer–to–salesman) relationship.

Lastly, JJ Electric requires that its suppliers submit their financial statements annually. Purchasing and production-control managers come to know each supplier's financial position intimately as future investment plans at the supplier are discussed, often requiring a loan from a bank which is willing to advance it on the basis of past trading records with JJ Electric. 'It would be troublesome if sub-contractors went ahead to buy expensive equipment and started asking for high prices to recover costs', said Site C's manager. JJ Electric may be able to obtain on the sub-contractor's behalf discounts on equipment purchase as well as low-cost finance. The fact that JJ Electric comes to know much of its sub-contractors' financial and internal management situation in part reflects the closeness of some customer–supplier relationships. It also reveals the power a large, reputable and resourceful company of JJ Electric's stature can command over its smaller suppliers in Japan.

Risk sharing

Another related service is a help-line for troubled SME suppliers in the form of an advice bureau at the HQ, established in 1969. A common problem is that of cash flow, which the bureau may tackle by asking various divisional sites if they can adjust their order levels. Thus, the bureau operates as a coordinator of orders between divisional sites. JJ Electric's concern to smooth out the level of orders given to SME suppliers and sub-contractors is a major aspect of risk-sharing. Suppliers may rely on such a consideration not because it is explicitly agreed but because it is a tacitly understood norm in trading relations with JJ Electric. In return, suppliers are asked to reduce costs through greater automation and other rationalisation as well as through making VA (Value Analysis) suggestions for changing component design, types of raw materials used, or processing technology. These aspects will be spelt out in greater detail in chapter 11.

In conclusion, JJ Electric appears to have merely followed the norm at various times in Japan in its dealings with suppliers and sub-contractors.

This impression that it is doing nothing unusual is obtained from JJ Electric's managers' self-assessment as well as my observation of other Japanese electronic manufacturers. JJ Electric has been pioneering in other respects, in R&D for instance, but not in its relationships with suppliers and sub-contractors. It is noteworthy, however, that the norm of long-term trading and relatively high transactional dependence, characteristic of OCR-type relations, has not been undermined despite major relocations of production facilities in the 1980s from the divisional sites in and around the Tokyo metropolitan area to more remote areas of Japan.

GB Electronics

Background[5]

GB Electronics was founded in 1917 to carry out jobbing engineering work. It expanded into the manufacture of radios, components and telephone handsets between the two world wars, and continued after the Second World War to design and manufacture electronic components, defence systems and telecommunications equipment. In the 1960s, the company became more vertically integrated, just like its competitors, through a number of acquisitions. But the advent of microelectronics eventually led GB Electronics to reconsider its highly integrated approach. As the investment required to adopt up-to-date production technology became relatively more expensive, GB Electronics' equipment investments came to trail behind those by specialist component manufacturers. Eventually, it became more cost-effective for the company to purchase than to make some of its components. This fact led the company by the 1980s to concentrate its component investment in semiconductors and to sell some of its component subsidiaries.

GB Electronics plc is a company with £1.3 billion sales turnover (in 1988), employing no less than 35,000 worldwide (about the same as JJ Electric's core workforce), of whom 27,000 work in the United Kingdom. Telecommunications equipment accounts for just under half, and defence electronics systems just over a third, of total sales. It is therefore not surprising that GB Electronics' principal customers have been British Telecom (BT) and the Ministry of Defence (MOD). The company tended to occupy a highly oligopolistic or even monopolistic position in certain areas of public contracting in Britain. Recently, however, the privatisation of BT and the liberalisation of the British telecommunications market increased the degree of competition GB

Electronics has had to face from non-British companies. The MOD has also come to rely more on competitive tendering and to move away from cost plus towards fixed price contracts. The financial pressure imposed by these changes contributed to the need to reconsider GB Electronics' overall company strategy including policies governing its relationships with suppliers. Even earlier, the company experienced several years of negative real growth in the 1970s and has only begun to grow in size with improved profitability in the 1980s.

The description below traces changes in GB Electronics' relationships with suppliers during the latter half of the 1980s by focusing on its telecommunications division which subsequently became a joint venture company partly owned by another company.

Preferred Supplier Policy (PSP)

GB Electronics had three product divisions, namely defence, tele-communications and components. Each might be divided further into more than one limited company. In particular, the telecommunications division consisted of four limited companies, each having more than one site. The company had the policy of devolving responsibility to the main divisional boards and through them to the operating subsidiaries for managing their businesses. At the same time, the control over the strategic direction to be followed by the group was retained by the main board of directors. The management of procurement followed this pattern of decentralisation, particularly as each division had different requirements for different products. For instance, the telecommuni-cations and defence divisions observed different quality standards. But even within a division, there was a tendency for autonomous procure-ment at each site, with a possible exception when bulk-buying standard memory chips.

An overall strategic direction provided by the divisional board in the area of procurement may be captured by the so-called Preferred Supplier Policy (PSP). This policy came into existence around 1985, and was formulated as a result of deliberations on how to combat overseas competition, not least from Japan. By forging closer relationships with fewer suppliers, GB Electronics wished to improve quality, reduce inventory and shorten leadtime. In turn, preferred suppliers would benefit from improved yields, greater stability in business levels, and potentially increased business volumes. As part of a seminar to familia-rise suppliers with the ideas behind PSP, GB Electronics (Site Y) listed the following as its procurement department's 'needs':

1 zero defects;
2 delivery on time;
3 competitive prices;
4 supplier has long-term strategy;
5 supplier has leading-edge technology;
6 supplier has necessary management skills;
7 supplier is profitable;
8 supplier is prepared to underwrite long-term commitments;
9 supplier is capable of being a market leader;
10 supplier had broad-based product range;
11 supplier is preferably based in UK.

To what extent is PSP a move from the ACR to the OCR end of the spectrum of possible trading patterns? And how successful is the policy in improving the company's performance? The ensuing analysis to answer these questions will concentrate on comparing the approaches taken by two sites in the telecommunications division which later became the aforementioned joint venture company. They will be referred to as Site X and Site Y, the two largest sites in the division, and two of the three sites in a much rationalised joint venture company (see Table 4.1 for summary statistics). Some components (e.g. relays, batteries and recti-fiers) are purchased centrally by the joint venture company HQ, but the management of purchasing remains largely site specific. Not surprisingly, then, the two sites have differed in their implementation of PSP. But the new Purchasing Steering Group of purchasing executives from all sites, which meets every six weeks, may tend to harmonise the policy throughout the company in the future.

The supplier base

Unlike a Japanese company involved in similar activities, GB Electronics does not use sub-contractors for assembly. The reasons for non-use include a dislike of losing direct control over the production process, a shortage of good sub-contractors, fear of leaking confidential technical information and, importantly, the wish to grant employment security to existing workers in-house who survived major redundancies in the recent past.

Table 4.2 summarises the basic facts concerning the suppliers at Site X and Site Y. The total number of suppliers, including 'indirect' suppliers such as doctors and travel agents as well as 'direct' suppliers of materials and components, is said to be as high as 3000 at each site. Despite a large

Table 4.1. *Site X and Site Y, GB Electronics*

	Site X	Site Y
Products	PABXs, terminals, telephones	Public switching systems
Production (1986)	£250m	£220m
Employees	4500	4000
Peak workforce in past	13,000	15,000

total number, there is a high concentration of orders placed on a few dozen suppliers. These suppliers have been elevated to the status of so-called 'preferred suppliers' after a rigorous selection process, and receive 65 per cent of the total order value at Site X and 92 per cent at Site Y.

At Site Y, 25 preferred suppliers supplied such components as integrated circuits (ICs), PCBs, cables, relays, resistors, hybrids, connectors, batteries and disk drives. Of the 25, 5 are subsidiary companies of GB Electronics. The non-subsidiary 20 suppliers (see Table 4.3) were said to take up 60 per cent of total orders in 1987/8, a proportion which five years previously was probably spread over 150 or so suppliers. By 1989/90, 92 per cent of Site Y's total expenditure was paid out to the 25 preferred suppliers (Table 4.2). Thus, the move towards rationalising the number of suppliers has been considerable. Site X had 24 preferred suppliers including one subsidiary, which accounted for a lower proportion, 37 per cent, of total purchasing expenditure in 1989/90 (see Table 4.4). The percentage is much reduced from 65 per cent in 1988/89 because more product lines were brought in from other sites which were shut down as part of rationalisation under new company ownership.

A difference in the situation before and after the implementation of PSP may be illustrated by the sourcing of PCBs. At each of the two sites, there are two preferred suppliers, one being the same recently hived-off

Table 4.2. *GB Electronics' Suppliers 1989/90*

	Site X	Site Y
Component suppliers	300	110
of which: preferred suppliers	24	25
of which: GB Electronics' subsidiaries	1	5
Purchasing spending	£54m	£135m
of which: % paid to preferred suppliers	37%	92%

Table 4.3. *Site Y's non-subsidiary preferred suppliers 1987/8*

Supplier company	Component types	% of supplier's total sales to Site Y	% of total Site Y purchasing expenditure
A	ICs	<1	10
B	PCBs	25	8
C	various components	0.1	4
D	cables	0.1	4
E	Porter blocks	0.1	4
F	IC	2	4
G	power supplies	10	3
H	relays, ICs	<0.01	3
I	ICs	0.01	3
J	PCBs	5	3
K	resistors, networks	23	2
L	resistors, hybrids	6	2
M	connectors	3	2
N	disc drives	20	2
O	ICs	<0.01	2
P	batteries	3	1
Q	connectors	<1	1
R	disc drives	10	1
S	passives, ICs	<1	1
T	ICs	<0.01	1
Total			61

The total value of orders placed at the above suppliers was £30 million which represented 60 per cent of Site Y's total purchasing expenditure in 1987/8.

ex-subsidiary company (B500(PCB)). The other preferred PCB supplier is B222(PCB) for Site X and B410(PCB) for Site Y (see chapter 5 for more details). Before PSP was implemented, there were around 10 suppliers of PCBs at Site Y but, since 1985, all the PCB requirement, with 292 different part numbers, is satisfied by the two preferred suppliers with a recent addition of a third in early 1989. At Site X, probably because of the greater variety of products being produced, there are six or seven suppliers of PCBs other than the two preferred suppliers, but even this number was said to be very much a rationalised figure.

The implementation of PSP at GB Electronics has not been without difficulties, particularly in rendering the new business norm of long-term trading credible in the eyes of suppliers. At Site X, for instance, thirty suppliers were asked initially to join the PSP, none of whom refused. But

Table 4.4. *Site X's preferred suppliers 1989/90*

Supplier company	Component types	% of supplier's total sales to Site X	% of total Site X purchasing expenditure
A(277)	key systems & phones (C)[*]	3.7	10.7
B(25)	PCBs (C)	10.3	3.2
C(5)	hybrids (C)	35.8	2.2
D(100)	ICs & discretes (S)	2.6	2.2
E(100)[**]	ICs (C)	1.7	2.2
F(150)	ICs, discretes, passives (S)	1.0	1.8
G(12)	power supply units (C)	10.4	1.6
H(3)	PCBs (C)	40.8	1.5
I(50)	connectors (S)	2.1	1.3
J(3)	coils, transformers, inductors (C)	32.7	1.2
K(160)	ICs (S)	0.9	1.2
L(100)	ICs, discretes (S, C)	1.3	1.1
M(100)	power supply units (C)	0.9	1.1
N(100)	ICs (S)	1.0	0.8
O)20)	capacitors (S)	2.8	0.7
P(185)	ICs (S, C)	0.5	0.7
Q(3)	coils, transformers (C)	17.8	0.7
R(55)	cables (S)	0.9	0.6
S(60)	ICs (S)	0.9	0.6
T(12)	resistors (S)	3.8	0.6
U(2)	cords, cable assemblies (C)	11.3	0.3
V(27)	connectors (S)	0.8	0.3
W(30)	moulding (C)	4.4	0.2
X(4)	connectors (S)	0.7	0.2
Total			36.8

NB The number in ( ) is total UK sales in £million.
[*] (C) = customised; (S) = standard components; [**] is a GB Electronics subsidiary.

subsequently, between 1985 and 1989, seven suppliers were taken off the preferred status due to either consistently bad quality (in the case of three suppliers), or in order to concentrate on fewer suppliers to cope with a falling production volume (e.g. in the case of a plastic injection moulding supplier). This latter reason for dropping preferred suppliers appears to have added fuel to some of the suppliers' (both preferred and non-preferred) scepticism about PSP; the advantage of being a preferred supplier is undermined if there is no guarantee of a long-term trading relationship. A junior sales manager of a PCB supplier, who used to be a

GB Electronics buyer, was of the view that a supplier is preferred only as long as it receives orders.

Projected length of trading

The PSP arose from the realisation that improved quality (as well as competitive prices) could only be achieved through offering longer term security of orders to a chosen few suppliers. With the new policy, GB Electronics has been trying to shift from a situation in which none of a vast number of suppliers was offered such security to one in which a selected few suppliers are, while retaining a periphery of other suppliers.

Both Sites X and Y work to an annual purchasing planning horizon. In August every year, each site estimates what the annual customers' requirement would be for the financial year starting in April of the following year. The MRP system is used to work out detailed material requirements for the estimated level of production. Requests for price quotations are issued in September, and negotiations take place between October and February on the basis of quotations received. By March, contracts, valid for twelve months in almost all cases, stating part numbers to be ordered, the agreed price for each and the estimated value of orders among other things, are issued. The rate at which quantities are called off depends on GB Electronics' production requirement, and are notified to suppliers using purchase order forms with a typical leadtime of six to eight weeks. There is no contractual guarantee that the total quantity ordered for the twelve-month period matches up with the estimated quantity.

The purchasing executive at Site Y described the pre-PSP purchasing strategy in terms of obsession with prices. According to him, GB Electronics used to regard purchasing as nothing but extracting the lowest possible price from suppliers. The supplier offering the lowest price was chosen every year, while giving only secondary consideration to quality and delivery. Thus, by concentrating on the only visible aspect of purchasing, there was a huge hidden cost which the company tended to disregard. This tendency was said to be due to the organisation and reporting structure of the company; buyers had to justify their decision on where to place each order to their superiors, and price happened to be the most tangible piece of evidence for such justification.[6]

Thus, the company had built up a reputation for being an aggressive negotiator using plenty of threats to withdraw orders. It came to be regarded also as fickle, switching away from a supplier when a contract came to an end, for a slightly lower price it managed to squeeze out elsewhere, only to go back to the same supplier the following year. A belief in the goodness of invigorating competition, at least from the customer's viewpoint, was reflected in GB Electronics' Director of Procurement's view in 1987 that no supplier was allowed to get into a cosy relationship with the company: 'we shake up our suppliers regularly; we even drop them periodically to show them that we have alternative suppliers'.

It is the stated intention of PSP not to shake up suppliers on a regular basis. But, in reality, not least because of stagnant demand from BT, no real commitment was said to be possible beyond a twelve-month period. At Site Y, there was talk of giving out three-year contracts, rather than annual ones, to key suppliers from 1988, with either a fixed-price schedule or the right of price renegotiation every year. Although the idea of a traditional marriage was evoked to encourage long-term commitment, old habits seem to die hard when the memory of past behaviour is still fresh. Suppliers apparently became nervous and wished to include all kinds of clauses to protect themselves from being locked into a long-term – and possibly fixed-price – contract. It appears to be a Catch-22 situation in the show of goodwill and commitment; the question is who starts the process towards making the projected length of trading go beyond each annual contract. For the moment, some suppliers reported that they remained suspicious of GB Electronics' intentions behind implementing PSP.

Transactional dependence

As part of PSP, Sites X and Y, and the defence electronics division, all mentioned a shift from multiple sourcing (i.e. of one part number from three or more suppliers) towards dual or single sourcing. At Site X, a policy of single sourcing is implemented for components produced by preferred suppliers. Similarly at Site Y, most part numbers are single-sourced, apart from very large batches such as the largest 3 out of 292 part numbers of PCBs, which were dual sourced.

How has the implementation of PSP affected the transactional dependence of preferred suppliers on GB Electronics? Little seems to have changed in terms of GB Electronics' stance which has traditionally been inimical to heavy dependence. According to the Director of Procurement, 'I would not like to think that a supplier was dependent upon our business, i.e. if I took the business away, then he would collapse and go bankrupt.' This meant in effect that taking up more than 20 per cent of any supplier's business was thought to be dangerous, at least in the defence electronics division. But there was no clear central guideline on the maximum threshold dependence. Site X's purchasing executive said, for instance, that 50 per cent would be the maximum dependence if it concerned a preferred supplier.

A low transactional dependence is thought to have the advantages of both the flexibility to vary the level of orders given out to any supplier as prices dictate, and of serendipitous discovery of know-how through other supply connections, as illustrated in Site X manager's view:

> There will be times when we have a change in mix of our
> requirements, and if we have too high a percentage of their
> output, then it will cause them significant problems. So we
> would like them to be doing business with others; we like them
> to be aware of competition; they may do something for
> someone else which is of benefit to us, something we never
> thought of.

There has to be a compromise, however, between the preference for a low transactional dependence and the need to command preferential treatment by suppliers particularly at busy times.

In reality, the maximum level of transactional dependence is 25 per cent by the ex-subsidiary company supplying PCBs at Site Y, and 41 per cent (increasing to 60 per cent by 1991) by another PCB supplier at Site X (see Tables 4.3 and 4.4). At the other extreme are preferred suppliers of ICs and other standardised electronic components, which depend on either site for less than 1 per cent of their turnover. Such low dependence reflects the large size of some preferred suppliers relative to GB Electronics. Although large size is not a criterion for being chosen as a preferred supplier, it is a characteristic consistent with another criterion that a preferred supplier must have a broad-based product range, which economises on transaction costs.

Contracts and contractualism

Purchase agreements, valid for twelve months in most cases and for up to three years in a very few cases, are signed between GB Electronics' operating company and its suppliers. Only those suppliers with large orders (with an annual value of £0.25 million or more) sign such an agreement. For smaller orders, purchase order forms suffice as contracts. In any year, there are 120–50 contracts signed at Site X and around 60 at Site Y.

The terms and conditions spelt out in any purchase agreement are highly substantive. Although there are common clauses which appear in most agreements, the content of an agreement differs from supplier to supplier because (a) each site negotiates its own contract drawn up by itself, and (b) each contract contains substantive clauses concerning agreed maximum prices, payment terms, warranty, delivery, quality checks and cancellation of orders among other things. This contrasts with standardised Japanese 'basic contracts', such as the one at JJ Electric, containing largely procedural rules.

As an example of substantive clauses, Site Y's purchase agreement with B410(PCB) states that in the event of goods being delivered late, the supplier shall offer price reductions of between 10 and 20 per cent, depending on whether the delivery is 7 to 21 days late. The clause is meant to apply to short leadtime orders, for which suppliers charge up to 300 per cent premium over normal leadtime orders. In reality, Site Y's purchasing executive said that the clause had never been invoked. Although late delivery was quite common for PCBs, it was partly caused by GB Electronics making last-minute changes in delivery schedules. The resolve to be contractual apparently falters when one is perceived to be in part responsible for causing the problem in question. Invoking the clause was also expected to make suppliers respond more inflexibly to GB Electronics' requests.

One purpose of specifying substantive clauses in purchase agreements is to leave no room for doubt about who bears the risk in the face of price and demand fluctuations. One such clause, which is also prone to opportunism (non-revelation) by suppliers, concerns price changes during the period of an agreement:

> 4.3   Should the Seller during the period of the agreement offer the same products in similar quantities or mix at lower prices than those attached to this agreement such prices will be passed onto the Buyer on a 'most favoured customer' basis.

In practice, the interviewed purchasing executives said that there had never been a supplier who volunteered to offer price reductions in the spirit outlined by the clause. The onus of discovery therefore lies with GB Electronics.[7] If, however, a supplier is over-keen to reduce his price due to excess supply, GB Electronics is quite happy to take it; the supplier is assumed to be the best judge of its own finances.

Site Y obtains a discount on price if, *ex post*, the total quantity called off turns out to be larger than the amount estimated in the agreement. But if the quantity is short of the initial estimate, as has been the case more frequently in recent years, the price stays the same as agreed. Site

X follows the same principle, but renegotiates prices in exceptional cases when its 'contract compliance' (as measured by the actual order as a percentage of the estimated value) is very bad, for instance 14 per cent in a recent case.

Quality: inspection on delivery and monitoring

Promoting quality consciousness, and 'zero defect', has been a major driving force of PSP. Until a few years ago, sample inspection was carried out on delivered batches which were either accepted or rejected with reference to an AQL (acceptable quality level) ranging between 0.5 per cent and 4 per cent. With the implementation of PSP, quality came to be measured in the – for some – unfamiliar concept of PPM (parts per million). GB Electronics' suppliers who had been used to monitoring their quality in percentage terms and having 2 per cent defects (i.e. 20,000 PPM) counted as acceptable had to do at least 40 times better now. The initial target PPMs were 500 PPM at Site X and 50–300 PPM at Site Y.

While emphasising the importance of 'inspection at source' i.e. by suppliers before delivery, Site X started monitoring the performance of its preferred suppliers on a PPM basis. They were ranked by grades: 'S' meaning satisfactory, with 95–100 per cent acceptance rate (i.e. less than 5000 PPM), then 'C', 'B' and 'A' in ascending order. According to Site X's record, the proportion of 'S' rated suppliers increased from 35.5 per cent in 1983 to 46.7 per cent in 1985 to 71.5 per cent in December 1986. More recently, the average PPM achieved by the preferred suppliers improved from 7584 in January 1988 to 695 in October 1989 by which time 6 suppliers had achieved zero PPM continuously over 12 months. Quality improved partly as a result of dropping bad-quality suppliers, and partly due to improving the performance of retained suppliers.

The next stage in PSP, which is still very embryonic, is so-called ship-to-stock delivery, i.e. delivery of components straight to the production lines without inspection. A strict procedure is followed by Site X before switching from inspection to no inspection on delivery. It is only when a particular component has achieved the level of 200 PPM consistently for 12 months that the supplier is asked to sign a memorandum titled 'Ship-to-stock terms and conditions', which is a two-page contract document. Among other things, it stipulates that the supplier must be willing to replace within 48 hours any faulty products, and that if a defect was spotted after assembly, then the supplier must be willing to bear the cost of labour and overheads incurred at Site X. By 1989, 854 items (15 per cent of all part codes) at Site X and 500 items at Site Y were delivered on this no inspection basis; they were mainly standard electronic components.

Communication: channels and intensity

As the major source of rejects in the past was found to be inadequate specification by GB Electronics and misunderstanding by suppliers of its requirements, improving communication became one of PSP's objectives as well.

At Site X, PSP activated both written and face-to-face communication between the company and its preferred suppliers. A monthly written feedback is given to the preferred suppliers (and to 75 other 'major' suppliers) on their quality performance as monitored by the site, and the exact faults of every component discovered to be defective. The suppliers are then expected to write a report on receipt of this information from Site X to indicate whether they agree with Site X's assessment or not. Moreover, two types of meetings are held on a regular basis with each preferred supplier. One is a quarterly quality meeting, attended by the supplier's quality personnel and GB Electronics' buyer and quality personnel. They discuss the monthly PPM data for each part number and every single defect on which someone is minuted to take action. The other is a commercial meeting, held every six weeks, to talk about the supplier's overall performance in quality, delivery and service, and to discuss what the supplier must do to get more business from the site in the following year. The meeting is attended by the supplier's sales director (or manager) and three representatives (a buyer, an expediter and a group contracts manager) from Site X's purchasing department. Both meetings are administered by the purchasing department which incorporates the quality and expediting functions.

At Site Y, suppliers have interface with four separate departments, namely purchasing, quality, scheduling and engineering. A monthly quality meeting is organised by the quality department. But it is the vendor performance review (VPR) meeting which has not only motivated suppliers to improve their performance, but also improved internal communication within Site Y by creating a forum for regular exchange of information on each supplier. The VPR meeting is attended by a purchasing manager, a quality manager, a production manager and technical personnel from Site Y, and normally the managing director, a quality manager and technical staff from the supplier. They discuss Site Y's assessment of the supplier's performance in price, quality, delivery and other aspects of business every three to four months. The first set of meetings in 1987/8 took 6 hours each, which amount to approximately 150 hours (4 weeks) of each participant's time. They constitute transaction costs (in part of an investment type) of a considerable sum imputable in terms of the opportunity costs of total person-hours spent at the meetings.

Besides the meetings described above, GB Electronics' buyers may visit some suppliers on a regular basis. But GB Electronics' normal level of communication, although becoming more multi-channelled, is less frequent and intense than at JJ Electric. At Site Y, the first of what is hoped to be a series of annual supplier conferences was held in May 1987. Of the twenty-five preferred suppliers who were invited to attend, fourteen visited the site for a whole day for presentations by GB Electronics on quality assurance, purchasing policy and the company's business projection. The suppliers were also taken for a tour of the factory. No such conference was said to have been held at Site X.

Related to the issue of buyer–supplier communication is the career development and the consequent professional identity of purchasing personnel. It was hinted earlier that the buyers' obsession with extracting low prices at the expense of ignoring hidden costs of bad quality and late delivery had something to do with GB Electronics' organisation structure. In particular, the purchasing department identifies most closely with the financial rather than the engineering concerns of the company. This basis is evident also in the career development of purchasing personnel.

In Britain, purchasing is a profession, although not a very high status one. Partly because of this primary allegiance to the profession, hopping from company to company is considered a good career move. Most senior buyers at GB Electronics are said to have worked for more than one company. More junior buyers at Sites B and L have been trained for a career in purchasing, having graduated in business studies or economics. Buyers are relatively young, most being between 25 and 30 years old, and leave GB Electronics at a rate of 10 per cent per annum at Site X and 12 per cent at Site Y (see Table 4.5). The purchasing executives considered such turnover too high but inevitable, as some graduate recruits are enticed to take up a job in sales (a sales job is apparently thought to involve more kudos, not least because it comes with a company car!). At the same time, it was considered good that a certain proportion of buyers turned over regularly. Besides the general talk of bringing in new blood and a fresh outlook, newly hired buyers were said to have proved useful as a source for identifying new potential suppliers known to them at their previous place of work.

Table 4.5. *Purchasing personnel at GB Electronics*

	Site X	Site Y
Total no. in purchasing department	40	40
Of which: buyers (incl. managers)	33	30
Modal age	25–30	27
Average length of service (years)	7	5
Annual labour turnover	10%	12%

Technology transfer and product design

The principle of supplier independence is one reason for less frequent communication at GB Electronics than at JJ Electric. At the beginning of trading with new suppliers, GB Electronics' quality personnel may provide advice to suppliers to enable them to be approved on the BS5750 standard. But it is assumed that no preferred supplier is in need of longer-term nurturing, as one criterion for becoming a preferred supplier is that it already has 'leading-edge technology'. There is no intention on the part of GB Electronics to transfer technology to its suppliers, as there is no longer in-house expertise in most component processing technology.

GB Electronics also expects little involvement by suppliers in its product design and development. In general, GB Electronics undertakes most of the detailed design on site with little input from suppliers. Exceptions to this rule are ASICs designed by the preferred suppliers, and plastic moulding parts and power supply units for which suppliers are consulted early.

Overall assessment

In terms of the features of ACR and OCR as listed in Table 1.1, GB Electronics had been an ACR customer company to all suppliers before the Preferred Supplier Policy came into existence. The PSP appears to be an attempt by the company to move from ACR-type to OCR-type trading relationships with its core suppliers, while retaining some other suppliers in the periphery. Evidence exists that preferred suppliers are achieving better and more reliable quality and that communication is becoming more frequent and multi-channelled. But there is also evidence that suppliers are not convinced of GB Electronics' commitment to long-term trading.

Ultimately, an interesting question is whether PSP is a viable half-way house between ACR and OCR. Although there is no single policy statement as such, PSP, as presented to suppliers, as noted earlier, has the following major objectives: (1) more reliable quality; (2) more assured deliveries, with lower inventory holdings and shorter leadtimes; and (3) more competitive (i.e. lower) prices. These objectives are to be achieved through longer term mutual commitments and better communication between the customer and the suppliers. A full OCR aims at the above objectives, plus: (a) a high degree of mutual interdependence; (b) sharing risks of market fluctuations; and (c) sharing costs, expertise, and risks in technical development.

GB Electronics is experiencing some difficulties even to achieve the stated objectives. Establishing mutual long-term commitment when the norm has been short-term arm's-length relations takes time. Moving a few suppliers in and out of the preferred supplier status due to GB Electronics' commercial reasons has been seen by suppliers as not honouring its half of the commitment. Moreover, PSP would not work well as long as some suppliers are suspicious that GB Electronics' major purpose in eliciting long-term open commitment from suppliers is to weaken their bargaining power over prices.

PSP, even if successful, cannot approximate OCR as it is never intended to develop 'goodwill trust' in relationships. One manifestation of this is the preference for relatively low transactional dependence, which may give GB Electronics insufficient leverage to be treated preferentially. In reality, a handful of good performing suppliers each have several major customers, all of whom are vying to be treated preferentially in return for recognising it as a preferred supplier. Given the competition, GB Electronics may have a hard time being treated as a preferred customer not least because its size relative to its chosen few suppliers is not very great. Thus, a transition from ACR to OCR relationships may be difficult when suppliers have greater market power than buyers.

Another manifestation is the lack of a sense of sharing risks. This results in part from a degree of contractualism as shown in the contract documents, but also from the mutual wish to preserve suppliers' transactional independence. Suppliers then rely mainly on risk-spreading by diversified customer outlets rather than on sharing inter-temporal risks arising out of unforeseen market fluctuations. Little risk is shared also because GB Electronics do not expect suppliers to make contributions to the design and development process.

In conclusion, PSP represents only a limited shift from 'arm's-length' relations, and that is bound to be so as long as the norm of supplier independence and minimum risk sharing continue to dominate business practices. Incentives for long-term commitment are harder to come by unless there exist other OCR features which promote a sense of mutual interdependence and risk sharing. In their absence, PSP is more vulnerable to fluctuations in market conditions which may easily undermine the stability of continued long-term trading.

Toshiba Consumer Products (UK) Limited

Background[8]

Toshiba Consumer products (UK) Ltd, or TCP for short, is a wholly owned subsidiary of Toshiba Corporation, established in 1981 after a brief two and a half year period of an unsuccessful joint venture with Rank Corporation. The TCP site in Plymouth is therefore a brownfield site, with a degree of continuity in personnel from the first phase when TCP was a minority shareholder of the joint venture to the current phase of 100 per cent Toshiba ownership.

However, 1981 marked a fundamental transformation in management philosophy and practices in all aspects of the factory (see Trevor (1988) for details). For instance, in the area of human resources, the rigorous selection procedure, the harmonisation of status and, above all, the signing of a single-union agreement and the establishment of a company advisory board to improve management–labour communication, were all part of a package to create a flexible and committed workforce. Since 1981, the company has more than quadrupled its workforce from 250 to just over 1000 in 1991, thus becoming a major employer in the area. Of these, only seven are Japanese nationals.

In the first ten years, the company has produced a number of products. VCRs were assembled from 1985 until 1989 when their production was moved to a greenfield site in Germany. Microwave ovens were also produced at Plymouth from 1985 until 1990 when they were shifted to production in France. By 1991, the production of air conditioners was under way. The account which follows concentrates, however, on colour television sets (CTVs) which have been produced continuously since the joint venture.

Most major Japanese electronics manufacturers have production facilities for CTV sets in the UK, and hence replicate in Europe the intense competition seen in the Japanese domestic market. TCP(UK)

Table 4.6. *Organisation of CTV production at TCP(UK) and Fukaya factory*

	TCP (UK)	Fukaya plant (Japan)
	1989/90	1987/88
Production started	1981	1965
Total employees	1000	2380 plus 500 *paato*[*]
CTV production (p.a.)	400,000	1,800,000
Number of models	80	20
Purchasing expenditure	£55m	¥11.5b
of which in-house:	13%	40%
(i.e. within TCP worldwide)		
Local content[**]	71%	n.a.
No. of suppliers	122	300

[*] Of the 500, 300 are full-time employees working continuously on rolling short-term contracts, while the rest are temporary and part-time workers who work at peak periods only.
[**] The proportion of total purchasing budget spent within Europe.

increased its production 5-fold during 1981–6, from 76,000 to 400,000 sets per annum. Since 1986, CTV production has levelled off, with a dip by 18 per cent in 1988/9. However, during 1990/1, CTV output at TCP increased 40 per cent, mainly to satisfy the non-UK European market.

How successful has TCP been in its relationships with its suppliers? The general impression obtained from the experience recounted below is that of eventual moderate success but after much trial and error. Complaints about bad quality standards and delivery records of British suppliers abound and are well documented (Jetro (1985, pp. 63ff); Arthur D. Little (1986, p. 12)). How, then, did TCP set about identifying suppliers which can satisfy its requirements? To what extent did TCP try to make British suppliers behave like Japanese suppliers? How do TCP(UK)'s relations with its suppliers compare with supplier relations at the Toshiba HQ factory at Fukaya? To what extent has there been guidance and direction provided by the Japanese headquarters on the issue of how to deal with suppliers? Attempts will be made to answer these questions.

The description which follows concentrates on UK suppliers which supply parts to the CTV operation of TCP(UK). Explicit comparisons with Fukaya factory in Japan will be made wherever appropriate. As Table 4.6 shows, TCP(UK) has had to cope with a greater number of models (to meet each European country's different requirements) at a lower level of overall production than at Fukaya plant. However, CTV sets are relatively mature products, whose number of components on a chassis has been reduced considerably over the years with development, from over 2000 in 1981 to 1300 by the late 1980s. Has this simplified the organisation of purchasing?

The supplier base

'The concept of subcontracting in the Japanese sense is not generally known in Western Europe . . . Japanese affiliates were trying to establish subcontracting relationships under the differing European business environment, where the very basis for such subcontracting relationship was nonexistent', declared a JETRO survey report on Japanese affiliates in Europe (Jetro, 1985, p. 67). The report defined sub-contracting as a special relationship formed through technical guidance, financial aid, management advice, or leasing production machinery. TCP(UK) managers referred to all component manufacturers as suppliers although, as we shall see below, TCP's willingness to transfer its know-how to some of its suppliers makes them more like sub-contractors in the JETRO sense.

The comparison between TCP(UK) and Fukaya factory highlights one major difference in the use of sub-contractors in assembly tasks. In Japan, Fukaya plant uses 12 assembly sub-contractors, each employing between 80 and 440 workers. This labour force works exclusively for Fukaya plant, some inserting components onto printed circuit boards, and others undertaking sub-unit assembly as well. These companies are typically located in the northern prefectures of Yamagata, Niigata and Iwate, where workers willing to do meticulous manual assembly tasks are available at a relatively low cost. Fukaya plant has been involved in specifying the factory layout, the equipment and detailed production methods for each of the twelve sub-contractors which are managed not by the purchasing department but by the production department. Thus, although Fukaya factory has to look after only 2380 regular workers plus 500 or so others on temporary contracts directly, there are another 2000 workers at assembly sub-contractors who do no other work but for Fukaya.

In Britain, the lack of availability of such sub-contracting companies and the low volume of production were given as reasons for not sub-contracting assembly tasks on a regular basis. TCP resorted to a sub-contractor temporarily during autumn 1989 for automatic PCB insertion as the internal facilities reached full capacity, but it proved to be expensive. The only regular assembly sub-contractor is a small work-shop in the local area. TCP helped to set up this company as a matter of service to the local community. It employs twenty-five workers, who are either retirees from TCP or handicapped, to make wooden fixtures for TV sets. A production supervisor at TCP, whose husband is employed in the workshop, is responsible for organising their sub-contract work.

Despite more sub-assembly work being put out at Fukaya factory, it is more vertically integrated than TCP(UK). Of the total annual purchasing requirements of ¥11.5 billion at Fukaya, 40 per cent were said to originate from within the Toshiba Corporation. For instance, all PCBs for CTVs come from other Toshiba factories, as do cathode ray tubes (CRTs), some of which are manufactured at Fukaya site (hence the relatively low purchasing expenditure at Fukaya in Table 4.6). At TCP(UK) by contrast, both TCP and European tubes were used, and as the CRT is by far the most expensive component, accounting for up to 70 per cent of the total material cost for a CTV set, the EC local content regulation of 50 per cent can be satisfied by purchasing European-made tubes. PCBs, accounting for just less than 10 per cent of total material cost, used to be imported from Japan but are more recently sourced from South Korea as the exchange rate movement has made it cheaper to do so. Thus, partly in order to meet the local content regulation and to adjust to currency fluctuations, the proportion of TCP(UK)'s expenditure on components which are made or purchased by Toshiba Corporation in Japan declined from 60 per cent in 1981 to 40 per cent in 1986, and further to 13 per cent by 1989.

Among European suppliers, a distinction is made between high technology 'designer manufacturers' and electro-mechanical suppliers. The former are generally large companies, typically not UK-owned, with which the Toshiba Corporation has collaborative development agreements. Because all major design and development work for CTVs has been done in Japan, TCP(UK) does not deal with these high-tech European suppliers directly; sample components are evaluated and approved by the HQ in Japan. The latter, electro-mechanical suppliers, provide such components as transformers, plastic parts, metal casings, and wiring. UK-based suppliers have been sought mainly for these relatively bulky and heavy parts.

There were in total 90 component manufacturers which supplied to the CTV section of TCP(UK) in 1987. Of those suppliers, 20 took up 90 per cent of TCP's total purchasing spending of £60 million, while the next 20 suppliers took up only 6 per cent of the spending. Of the top 20, one is the parent company, Toshiba Corporation in Japan. The other 19 may be classified as follows:

Suppliers with:	No. of suppliers
(a) TCP(UK) as the largest customer	6
(b) TCP(UK) as a major customer (i.e. 15–30 per cent dependence on TCP(UK))	4
(c) less than 15 per cent dependence on TCP(UK)	5
(d) Toshiba Corporation's equity holding in the Far East	4

By 1989, the total number expanded to 122, mainly because components which used to be supplied by Toshiba Corporation in Japan came to be procured directly from Far Eastern suppliers. Of the 122, 65 are located in the UK, accounting for 18 per cent of total purchasing expenditure. The majority of these UK suppliers employ less than 1000, and some are considerably smaller. Many (40 out of the 65) manufacture customised components to TCP(UK)'s proprietary design.

Only a handful, though an increasing number, of UK component manufacturers can meet TCP(UK)'s quality requirements or those of other Japanese companies in the UK for that matter. Consequently, many of the major suppliers of TCP(UK) trade with other Japanese manufacturers located in the UK. This has implications for the relative bargaining power between the customer and the supplier, as we shall see later.

Transactional dependence

As a rule of thumb, there are two suppliers per particular component type, but each with a different speciality. An extremely small number of part numbers for the 'industry's staples' (i.e. standard electronic components) are multiple sourced, while customised part numbers are single sourced as the small volume does not warrant splitting an order. This is in contrast to the practice at Fukaya factory which multiple sources customised components required in large volumes. For instance, even plastic parts, which involve using expensive tooling, were said to be dual sourced at times when working one tool twenty-four hours a day is not sufficient to meet the production scheduling requirement.

One reflection of the obligational contractual (OCR) nature of TCP(UK)'s relations with its suppliers is the fact that the avoidance of high transactional dependence was not accorded high priority by the company. In fact, a company policy on the upper threshold of supplier dependence was said to be unnecessary as relationships are close and evolve on trust.

In reality, not many suppliers were dependent on TCP(UK) for much more than 25 per cent of their business. This may partly reflect some suppliers' preference for transactional independence. At the same time, some remarkable examples of high dependence have emerged, situations which just evolved rather than being created by design, as TCP(UK)'s business grew very rapidly. One is a polystyrene supplier which is 99 per cent dependent, and delivers three or four times a day, and another a small metal pressing company, around 80 per cent dependent and delivering at least once a day. Both are located very close to TCP's factory. In the meantime, the Fukaya site in Japan was encouraging its sub-contractors to reduce their dependence on it, just as other companies such as JJ Electric had done.

Contracts and contractualism

It is not necessary to be overly concerned with suppliers' transactional dependence, according to TCP's purchasing manager, because long-term relationships have been established with suppliers. Long-term commitments from suppliers, however, are secured not by making them sign longer term written contracts, as GB Electronics was attempting to do. In fact, TCP(UK) decided not to have written agreements from the start in 1981. The standard European terms and conditions of trade would apply, but they are hardly referred to explicitly. In effect, purchase order forms setting out a rolling 12-week schedule – one month firm, 2 months tentative – are the contract. The absence of a contract document, other than purchase order forms, was explained in terms of its non-utility. What are required by TCP are long-term reliable sources of supply, which cannot be secured by merely signing a piece of paper. Moreover, a contract would be referred to only in dispute, and if a relationship had come to involve solicitors, then it is a sign of irreversible failure. TCP(UK)'s purchasing manager, a British national, believes that the mere existence of contracts may give rise to conflict. In particular, get-out clauses such as the supplier not bearing consequential losses would encourage antagonistic attitudes and avoidance of responsibility.

The practice at Fukaya factory, which might have served as a model for TCP(UK), was studied but not followed. The 'basic contract' in use at Fukaya, similar to JJ Electric's, was translated into English. But TCP decided not to create a similar contract because signing such a document was nothing more than a ritual and, anyway, there was nothing in the contract which one would not do without it.[9]

Projected length of trading and ordering procedure

Without written contracts, the viability of long-term trading relationships was said to rest on good faith. How did TCP(UK) come to trust its suppliers, and vice versa? What triggered the virtuous circle at the beginning in 1981?

During the joint venture period, contracts were given out every 12 months. Every supplier was on tenterhooks once a year, as the company constantly changed suppliers; a contract might be renewed with the same supplier, but just as likely, it might not. When the joint venture folded, all suppliers lost their business, just as all employees were formally made redundant. After the announcement of the closure, three months passed before the TCP(UK) purchasing manager approached old suppliers who had by then written off their business with the company for the forthcoming year. The occasion for approaching them and some new potential suppliers was a suppliers' conference, at which the Managing Director made 'loud and provocative statements' to impress upon them that TCP(UK) was a completely different company from the joint venture company. During the conference, TCP(UK) set out its requirements, among which was the need for both suppliers and TCP(UK) to make long-term commitments. The suppliers which remain to date are the ones which absorbed the new mode of thinking on buyer–supplier relations. With the benefit of hindsight, the recession in the early 1980s may have helped some companies to alter their attitudes fundamentally.

A new business culture helped to establish good mutual faith particularly when accompanied by TCP(UK)'s ability to honour its commitment; the total absence of cancellation of orders created an atmosphere of confidence and success. At TCP(UK), a strict internal planning system backed up by market research enabled it to hand down firm delivery schedules to suppliers. TCP's ability to keep to the schedule was helped by an ever-growing volume of output, similar to the situation in 1960s' Japan. Thus, TCP's attempt at creating shared expectations in long-term trading, its emphasis on rational planning to create a self-image of competence, and rapid expansion in business all contributed towards developing trust relations with selected suppliers.

Advantages of long-term commitments are non-trivial particularly for consumer electronic goods, whose product development cycle is getting shorter and shorter. TCP(UK) works to a two-and-a-half-year cycle for colour TV sets: six months of gradual phase-in, followed by eighteen months' full production and then six months' phase-out. This cycle is said to be getting shorter. In Japan, Fukaya factory worked to an even shorter cycle; an annual major model change, with minor changes once a quarter, which is seemingly unnecessary but a vital part of staying ahead in the competition. According to the vice president of Matsushita Electric Industrial (*Asahi Shinbun* 12 August 1988), the 9 Japanese manufacturers of CTVs together accounted for the announcement of 155 different models in 1987 alone, compared to 105 in 1985.

TCP requires from its suppliers not just reliable supply but also flexible and speedy responses to design changes which can be handled only by long-term suppliers. Part of the saving in transaction costs is that the suppliers can take a lot of things for granted and assume that unless specified differently the normal practice for TCP applies. According to the TCP purchasing manager, there is still the following attitudinal difference between British and Japanese suppliers:

> ... a UK manufacturer requires a dogmatic statement of
> requirements. He wants a fully specified drawing with every
> single line in place and a fixed design ... He wants to start to
> manufacture something, a tool for something, knowing that
> that is it, it's finalised, fixed and there will be no substantial
> change. We will never survive with that ... Yes, we must have
> the essential details there. But if we waited until we were
> absolutely sure of every final detail, and we drew it up
> beautifully so that anyone could read it, we would be 6 months
> or 12 months later than the market place. What is the point?

This pressure of time also affects TCP's mode of placing orders. In effect, TCP may not have all the essential details to ask suppliers for price quotations, and therefore may proceed to prepare for pilot production with the designated supplier without a negotiated price. This is done, however, with an understanding of a target price range which the supplier is deemed technically capable of achieving. Although a definite price may not be settled until just before mass production starts, there is no expectation of 'post-contractual opportunism' (of suppliers asking for high prices) on the part of TCP.

Risk-sharing

TCP managers agreed that its UK suppliers were generally keen to start business with TCP. But, thereafter, frequent requests to pass on cost increases to the customer were said to have been made. This British norm is contrary to the Japanese norm of cost reduction, and is difficult to sustain, particularly as CTV prices never rise and can only fall in the fiercely competitive consumer market.

In practice, the price is agreed between TCP and its suppliers at the beginning of each project for a model, which typically lasts for eighteen months to two years. The price remains unchanged for the duration of the model unless there is a significant change in specification, or a significant rise (tacitly understood to be over 5 per cent) in raw material prices. TCP reluctantly accepts the British norm of suppliers passing on cost increases beyond their control, normally due to raw material price changes, although TCP may attempt to delay approving price increases.

TCP seeks a reduction in prices towards the end of each project, justifiable on the grounds of (a) the learning curve effect, lowering the unit cost of production at the supplier's end, and (b) a lower design status of a model in the last six months' phase-out period, during which time design functions are lowered in order to sell off the model while new models take over in the market. Both (a) and (b) are used as counter-arguments against suppliers' claims that prices ought to rise during phase-out because of reduced order quantities. Moreover, a little cross-subsidisation of components for the old model by those for the new is expected by TCP, such being the advantage of continuous over one-off trading.

Overall, TCP(UK) has a harder time trying to keep down its suppliers' prices than Fukaya factory, where price changes – always in the downward direction – take place every six months as is the normal practice for JJ Electric and other manufacturers in Japan. TCP(UK)'s difficulty lies in its relatively weak bargaining position because of at least two factors. First, there is a relative lack of competition between suppliers as only a handful can meet the requirements of TCP and other Japanese companies. Second, the transactional dependence of suppliers is not high enough for TCP's pressure to be effective. Moreover, temporarily in the late 1980s, the yen appreciation, the very reason for Fukaya suppliers' keen compliance with the cost reduction drive due to fear of losing orders to NIC suppliers, gave an extra scope for UK suppliers to raise prices, because TCP's opportunity cost of not sourcing in the UK (i.e. of importing similar components from Japan) had risen.

The UK suppliers' orientation in not wishing to share the burden of cost adjustments is also a reflection of their non-involvement in the product design and development process. In practice, it is difficult for UK-based electro-mechanical suppliers to make contributions to product development, as the chassis development for new models has been undertaken at Fukaya factory, and not many have the resources to make regular visits to Fukaya to collaborate on design and development. TCP(UK) has begun to feed back more local marketing information to be taken into account in the design process in Japan, but so far it has local autonomy only in post-development design of outer appearances of TV sets. Thus for the moment, TCP's UK suppliers do not have the opportunity to share risk in product development, nor to supplement their tight profit margins by earning development fees.

Quality inspection on delivery

Just as at Fukaya, all components delivered to TCP go straight onto the CTV production line without inspection. This is different from TCP's microwave division which sample checked all components on delivery. The rationale behind the difference lies in the larger production level (400,000 CTVs vs 200,000 microwave ovens) and a greater number of components (1300 vs 150) for CTVs than for microwave ovens. It is thus more cost effective for TCP to ensure good quality at source by selecting good suppliers and providing technical guidance rather than employing personnel to inspect goods on delivery.

In the event that a component fault is discovered on the assembly line, the problem is dealt with on a case by case basis, as there is no formal procedure agreed in writing. Normally the supplier is expected to go to the TCP site immediately to conduct a 100 per cent batch inspection if a fault is discovered on the assembly line. With a large supplier, the problem is resolved amicably by the supplier offering a discount for the next month's delivery. The extent of the discount is equivalent to the direct cost to TCP of rework labour time and extra transportation. There is no attempt by TCP to obtain full compensation as the true cost of line stoppages, the rescheduling of lines, etc. would be very great.

Communication: channels and intensity

TCP keeps a detailed record on the quality of each supplier's delivered goods. Even if it is not making a claim, TCP makes a habit of sending an example of any defects back to the supplier every time it occurs. TCP's quality personnel make regular visits to suppliers to discuss quality improvement. There is also intensive technical guidance at the initial stage, when TCP engineers may be involved in laying out the lines, installing expensive tools owned by TCP, and setting up the quality control system, which may all take four to five months. Thus, the quality personnel and engineers as well as purchasing personnel are involved in dealing with suppliers directly.

Good communication between TCP and its suppliers exists not only to improve quality but also to allow TCP to vary the mix of components rapidly according to market demand. TCP holds meetings on average every four weeks with each of its top twenty suppliers to discuss scheduling. Other suppliers with £50,000 or more order value per annum have meetings at least twice a year.

Similarly at Fukaya in Japan, close communication was said to be essential to make last-minute changes, often by telephone, in production scheduling and the time of delivery. Suppliers' salesmen are said to come into Fukaya's purchasing department more or less daily, to pick up purchase order forms placed by buyers in supplier-specific pigeon holes. Daily visits are made possible as large suppliers have local offices in the vicinity of Fukaya where salesmen are based, while smaller suppliers are situated locally. On the whole, the frequency of communication with suppliers is greater at Fukaya factory than at TCP(UK).

We already noted in the case of GB Electronics that the nature of communication with suppliers is affected by the buyers' career development. Of the twelve purchasing personnel working at TCP, only one, the Far East liaison manager, is Japanese, who is on a three to five year rotation presumably as part of an integrated career development at the Japanese HQ. British middle managers and buyers tend to move on after three to four years also, as there are limited opportunities for internal promotion or for inter-departmental rotation to develop general management skills at TCP(UK). Stability is provided only at the top, which is the cause of promotion blockages. For example, the British purchasing manager interviewed had worked for the joint venture company, and knows his opposite number in other Japanese companies located in the UK. They might ring him, or he rings them, to consult on suppliers' performance as frequently as once a month: 'I'm having a terrible problem with this supplier; is he doing the same to you?' or even 'the delivery is late, can you lend me some of those components?'[10]

As already mentioned, TCP(UK) has organised a suppliers' conference since 1981 every two years or so. This is the occasion when TCP gives a projection of where the company is going, and the target sales in two years' time. Although the top twenty suppliers would not learn anything more at the conference than what they know from their monthly meetings, TCP seeks an added benefit in cross-fertilising suppliers. They can talk about their problems to each other; they might jointly think of solutions to deal with TCP; and they can introduce other customers to each other. This is a relatively hands-off approach compared with the practice at Fukaya factory, where each of the four sub-groups of the suppliers' association formed in 1984 with 80 members meets monthly to discuss how to improve quality and delivery, or to consider how to achieve requests made by Fukaya factory such as halving leadtimes. Someone from Fukaya site is always present at these study group meetings.

Technical guidance

At TCP(UK), technical guidance is strictly bilateral. But it is a common feature of forging relationships with most electro-mechanical component suppliers. TCP's experience in sourcing plastic injection moulding parts best illustrates its willingness to provide technical assistance in the belief that benefits may be reaped in the distant future. TCP currently has four UK plastics suppliers, two of large high-volume components, and the other two of smaller low-volume components. To arrive at this situation, much effort was expended on the part of TCP.

To start with, TCP encountered some fundamental differences in Japanese and UK techniques in plastic moulding for consumer electronic goods. First, it was highly unusual for British plastic suppliers also to decorate (eg. paint), finish and assemble non-moulded parts, as was the norm in Japan. Secondly, the metal used in tooling was different and reflected a different philosophy. In Japan, tools were made of soft metal, which was cheaper overall even after taking account of higher maintenance costs requiring more sophisticated operators than for hard metal tools. In Britain, by contrast, tools were made of high-precision hard metal, requiring low maintenance and were certain to be 'idiot proof'; the technology was totally in the tool and the press, while the operator was incidental.

The Japanese approach faced resistance in Britain. Either out of management choice and/or lack of otherwise suitable workers, British firms did not employ operators who knew the operating efficiency and the quality level which had to be achieved and how the tools were interacting with the resin at different temperatures. Japanese operators, by contrast, were trained to think and know all these things, made easier by generally higher levels of education.

TCP decided to start by using UK tools, as importing moulds from Japan would give UK suppliers an opportunity to blame the moulds for any faults. The technical guidance in concrete terms involved sending the UK plastic-moulding suppliers to Japan in order to study how tools were made by Japanese tool-makers. Moreover, engineers and quality personnel were posted at the suppliers for periods to check that tools were being used correctly, to assist in the unfamiliar area of assembly and decoration methods, particularly in spray technology.

At the outset in 1981, TCP identified two plastics suppliers, referred to as L Plastics and K Plastics, both of whom were keenly sought after by other Japanese CTV manufacturers in the UK. L Plastics became a successful supplier to TCP, but only after its business was shaken when another Japanese manufacturer carried out its threat to cease trading with what it considered a hopelessly incapable supplier. The supplier's commitment to improvements coincided with TCP's determination to succeed, particularly at a time of complete failure with K Plastics, rendering L Plastics the sole UK source for a while.

K Plastics was a high-volume manufacturer of injection moulding parts. The company was known to TCP's purchasing manager who had placed an order before. It was also attractive in being a private company with plenty of capital, the willingness to invest, and control over its own finances. At its height, 90 per cent of K Plastics' business was with Japanese companies, the largest customer being TCP, taking up 40 per cent, followed by the second largest with 30 per cent.

Assistance started modestly, in assembly, in spray technology and in getting the company to produce at higher than necessary volumes in order to obtain better quality. The breadth of assistance and intervention widened with time to the extent that in 1982 the general manager of the TV operation and the purchasing manager both worked on K Plastics' shopfloor, running the press themselves. For another two years, TCP continued to provide assistance, setting up the production line for K Plastics and staying with them until the required standard was reached. But every time TCP personnel left the factory to be run by K Plastics' staff themselves, the quality deteriorated. K Plastics apparently developed a degree of passivity waiting for TCP to come up with solutions. The longer TCP stuck with K Plastics, the more difficult it became to pull out, as it had already invested a huge amount of resources. In 1984, however, TCP finally decided to quit, taking away its tools. According to TCP, K Plastics, which went bankrupt eventually, was a case of well-intentioned but incompetent management.[11]

By 1984/5, TCP was also instrumental in setting up a moulding company in Ireland which reached a technical collaboration agreement with a Japanese tool-maker. This company, for which TCP is one of the large customers, supplies large high-volume plastic parts to several other Japanese companies in the UK.

The three customer companies

For smaller plastic parts, TCP decided to concentrate its efforts on one supplier, S Plastics, which employed around 100. But, with rapid expansion, TCP decided in 1985 to look for a second supplier ideally located nearby. When informed of this, S Plastics' senior management showed a desire to set up a satellite company. When this wish was vetoed by the holding company of the group to which S Plastics belonged, two senior managers decided to leave the company to set up their own plastic-moulding business near TCP.

TCP did not give outright support to this idea, but said that if S Plastics did not want to set up a satellite, then TCP would continue looking for a local company, and therefore a hive-off would have an advantage in obtaining TCP orders if it were to be set up. By 1986, all the equipment was installed at the newly established company, T Plastics, to which the TCP purchasing manager wrote a letter marking the commencement of a trading relationship. In this letter, he mentioned that given T Plastics' projection for growth, 25 per cent of total business 'should and could be sourced locally' (i.e. taken up by TCP). By 1987, the purchasing manager and T Plastics' Managing Director agreed that 30 per cent was taken up by TCP's CTV and microwave divisions combined, with a projection for it to increase to 45 per cent for the year 1988/9. In reality, in 1989, only 20 per cent of T Plastics' total business was taken up by TCP as it had been successful in developing business with other customers.

Trading between TCP and T Plastics is based on a relationship which most resembles a Japanese sub-contracting relationship. TCP's purchasing manager and T Plastics' MD have known each other for fifteen years. Communication is at a rate of twice a week; often the TCP manager pops in at 9 p.m. from T Plastics' shopfloor entrance. However, T Plastics is a British company run by British managers who are used to British norms of business practice. For instance, T Plastics' marketing director opined that TCP people appeared a bit too often on T Plastics' site. A discrepancy between the TCP purchasing manager's assessment of transactional dependence at 60 per cent (he underestimated the growth of orders from the other 10 customers) and the correctly estimated figure of 30 per cent evoked a joking, but telling, response from T Plastics' manager: 'TCP wants to take us over, you see!' T Plastics has had a clear objective to retain eleven customers and to maintain the company size to below fifty workers and fifteen press machines.

T Plastics feels that it has not received any explicit help from TCP in setting up the company. For example, it was not necessary to ask for financial help as the company managed thus far with bank overdrafts. It was interesting to hear, however, that T Plastics thought correctly that

TCP would have given them low-interest loans if they had asked. Such convergent expectation is a good sign for sustaining a long-term relationship.

In conclusion, TCP(UK) has clearly attempted to develop OCR-type relations with its UK suppliers since 1981. A number of factors contributed to its relative success. These are (a) a clean break in 1981 to establish a new culture; (b) the decision not to have any written contractual agreement; (c) a rapid expansion in production; and (d) the company's competent forecasting capability. However, a number of inimical circumstances also exist, in terms of (a) a lack of competition among suppliers; (b) relatively low transactional dependence of suppliers; and (c) a lack of local autonomy in product development which precludes UK suppliers from contributing to it. How these factors change would significantly affect the nature of TCP's relationships with its suppliers in the future.

Summing up

The preceding discussion makes clear that all three customer companies' relationships with their suppliers are evolving over time. However, JJ Electric has preserved the obligational contractual (OCR) essence of its relationships with core suppliers despite changes in its product mix and plant relocations in recent years. GB Electronics had realised the costs associated with its arm's length (ACR) purchasing strategy in the past, and is in the process of shifting towards OCR, although it is not willing to develop high dependence by, or to share risk with, suppliers for the moment. Lastly, TCP has been blessed with favourable conditions to establish OCR-type relations with UK suppliers initially, but the long-term viability of these relationships appears to depend on Toshiba Corporation's global strategy towards the localisation of design and development functions.

5

The analysis of supplier companies

We will now turn to the thirty-six suppliers (see Table 3.2) and their views on links with their customer companies. This chapter analyses the nature of these relationships by examining each of the eleven features of ACR–OCR patterns identified in chapter 1 (see Table 1.1). An overall assessment of how the ACR–OCR features fit together will be given at the end.

Transactional dependence

We start with an examination of the most tangible data, namely the number of customers each supplier trades with, and the related issue of transactional dependence. It was stated in chapter 1 that a heavy transactional dependence on a few customers is a reflection of the company's willingness to be locked into a relationship, which is a feature of OCR. By contrast, a broad customer base with minimum dependence on any one customer is a characteristic of ACR.

As Table 5.1 shows, the degree of transactional dependence is higher and the number of customers less on average in Japan than in Britain. This is consistent with interviewees' responses on the optimal situation: in Britain, 15 per cent in the PCB industry and 25 per cent in electronic assembly were often cited as the maximum allowable threshold dependence, while in Japan, having three major customers with each taking up a third of the business ('the three pillar principle') was offered as the ideal by many. The British–Japanese contrast in the number of customers per supplier is marked, particularly when we take into account the fact that the size of the population of potential customer enterprises in Japan far exceeds that in Britain.[1]

Sectoral differences are also of note. In each country, electronic assembly sub-contractors had fewer customers and higher transactional dependence on average than PCB suppliers. In particular, the maximum

Table 5.1. *Number of Customers and Transactional Dependence*

Company	Customers	Transactional Dependence (%)	Company	Customers	Transactional Dependence (%)
B38(PCB)	80	8	J17(PCB)	20	30
B50(PCB)	228	12 ·	J65(PCB)	90	20
B107(PCB)	220	12	J120(PCB)	30	55
B118(PCB)	100	10	J140(PCB)	50	30
B120(PCB)	150	12	J150(PCB)	200	30*
B203(PCB)	407	9	J220(PCB)	200	30
B222(PCB)	150	14	J480(PCB)	100	13
B300(PCB)	60	12	J650(PCB)	100	85
B410(PCB)	100	25	J700(PCB)	60	30
B500(PCB)	180	35	J1210(PCB)	400	15
Average	168	15	Average	125	34
B10(EA)	37	25	J30(EA)	1	100
B15(EA)	40	30	J71(EA)	11	60
B90(EA)	15	35	J160(EA)	1	100
B205(EA)	10	18	J170(EA)	20	30
B230(EA)	50	33	J240(EA)	17	30
B350(EA)	20	35	J250(EA)	3	67*
B750(EA)	20	18	J265(EA)	10	65
B1100(EA)	21	15	J360(EA)	4	99*
Average	27	26	Average	8	69

* = dependence on parent company
N.B. Transactional dependence refers to the percentage of the supplier's annual sales turnover taken up by the largest customer.

number of customers in electronic assembly – 50 in the British sample and 20 in the Japanese sample – contrasts sharply with the maximum number – around 400 in both countries – in the PCB industry sample.

Despite these country and sectoral characteristics, company-specific strategies are varied. Each company has a target dependence ratio which in turn dictates the preferred market niche and a typical batch size associated with it. For example, J65(PCB) has adopted a strategy, considered unusual in the Japanese PCB industry, to remain small, independent and profitable by concentrating on the production of small-batch high-technology PCBs. It consequently has a large number of customers for its size and a lower than average dependence. B203(PCB) has similarly concentrated on small batch production, but decided to grow.

For some other suppliers, there may be a divergence between the desired degree of dependence and the reality. This is unfortunately not captured in Table 5.1, which is a mere snapshot. Such divergence may have been caused by (a) constraints imposed by the customer, as in the case of J160(EA) whose sole customer forbids it from supplying any other; or (b) past events which exposed the company to the dangers of a high-dependence strategy, as in the case of J71(EA), J250(EA) and J120(PCB) which ceased to be 100 per cent dependent on a single customer after a drastic cut in demand during the first oil shock. J120(PCB), 55 per cent dependent at the time of the interview on what was the sole customer in the 1970s, aims to reduce its dependence to 15 per cent. Thus, all changes in the Japanese sample have been in the same direction towards lesser dependency. Similarly, B1100(EA) and B410(PCB) both suffered from the 1985 computer market recession. This resulted in lowering their transactional dependence from 90 per cent (in 1984) to 15 per cent, and from 40 per cent to 25 per cent respectively.

Those companies which prefer to spread risk may do so either across many customers or with a few diversified customers. Many PCB suppliers with low transactional dependence are making sure that their customers' final markets are spread across telecommunication, data processing, instrumentation, defence equipment, etc. in order to maximise the chances of counterbalancing order levels. B107(PCB), among others, pointed out the company's weakness in the past of supplying to a handful of customers who were all ultimately satisfying the same monopsonistic market, namely that of British Telecom contracts. By contrast, J120(PCB), although 55 per cent dependent on JJ Electric, is supplying to its 9 different sections manufacturing a diversified range of products.

For those suppliers who prefer relatively high transactional dependence, the rationale behind their preference is two-fold. First, there is the practicality of servicing each customer well; transaction costs would be prohibitively high with too many customers (see the later section on communication intensity for more details). Second, risk-spreading is less necessary for the suppliers whose customers give a more-or-less trustable assurance of a steady, continuous level of orders.[2]

Procedure for obtaining orders

How do the sample suppliers go about obtaining business from their customers? For new orders (i.e. newly issued 'part numbers'), suppliers always submit price quotations for a competitive bid in ACR–type relations. In OCR, by contrast, suppliers do not have to bid for new orders because it is up to the customer to commission work. The procedures under the ACR and OCR ideal types respectively are as follows:

ACR

1 Development and design undertaken by the customer.
2 Customer invites suppliers to bid.
3 Submission of price estimates by suppliers.
4 Price negotiation.
5 Customer chooses the supplier who is to receive the order.
6 Supplier receives and accepts the order.
7 Production of ordered parts at the supplier commences.

OCR

1 Initial development undertaken by the customer.
2 Customer decides which supplier is best suited to produce a particular type of component and commissions to a chosen supplier which may become involved in design specification.
3 Price is discussed and agreed upon.
4 Supplier agrees to the order.
5 Production of ordered parts at the supplier commences.

Subsequently, after the initial contract is up, the competitive bidding process is repeated in ACR. The buyer invites bids for the same design specification from several suppliers, including the one which has been supplying already. Whoever submits the lowest price wins the repeat order. In OCR, the buyer places a straight commission to the same supplier who has been producing the part number in question, while prices are reviewed at a regular interval. In both new and repeat orders, the central ACR–OCR difference is this: in ACR, prices are settled before a supplier accepts an order; in OCR, a supplier accepts an order before price negotiations take place on the assumption that a consensus can be reached. From the buyer's viewpoint, in ACR, the selection of a supplier and price negotiation are collapsed into one step in the competitive bidding process, which is the only occasion when the buyer can exercise its bargaining power. In OCR, by contrast, the buyer's power is more all-encompassing, for example, through its access to suppliers' costing and other financial information.

British practices

Generally, a procedure close to the ACR ideal type was followed in the case of new orders from new customers, although only those suppliers which passed the initial vendor appraisal are asked to quote. Where it differs from pure ACR is in dealings with existing customers which we expect contain some relational elements arising out of previous transactions. As described below, some relationships attempt to minimise the impact of past choices, experience, and information on future repeated transactions, thus giving a semblance of discrete exchanges with no interconnection between them. Other relationships not only acknowledge the experience in previous transactions but the customer makes it the major source of information in deciding where to place future orders.

For new orders, the number of suppliers asked to bid was said to be at least three. B107(PCB) mentioned that asking three suppliers to bid is a stipulation for government contracts, and has been adopted as a rule of thumb in the private sector. However, there were some exceptional cases in the past, when B120(PCB) found itself bidding against forty other quotations, and B107(PCB) against twenty. Such purchasing practice was said to be on the decline, as more and more customers have come to adopt a philosophy similar to GB Electronics' Preferred Supplier Policy.

The chances of winning a new order varied from company to company. The quotation-to-success ratio was said to be as low as 30 per cent even from existing customers at B120(PCB), while at B107(PCB) there was 65 per cent success, and at B10(EA) as high as 80 per cent success rate, if requested to quote. The probability depends on the mode of price determination and the information imparted to the suppliers around the time of the price quotation. At one extreme, British Telecom was named by B205(EA) and B230(EA) as a customer which adheres strictly to the principle of 'one-shot' open tendering with no prior information being passed on about its target price. Nor is there price negotiation: 'you get one crack to get the price right, and that's it', according to B205(EA)'s Managing Director. Although exasperated by being kept in the dark, the MD thought that one-shot tendering was more ethical than the practice of some private-sector customers who may pass on prior information to give some companies unfair advantage over others in winning orders.

At the other extreme are a few suppliers (namely B15(EA) and B50(PCB)) which, even if offered the chance, would refuse to negotiate, quoting prices on a take-it-or-leave-it basis (there was no such practice in the Japanese sample). At B50(PCB), non-negotiable prices were quoted on the telephone or in writing by clerks in the sales department. The Managing Director at B50(PCB), which specialises in supplying prototype PCBs, justified its practice by referring to the unmanageably high costs in terms of time and effort if it were to negotiate with a large number of customers (200+) all with one-off orders.

Between the two extreme practices of refusal to negotiate by either party are cases where negotiations do take place. Suppliers may well be given an explicit indication of what would be an acceptable price prior to the submission of estimates. For example, large customers to B410(PCB) give a price marker through verbal communication; if this is an acceptable target, B410(PCB) simply submits a quotation identical to the customer specified price; if not, B410(PCB) submits a different quotation which becomes subject to negotiation.

Lastly, although not common in our sample, a practice close to OCR, i.e. straight commissioning for new orders, was found in three of the British electronic assembly sub-contractors. B350(EA) always has 100 per cent chance of winning an order from its largest customer by virtue of being the sole supplier of wiring harnesses to the customer. B230(EA) said that if there has been continuous trading with a particular customer, the latter tends not to go out for other quotations; only if there has been a time gap in trading would customers go out for bidding. Similarly, B750(EA)'s customers with whom it has long-term relationships were said quite often to place orders straight. Moreover, according to the plant manager, 'we have been known to have agreed on a price two months after delivery'. Disagreements over price are rare due to the customers knowing B750(EA)'s costs very well. Not surprisingly, straight commission for repeat orders is common practice in British electronic assembly.

In the PCB industry, repeat orders occur rarely for some suppliers (especially B230(PCB) and B50(PCB)) whose business is one-off orders with short leadtime. For those companies which deal in long-term orders lasting at least one year (e.g. B500(PCB), B410(PCB), B300(PCB)), repeat orders tend to be straight commission. B410(PCB) mentioned, however, that it is only a recent tendency for customers not to go out for quotations if they are satisfied with the existing supplier. Even recently, B300(PCB) won a major contract with GB Electronics worth £0.75m (just over 5 per cent of its total sales turnover), which was whittled down to one-fifteenth in value the following year due to loss of repeat orders.

Japanese practices

Whether for new orders or for repeat orders, the modal practice in the Japanese electronic assembly industry was for customers to give out straight commission orders. Typically, the customer is said to have mapped out, in consultation with the core sub-contractors, an overall plan of which sub-contractor would do what type of work. For instance, J160(EA), being one of the four suppliers to its sole customer doing similar tasks, is handed down the customer's six-monthly plan of production for J160(EA). These production schedules come as no surprise to J160(EA) as there is regular communication with the customer which discloses its longer-term future business plans.

The sub-contractors submitted price quotations, but only as a matter of formality and, typically, after orders are firmly placed and accepted. Customers commonly have information on their sub-contractors' labour rates, overheads and other relevant financial statistics, so that they have a relatively good idea of how much an assembly task may cost at a particular sub-contractor's. There is therefore little scope for disagreement on the price which may be finally determined after production starts or even after delivery is made. Thus, the steps taken in the ideal type OCR procedure are often overlapping or even changed around in some cases.

Such flexibility in the procedure, permitting short leadtimes, is afforded by mutual expectations in the lack of post-contractual opportunism. Sub-contractors would not betray their customers by refusing to produce or deliver due to, say, a disagreement over price. But the extent to which this may be due to 'goodwill trust' rather than unilateral control varies from company to company. For some sub-contractors, the spirit in which prices are agreed is not that of antagonistic zero-sum negotiation but more of amicable discussion and compromise. The manager interviewed at J250(EA), for example, said that a genuine consensus on a 'fair' price, or at least a mutually acceptable compromise, was always reached. By contrast, J30(EA) and J71(EA) both disliked their customers' unilateral imposition of low prices in 'price notification forms', but were resigned to this predicament resulting from their high transactional dependence.

Deviations from the above procedure of straight commissioning in the Japanese electronic assembly sample were found at J170(EA), J240(EA) and J264(EA). All three bid for new orders against several other sub-contractors. J170(EA) and J265(EA) in particular said that they only had a 50:50 chance of winning new orders if asked to quote.

Practices also varied in the Japanese PCB industry sample. At one extreme, J1210(PCB), J480(PCB) and J65(PCB) are given straight commissions but on different grounds. For J1210(PCB), straight commissioning is due to its sheer size; being the largest company in the industry capable of manufacturing large batches, its customers simply reserve a certain level of capacity at the supplier's. J480(PCB) receives orders for prototype boards on the tacit understanding that the ensuing production board orders will be placed subsequently. A quotation is submitted for an all-in-one price for both prototype and large-batch production put together; in effect, J480(PCB) carries the higher cost of prototype production as a service. The final price is not likely to get settled until large-batch production commences. J65(PCB), which prides itself on its good technological capability, gets involved at the prototype development stage, which gives it a head start in obtaining subsequent large-batch orders. However, orders are known to have been lost after prototype development. All other sample PCB suppliers bid for new orders, competing against at least two other suppliers, and up to six others in the case of J150(PCB). The success rate varied from supplier to supplier, with J220(PCB) mentioning near certainty if asked to quote, and J700(PCB) as low as 60 per cent.

Repeat orders remained straight commissions for most Japanese PCB suppliers, although J150(PCB) and J700(PCB) mentioned a recent shift towards bidding for some customers. There was apparently greater uncertainty in winning orders, both new and repeat, for some suppliers. The clearest shift was in the case of J150(PCB) which used to receive straight commissions until a few years ago, when many customers switched to soliciting multiple quotations in an attempt to extract lower prices. The appreciation of the yen after the September 1985 Plaza Accord and competition from overseas (especially from NIEs) were the major force behind this shift in practice.

To summarise, a variety of practices exist among sample suppliers and sub-contractors in securing orders. The British modal practice in the PCB industry was closest to the ACR ideal type, although even in this industry there was evidence that the practice is moving towards OCR, reflected in the tendencies to request quotations from fewer suppliers. In the British electronic assembly industry, a number of sample suppliers had OCR-like practices, agreeing on prices after orders are placed. The Japanese electronic assembly industry had more pronounced OCR practices, including the settlement of prices after production started. The modal Japanese PCB industry practice was less OCR than in electronic assembly. Here, straight commissioning was found to be a declining practice, and the chances of quotations leading to success were said to be becoming more uncertain due to the competitive pressures exerted by a strong currency.

Projected length of trading

Related to the procedure for securing orders is the 'projected length of trading', short and discrete in ACR and long beyond the current contract in OCR. There are clearly a number of factors which affect how long 'long term' is and whether continuous trading (*à la* JJ Electric) is easily achievable or not. First, there is the likelihood of repeat orders, more common in large-volume scheduled orders than in prototype or one-off orders. Second, the higher the customer's prioritisation in giving repeat orders to the same supplier – a factor considered in the previous sub-section – the more continuous trading will be. Third, beyond repeat orders, a supplier is likely to have a continuous long-term trading relationship with a customer if the supplier produces a large number of part numbers with overlapping product life cycles.

One indication of whether long-term relationships are considered desirable or not is given in responses to the questionnaire. Almost all suppliers agreed with the statement (O in Question 4) 'We start trading with a customer always in the hope of establishing a long-term relationship.' There was, therefore, no significant British–Japanese difference in the *desirability* of long-term relationships.[3] But a clear difference emerged when it came to achievability. Given a pair of statements (Q.1(iv)), (A) 'our customers give consideration to placing continuous stable orders', and (B) 'our customers change their order levels as it suits them', 14 out of the 17 Japanese suppliers, but only 2 out of the 16 British suppliers, chose the former.[4] Thus, there appears to be a significant difference between Britain and Japan in the behaviour of customer companies. One reason for this difference is presumably the legacy in Britain of using suppliers and sub-contractors intermittently to cope with spill-overs whenever in-house capacity is full.

In Britain, long-term continuous trading was found in the electronic assembly sector. At one extreme, B350(EA) is a sole supplier to its largest customer and is therefore obliged to act as an extension of the customer's production facility. Even without sole sourcing, B205(EA)'s marketing director said that there were customers with whom the company had traded for over 20 years, and that there had not been a time when their products were not passing through the factory. At the other extreme, B118(PCB), most of whose business is in non-scheduled one-off orders, actually preferred short-term commitment; as long as reasonably high profits were earned, it was not concerned that there was 'not a lot of visibility even with customers we work closely with'. The company recognised the trade-off between long-term 'visibility' (a trade term for certainty of future prospects for orders) but low profit in large-volume scheduled orders on the one hand, and short-term 'visibility' but high profit in small-batch orders on the other. For B50(PCB), which specialises in one-off orders, long-term customers were those

115

whose names were on a computerised list, who come and go as required. 'We don't part company with customers . . . We are still friends; we still know each other', said the MD, even if changes in products or technology meant that there had not been orders from specific customers for some time.

In between, more sample PCB suppliers than assembly sub-contractors complained that their customers were unwilling to make long-term commitments. Short-termism was due to a combination of (a) switching suppliers for a small price advantage and (b) uncertainty about future order levels due to non-disclosure of future production plans by customers. With respect to (a), B120(PCB)'s Managing Director, for instance, lamented its customers' proneness to flit from it to another supplier offering a 'silly price', only to come back to the company having been let down in either quality or delivery (see NEDO (1983, p. 6) for a similar point).

With respect to (b), customers' non-disclosure of future business plans created a sense of uncertainty in the British PCB suppliers. To the pair of statements (Q.1(vi)), (A)'our customers always let us know in advance their future production plans', and (B) 'our customers tend not to let us know their future production plans', all the British PCB suppliers chose the latter while all the British electronic assembly sub-contractors chose the former. Such uncertainty was said to be either created deliberately by customers who wished to appear to call off greater quantities than actually planned so as to extract lower prices, or due to their inability to forecast future demand themselves. Neither opportunism nor incompetence is conducive to creating an atmosphere of trust.

B410(PCB)'s sales manager also talked in terms of customers having a 'narrow window approach', and how 'orders die a sudden death'. At this supplier, there are two ways in which customers' commitment beyond the next twelve months is sought. One is through a letter of intent, which states only the estimated annual level of order. The other is through lengthening the contractual period beyond one year, e.g. up to five years.[5] The Managing Director of B500(PCB), which has agreements lasting up to three years, prefers long-term contracts because less time is wasted in negotiation of contractual terms (in particular, he noted, over who bears the cost of stock-holding in JIT delivery).

In Japan, as the questionnaire results indicate, long-term continuous trading is both desirable and achievable. Many of the sample suppliers have been trading with their major customers for the last twenty years or longer non-stop. In the case of J120(PCB), the trading relationship with its major customer dates back from even before the company started manufacturing PCBs. In fact, it was the customer who suggested that J120(PCB)'s in-house skill in painting and sheet-metal processing might be a good foundation for diversifying into PCB production.

One would expect relatively heavy transactional dependence and long-term commitments in customer–supplier relationships to go hand in hand. At the extreme, companies such as J30(EA), J160(EA), J360(EA), and J650(PCB), which are 100 per cent or nearly totally dependent on a single customer, are in effect trading on the assumption that the relationships will continue, if not for ever, for a long time. They also had very good access to their customers' future production plans.

But it is not just for the heavily dependent suppliers that this working assumption applies. Even J65(PCB), which prides itself on being exceptionally independent in the Japanese industry, has not been able to refuse an order from NTT (and its pre-privatised Denden Kosha) of an identical part number which has been continuously placed for the last twenty years. Thus, just as some British customers' fickle behaviour of light-heartedly breaking off relationships as prices dictate can be a constraint on British PCB suppliers, the Japanese trading norm of long-term relationships may act as a constraint on both customers (as we saw in the case of JJ Electric) and suppliers.

In sum, long-term continuous (with an emphasis on continuous) trading is more of a norm in Japan than in Britain. There is evidence that Japanese suppliers are given more access to customers' future production plans than British suppliers. Some British suppliers complained about the short-termism of their customers (no such complaints were encountered in Japan), which they tried to rectify by both contractual and more informal methods. A minority of British PCB suppliers, however, regarded short-termism as a small price to pay for obtaining orders with high profit margins.

Documents for exchange and contractualism

So far, we have referred very loosely to an 'order' or a 'contract' as a show of commitment on the part of the customer to purchase components. What kinds of documents are used to underpin such commitment between the customer and the supplier? Broadly classified, three levels of transaction exist.

(i) A 'framework agreement', setting out basic rules and procedures which govern a trading relationship, such as inspection procedures, cancellation charges, payment terms, packaging and transportation arrangements. These terms may be bilaterally negotiated and agreed between a customer and a supplier, or they may simply follow the industry standard if it exists.

(ii) A 'framework order' which specifies the total quantity to be called off of each part number over a period, issued when prices are negotiated and agreed.

(iii) A 'calling off' of the order with a purchase order form, which specifies exact quantities to be delivered and delivery dates.

Trading relationships are more ACR the greater the extent to which (i)–(iii) above are detailed in written form rather than left as oral or tacit understanding. In particular, the more completely each partner's obligations in every conceivable contingency are stipulated, and the more closely they are applied in reality, the more ACR relationships are deemed to be. As all contracts contain non-contractual elements (Macaulay, 1963), the ACR–OCR distinction, in this respect as in others, is a matter of degree.

British practices

B300(PCB) typifies the most documented of British suppliers. With all major customers, the supplier signs a one-year agreement which is renegotiated and signed every year. It mentions the value of the annual contract, broken down into an estimated quantity for each part number, as well as details on payment terms, delivery arrangements, procedure for price changes, etc. The legal contract is a rolling monthly purchase order form, which gives a firm order for the first four weeks, an indicative order for the next four weeks for which materials can be procured, and a forecast for the third four weeks. There is also B300(PCB)'s own terms and conditions of sale printed at the back of the price quotation form; the safeguard it provides on not bearing any consequential losses was said to be important.

At the other extreme, both B10(EA) and B15(EA) rely in the main on only purchase order forms as contractual documents. Orders are one-off, and the indication of repeat orders is generally absent. Only large orders have some terms and conditions of purchase (e.g. penalty for late delivery) at the back of the form. They also stipulate no terms and conditions of sale of their own, so that many aspects of trading, such as payment terms, remain oral agreements.

In Britain, therefore, a 'framework agreement' may consist of the supplier's terms and conditions of sale and the customer's own terms (spelt out in an 'agreement' or at the back of the request for quotation (RFQ) form and/or the purchase order form). The two documents may well stipulate different terms. With the exception of B10(EA), B15(EA) and B90(EA), all the British suppliers had their own terms and conditions of sale. They were said to be there as a safeguard just in case. In reality, not many suppliers expect their customers to have studied the terms and conditions of sale. In the majority of cases, the suppliers accept their customers' conditions. On the rare occasions when these conditions are regarded as unacceptble, negotiation ensues. The most commonly negotiated term appears to be the payment period, invariably longer in the customer's than in the supplier's terms and conditions.

The next level of refinement, a 'framework order' for scheduled orders, may be written or oral. If written, it takes the form of an annual 'blanket order' contract, which is a written list of total quantity against each part number which is likely to be called off during the year. However, this was treated as indicative, and in no sense contractual; B300(PCB)'s Managing Director called it a 'contract of intent'. B350(EA) and B1100(EA) rely on oral communication as their customers show reluctance to give written indications of future orders.

A further level of refinement, the actual call-off, has a firm contractual element and a forecast element, the latter being necessary to procure materials in advance. It is quite common for orders to be made monthly – a firm order for the next month and a tentative order for the following two months. B350(EA), whose customers' forecasts over three months are relatively accurate, reasoned thus; 'they [customers] are trying to make us bear the risk of buying materials in advance, and then cut down the actual leadtime for orders to the absolute minimum'. If, however, there is a shortfall in calling off a particular part number, some customers attempt, if possible, to balance this out by increasing other orders in the same contract period or to make it up the following year (mentioned also by GB Electronics).

A flexible case-by-case resolution was also said to be necessary because late delivery or quality defects may be caused by a combination of reasons. For example, late delivery by a supplier may be due to last-minute changes by customers in the mix of part numbers to be delivered (mentioned by B410(PCB)), or due to the delayed supply of free-issued materials from customers (mentioned by B1100(EA)). Even if it may be possible to hide behind the contractual terms of accepting no consequential losses, B300(PCB) would admit responsibility for a quality problem; the Managing Director recalled a particular incident when it offered to pay the customer for the cost of reworking after assembly.

Similarly, B50 (PCB)'s MD said he would 'do what is right' in each circumstance.

Japanese practices

The major documents which are exchanged between Japanese suppliers and their customers are: the basic contract (*kihon keiyakusho*), the purchase order form (*hatchusho* or *chumonsho*) and, in some cases, production-scheduling plans (*seisan keikakusho*) provided by the customer company. A further refinement in delivery schedule may be made by telephone or by computerised links.

The basic contract, such as the one at JJ Electric, is a legal requirement for trading between large customers and smaller suppliers. Such regulation derives from an attempt to protect suppliers from unfair trading practices by customers, which were considered to be sufficiently prevalent to warrant government action in post-war Japan (see chapter 7). Most sample suppliers regarded it as a matter of course that they sign a basic contract with large customers. It is a highly standardised 'framework agreement' which spells out procedural rules, while leaving substantive matters to be settled separately. Moreover, once signed (almost as a ceremonial gesture to mark the start of a trading relationship), the basic contract is automatically renewable annually unless either side indicates otherwise. Unlike in Britain, no sample supplier has its own terms and conditions of sale.

A 'framework order', which gives an indication of the total level of orders for a year or six months, is totally separate from the basic contract (cf. in Britain, some annual agreements are a combination of both a 'framework agreement' and a 'framework order'). The most common method of placing framework orders in Japan was through customers' semi-annual or annual meetings at which future business strategies and forecasts were disclosed to the suppliers. A firmer, yet oral, agreement of the total annual order value was said to be made at the top level when suppliers' Managing Directors visited their major customers.

Some assembly sub-contractors (namely J30(EA), J160(EA), and J360(EA)) received written production scheduling plans over six months instead of purchase order forms. These plans were said to be relatively accurate. J360(EA) received a monthly firm order with delivery schedule, plus daily modifications to the schedule, over a direct computer link with the customer. Both J30(EA) and J160(EA) have monthly meetings with their customers at which the following month's daily production schedule is discussed and firmed up.

At the PCB suppliers and the other assembly sub-contractors, monthly purchase order forms were treated as legally binding. Indeed, in trading between smaller customer companies, purchase order forms constituted the central document being exchanged, in the absence of basic contracts or production-scheduling plans. Unlike highly dependent assembly sub-contractors, the other suppliers considered customer forecasts as only tentative projections increasingly subject to sudden changes.

Just as in Britain, there was a general view that much flexibility exists in responding to problems and last-minute emergencies. The difference from Britain lies in the Japanese companies' belief that non-contractual responses are typically Japanese and have both good and bad points. Japanese customers are said to muddle through, fudging their immediate contractual obligations by referring to more diffuse obligations within their long-term relationship of give and take. Appeals are made to the idea of 'swings and roundabouts' or sharing good times and bad. A conversation with J77(PCB)'s sales director gives a flavour of variations among customers: 'our customers may end up calling off much less than was originally indicated, but they are likely just to apologise curtly and pay no compensation even if there are some tied materials'. This practice was contrasted with an exception, namely IBM Japan's meticulous conscientiousness in fulfilling contractual obligations. For instance, it pays without fail by cash for all 'IBM unique' materials and tools already purchased by J700(PCB) but unused or not fully amortised. Is IBM's code of practice preferable over Japanese customers' practices? J700(PCB)'s sales director thought not, as a *quid pro quo* for IBM's contractualism is that J700(PCB) itself is expected to be strictly contractual also, for instance by paying full penalties for late delivery which may cause severe cash-flow problems. At the same time, he felt that Japanese customers could learn to be a little more business-like and *dorai* (dry) in their dealings.

In both Britain and Japan, strictly contractual relationships are difficult to maintain because of (a) unpredictable future demand; (b) short leadtimes and last-minute changes in order scheduling; and (c) the need to apportion blame for late delivery and quality defects case-by-case. There is also another reason in Japan, which is due to the norm of long-term trading and unequal financial resources between large and small companies. As mentioned by J120(PCB), a large customer may well lead a smaller supplier into bankruptcy if it insists on the supplier paying the full compensation it is contractually entitled to for quality defects. In return for receiving only partial compensation, however, the large customer is allowed a slightly larger reduction in component prices. Such is the logic of give and take in power-unequal relationships in Japan.

Trust

Three kinds of trust, as discussed in chapter 2, are states of mind which, given the present methodology, can only be measured indirectly through their manifestation in certain types of behaviour. This sub-section looks at the following aspects as *prima facie* evidence of trust. First, 'contractual trust', i.e. trust in keeping promises made, is presumed to exist if suppliers are willing to proceed with production of customised components before a 'contract' (i.e. purchase order form) is received. 'Contractual trust' is low if suppliers insist on receiving a written contract first.

Second, 'goodwill trust' is trust in mutual open commitment to the relationship, including the expectation of not being taken advantage of. It is postulated that the existence of mutual dependence – namely high transactional dependence by the supplier combined with single-sourcing by the customer – is a reflection of goodwill trust in relations. There is a two-way causation at work here: the existence of 'goodwill trust' leads to the willingness to enter into a mutually dependent relationship; but a high degree of mutual dependence, with trading partners being 'locked in' to a relationship, requires a careful cultivation of the relationship, which in turn is likely to breed trust. If the buyer exercises dual or multiple sourcing, goodwill trust is inferred to be lower, although, of course, large production volumes relative to suppliers' capacity may be a reason also.

Third, 'competence trust' is deemed to exist if customers practice so-called ship-to-stock delivery straight onto the customer's assembly line. A thorough inspection on delivery is undertaken by the customer because (i) the onus is on the part of the recipient to detect faults (the principle of *caveat emptor* applies), and/or (ii) it does not trust the supplier's competence to manufacture to the stipulated quality standards. The practice of inspection on delivery may not necessarily imply lack of trust, as it may reflect a mere norm concerning the division of tasks between the customer and the supplier. But its absence reflects the presence of trust.

The analysis of supplier companies

Production before written purchase order forms?

The requirement of short leadtimes is often a major factor behind suppliers in both Britain and Japan having to produce on the basis of oral commitment. In fast turnaround and prototype business, the leadtime is sometimes as short as twenty four hours. J65(PCB), whose strength is in prototype board production, said two to three days' leadtime is rather common. The paperwork takes longer than the required leadtime, so that production precedes the receipt of purchase order forms. J65(PCB)'s owner-manager thought this was a perfectly acceptable practice for customers with long-term open relationships. Even for new customers, J65(PCB) produces before written contracts as long as they are acquaintances.

Similarly, it is normal practice for a 'fast turnaround' specialist, B50(PCB), to commence production immediately after the artwork is delivered by the customer or picked up by one of its sales engineers. According to the company's Managing Director: 'this fast turnaround business runs very much on trust. Many times, the orders don't arrive until after the goods are shipped. Just as the customer has got to trust us that we deliver on time, we must trust the customer that what he tells us, the exact information, is what he really wants.' For a new customer, a telex or a fax is requested as written evidence before production commences. The MD said that six months or so of regular trading must elapse before trust is built up with a new customer.

For other British suppliers which receive only occasional short lead-time orders, a faxed or telexed purchase order number was generally said to be sufficient to start production. Similarly in Japan, the receipt of a drawing or an artwork was considered adequate before producing prototype development boards. J120(PCB)'s manager thought that such practice was peculiar to Japan, and proceeded to say: 'it's also against the sub-contracting law, but we wouldn't be getting any business if we were to observe the law always'.

B120(PCB) was the only supplier which recounted the bitter experience of being caught out once or twice when the boards were produced but delivery refused without the customer offering any cancellation charges. Such an experience has not stopped B120(PCB) from continuing to produce quick turnaround boards on the basis of oral agreement, presumably because each order does not constitute a large part of their business.

For scheduled orders of larger batches, the principle of not producing until a firm written order is placed was advocated by most sample suppliers. The need to produce before receiving a firm written order seldom arose for some suppliers, such as the Japanese assembly sub-contractors receiving production scheduling plans. But, for others, last minute scheduling changes by customers may require that the supplier exercise discretion to produce ahead of plan on the basis of forecasts. Among the British suppliers, such advance production based on projection was found to be rare, although materials may have to be procured on the basis of forecasts. In Japan, some suppliers produce in advance of firm orders in order to respond flexibly to customers' requirements. There are variations, however, in who bears the risk. Both J220(PCB) and J1210 (PCB) had persuaded their customers to buy up left-over boards which are not called off, thanks to skilful salesmanship. But J480(PCB) is made to bear the full burden of being left with excess stocks of unused boards.

Combination of high supplier transactional dependence and single sourcing?

Customer companies may exercise single-sourcing for a particular part number for various reasons, but chiefly to save on transaction and production costs (if economies of scale exist).'[6] A necessary condition for single-sourcing to constitute a saving on transaction costs for the bilateral relationship is high trust of both competence and goodwill types, so that there is little need to insure against late delivery, bad quality and opportunistic requests for price increases. In reality, a customer may choose a supplier as a single source not so much because of high trust but primarily because of a very small order volume. Conversely, dual or multiple sourcing may be exercised by a customer company not due to low trust but because of the sheer high volume of some orders.

Several British PCB suppliers noted a recent decline in the total number of PCB suppliers used by their customers and an accompanying increase in single-sourcing. For instance, B222(PCB)'s two largest customers reduced their PCB supplier base from a dozen to two or three, and a customer of B118(PCB) from seventeen to three. Suppliers' reactions to this diffusion of a preferred supplier-purchasing philosophy are varied. On the one hand, some doubt the customers' motives. For instance, B120(PCB) thought that single-sourcing can be used as a ploy by customers to obtain lower prices by placing higher volume orders. On the other hand, a few suppliers were aggressively promoting themselves as sole suppliers. For example, B750(EA) is said to be a sole supplier to most customers, or else it is competing against some customers' in-house facilities for assembly. Similarly, B500(PCB) has so far succeeded in becoming a sole source from a situation of one of multiple sources for eight large customers. Neither B750(EA)'s nor B500(PCB)'s transactional dependence, at 18 per cent and 35 per cent respectively, is very high, however, so that dependence is not mutual. (In fact, 35 per cent is quite high by British standards, but the largest customer does not treat B500(PCB) as a sole source.)

Against this background, other suppliers (B15(EA), B118(PCB), B120(PCB), B203(PCB), B410(PCB), and B1100(EA)) said that multiple sourcing – splitting a part number – was the norm for all longer leadtime orders. The capacity constraint, the volume being too large if part numbers were not split, was mentioned more often as a reason for multiple-sourcing than the customers' need to protect against the failure to deliver.

In Japan, J700(PCB) was exceptional in being subjected constantly to dual sourcing – sharing a part number with another supplier – due to large volumes. Both J140(PCB) and J150(PCB) used to have split-up part numbers in the past (in the rapidly growing 1960s), but not any longer. J250(EA) and J120(PCB) still faced multiple-sourcing from time to time when the required volume was beyond the company's capacity.

For all other sample companies, the practice of splitting a part number was not encountered. Thus, in Japan single-sourcing has been the norm, but not sole-sourcing. All sample suppliers were competing against other suppliers making similar components for the same customer; even J160(EA), whose sole customer forbids it from taking on work from other customers, has always competed against three other sub-contractors doing similar assembly work. The closest to the situation of high mutual dependence was encountered in the case of J650(PCB), 85 per cent dependent on the customer which in turn sources 35 per cent of all bought-in PCBs, rendering J650(PCB) the largest PCB supplier to this customer.

Quality inspection on delivery?

In ship-to-stock delivery, the supplier assures quality by carrying out its own quality checks and delivers straight onto the customer's assembly line. This delivery mode is often regarded as a first step towards achieving just-in-time (JIT) delivery. Despite the received wisdom that JIT production is equally suitable for large and small batches, ship-to-stock delivery usually applies only to delivery of parts required in large volumes over time. This is due to (i) the fact that savings on transaction costs of inspection on delivery is not much in small batches compared to large batches; and (ii) trust in the supplier's quality standards is built up more easily over long runs than over a series of shorter runs.

The highest level of competence trust was manifested by the customers for J240(EA), J250(EA), J265(EA) and J360(EA), all of which assembled final equipment ranging from telephone handsets, TV sets, banking terminals and mainframe computers, which were tested, packaged and delivered straight to customers' warehouses. A more common practice was for suppliers to conduct their own electrical, mechanical and thermal tests on sub-assemblies before delivering them to their customers' production lines. Many suppliers, but more in the Japanese than in the British sample, had part of their orders which became subject to no customer inspection after an initial period of monitoring; they included J17(PCB), J120(PCB), J150(PCB), J220(PCB), J480 (PCB), J700(PCB), J1210(PCB), J160(EA), B50(PCB), B120(PCB), B222(PCB), B300(PCB), B410(PCB) and B750(EA). The rest had their customers conduct sample or 100 per cent checks on delivered parts, although there was talk of some switching to ship-to-stock delivery.

Getting to be trusted is costly for suppliers, both in the process of ensuring high quality using expensive testing equipment and in the event of defects being discovered after components are assembled. One extreme reaction to this onus was by B15(EA) which would dissuade any customer wanting to implement ship-to-stock delivery; in the end it is the customer's brand which goes on to the product, and the customer's reputation which is at stake. A more common reaction was to regard ship-to-stock delivery as something progressive, even if many suppliers explicitly acknowledged the undesirable aspect of customers passing on the cost of testing and inspection to the supplier. Ultimately, the technical capability worthy of trust becomes a condition for receiving future orders. At GB Electronics, for instance, the practice of ship-to-stock delivery earns points on the monthly vendor performance review (VPR), and the higher the VPR score the more assured the supplier is of long-term business with the customer.

Communication channels and intensity

The three types of trust may develop through various modes of communication, the next feature to be examined in the ACR–OCR framework. This sub-section begins by examining the organisation of the sales department, as it constitutes an important interface for customer–supplier communication.

Organisation of sales personnel

The functions of the sales department involve both search for new customers and liaising with existing customers over current and future orders. The task of calculating, quoting and negotiating prices given customers' specifications, and sometimes of discussing customers' drawings, falls within the sales department's duties, as does the task of progress chasing and of responding initially to any defects discovered after delivery. Beyond such generality, variations exist along a number of dimensions.

First, some small owner-managed companies do not have a sales department nor a salesman because they have not developed the functional division of labour more common in larger organisations. Typically, the managing director or plant manager takes on the role of a salesman as in the case of B10(EA), B15(EA), B90(EA), J30(EA) and J71(EA), reflecting the importance, in the eyes of top management, of sales activity to the survival of these companies.

Second, production managers tended to be more directly involved in customer liaison in the electronic assembly sector than in the PCB sector. J160(EA), for instance, had one worker specialising in coordination of production scheduling with the sole customer. Similarly, production managers in some assembly sub-contractors took on the role of coordinating production scheduling and progress chasing, as in the case of J240(EA) with no specialist sales personnel but seven such production managers. By contrast, the sample PCB suppliers all had a sales department whose task it was to seek new customers and to service existing customers. The most common division of labour among PCB companies' sales personnel was between sales engineer 'in the field' operating from regional offices (or private homes in Britain) and internal sales clerks who are responsible for the paperwork in quotations, acknowledging orders and invoicing.

Third, sales personnel moved between companies more commonly in Britain than in Japan. In both countries, the sales workforce consisted of people who were recruited into the sales department from the beginning and those who were transferred from other departments in the same company. The most preferred internal transfer, given the increasing need for salesmen to be able to discuss technical aspects, was from the design engineering department. Job rotation was more institutionalised in Japan, where the norm of lifetime employment operated among the male workforce of a few large Japanese PCB companies. In particular, J1210(PCB) recruits university graduates who are given induction training on the shopfloor for six months to learn the production processes before starting work in the sales department. Other PCB companies are small or medium sized, and have had quits as well as mid-career hires. Well-qualified technologists are the most coveted category of workers some Japanese PCB suppliers wish to attract (see chapter 9). But no Japanese sample company mentioned the desire to poach salesmen for their expertise. As will become clear in subsequent discussion, this is because the expertise required of Japanese salesmen is not in codifiable occupational knowledge, but in more particularistic, tacit knowledge of not only customer companies but of how specific relationships operate.

By contrast, the British PCB suppliers rely in part on a mobile tribe of salesmen who have had work experience in more than one company, not necessarily in PCB manufacturing. For instance, one salesman for B120(PCB) used to work as a buyer at GB Electronics, a customer to B120(PCB). Another salesman, who also started his career in GB Electronics' purchasing department, worked for B410(PCB), and has recently moved on to an electronic assembly company. B222(PCB)'s chairman expressed the general sentiment in the British PCB industry that a company needs both a stable core of salesmen and a mobile element who bring in new ideas from outside. Mobile salesmen are considered beneficial to a company for all the contacts they bring into the company, in particular, in establishing business with new customers known to a salesman personally in his previous job. However, no cases were acknowledged of customers being lost as a result of a salesman leaving a PCB company.

Thus, salesmen in the British PCB industry are made to rely more on personal informal networks to cultivate new customers. They are hardly a profession (in the sense that lawyers and accountants are) despite the existence of the Institute of Purchasing and Supply which is a professional association conferring qualifications. But they are less well integrated into companies they work for than their Japanese counterparts who are more willing to take on the accumulated obligations of the company they work for. For these Japanese salesmen, career development is not through accumulating experience in different companies but through job rotation within the company. J700(PCB) mentioned that each salesman dealt with a different set of assigned customers every five years or so, in order to avoid too close an identification with the customer's interest which may result from too much familiarity.

Lastly, one may hypothesise that the Japanese suppliers devote fewer resources to sales activities than the British suppliers because they have fewer customers to deal with. Table 5.2, which shows the ratio of the

Table 5.2. *The Size of Suppliers' Sales Department*

Company	Sales empl.	%TE	C/S	Company	Sales empl.	%TE	C/S
B38(PCB)	1	2.6	80	J17(PCB)	1	5.9	20
B50(PCB)	3	6.0	76	J65(PCB)	6	9.2	15
B107(PCB)	4	3.7	55	J120(PCB)	7	5.8	4
B118(PCB)	5	4.2	20	J140(PCB)	25	17.9	2
B120(PCB)	10	7.3	15	J150(PCB)	12	8.0	17
B203(PCB)	15	7.4	27	J220(PCB)	13	5.9	15
B222(PCB)	4	1.8	38	J480(PCB)	13	2.7	8
B300(PCB)	13	4.3	5	J650(PCB)	20	3.1	5
B410(PCB)	10	2.4	10	J700(PCB)	24	3.4	3
B500(PCB)	16	3.2	11	J1210(PCB)	80	6.6	5
B10(EA)	1	10.0	25	J30(EA)	1	3.3	1
B15(EA)	1	6.7	30	J71(EA)	1	1.4	11
B90(EA)	1	1.1	35	J160(EA)	1	0.6	1
B205(EA)	6	2.9	3	J170(EA)	3	1.8	7
B230(EA)	8	3.5	4	J240(EA)	7	2.9	2
B350(EA)	2	0.6	18	J250(EA)	1	0.4	3
B750(EA)	14	1.9	1	J265(EA)	4	1.5	3
B1100(EA)	9	0.8	2	J360(EA)	1	0.3	4

N.B. % TE = Sales employees as per cent of total employees
C/S = Average number of customers per sales employee.

number of customers per sales employee, does not support this supposition. The ratios are lower on average among electronic assembly sub-contractors than PCB suppliers, and among Japanese suppliers than British suppliers, reflecting a higher intensity of communication and service offered by some suppliers to each of their customers. We will now turn to the exact nature of communication with customers.

Communication channels and intensity

As discussed before in chapters 1 and 2, an OCR-type relationship is carefully cultivated through (a) multi-channelled communication so as to make it 'thick' and not easily breakable; and (b) frequent communication, often extending beyond the immediate business into socialising which may breed friendship among people working for the two separate organisations. By contrast, trading partners in ACR attempt to minimise dependence on each other. This is achieved through (a) maintaining a narrow channel of communication, often only between the customer company's purchasing department and the supplier's sales department, and (b) minimising communication to what is strictly necessary, and ensuring that social relations do not affect company-to-company relations.

British practices

In the British sample, the most ACR-like frequency of communication was mentioned by B38(PCB) and B50(PCB) whose salesmen are said to visit each customer only once or twice a year. More common was a frequency of once a month generally, and once a week for major customers. At the OCR end of the British spectrum was B90(EA) whose Managing Director visits the major customers two to three times a week. The purpose of the visits may be to solicit new orders, pick up an order, make deliveries, or discuss quality problems. B15(EA)'s MD visits customers two to three times a month, but only for a definite purpose; 'one thing I never do', according to him, 'is to go and pester them [customers] for work.' Some customers do indeed regard too frequent a visit from their suppliers as a nuisance; B410(PCB) recalled being told by a customer that it is too busy to receive salesmen.

Sales-to-purchasing communication gives only a partial picture. As an example of multiple channels of communication, B300(PCB) had the following regular occasions to see its customers. First, annual negotiations with major customers take place either at B300(PCB) or at the customer's site, at which the Managing Director, a sales manager, a quality manager and an engineer from the supplier would be present. Within the year, there is a monthly performance review meeting at the customer's site, which the sales engineer in charge attends. Moreover, the head of the sales department visits each major customer twice a year, and the Managing Director once a year. Customers also visit B300(PCB) at least once in two months, but the major customer visit is a yearly quality audit which takes a whole day.

With other suppliers, monthly quality review or performance review meetings are becoming more common, and are practised at B500(PCB), B410(PCB), and B750(EA). These meetings are occasions when technical and quality personnel besides salesmen become involved on a regular basis with customer liaison. Some companies are also altering the norm of 'no news is good news' to regular communication for preventing quality defects.

Varying views were expressed by the British suppliers on how best to cultivate good business relations with their customers. At one extreme was B203(PCB) whose Managing Director had a deep suspicion of the motives of anyone who wished to entertain or to be entertained; he would not feel comfortable if his sales engineers were throwing money at individuals, nor would he feel relaxed if he were being entertained. Similarly, B500(PCB)'s Managing Director said that besides having no time for socialising, he dislikes buying favours by entertaining. Their views, associating 'mixing business with pleasure' automatically with the potential danger of being unethical (including accepting and giving bribes) tallies with the IBM philosophy[7].

At the other extreme, B300(PCB)'s managers believe strongly that socialising, such as having dinners and playing golf with customers, helps establish a relationship of trust. A regional sales engineer of B300(PCB) invites customers' buyers home to have a good chat until the early hours, out of which friendship may grow. He evidently regards 'getting to know them [buyers] really well' as important. His boss, the sales manager agrees; if several suppliers are equally competent, what swings a customer's decision, as a customer once told her, 'depends much on how you and I get on'.

Japanese practices
It is more of an accepted norm in Japan that suppliers socialise not only with their customers but also with their main banks. Playing golf is more or less obligatory. Moreover, large customers provide a focus for end-of-the year parties and visits to hot springs, which may be organised by the suppliers' association (*kyoryokukai*). Indeed, some suppliers' associations are said to exist for nothing more than to organise these social gatherings to cultivate mutual intimacy (*shinboku*) within a group. The exception in accepting this Japanese norm was J170(EA) which has no entertainment budget; the MD plays golf but only with personal friends, and he does not much like drinking. He concluded that there was time and money to entertain customers if need be, but orders rolled in without it, so why bother.

A more common view was that of J140(PCB) whose managers showed a preference for socialising with customers, but regarded socialising as a consequence of, rather than as an instrumental means to, establishing trust relations. How, then, do suppliers go about establishing trust (of all types)? The answer is, by frequent communication, getting to know the customers personally, and offering good service to them, responding flexibly and promptly to their requirements.

In this regard, the majority of Japanese respondents agreed to the statement in the questionnaire that 'socialising with the customer helps to deepen relations and establish a relation of trust' (Q.4M), and another that 'socialising is a good way of getting information about competitors, supply and demand, etc,' (Q.4N).[8] But, regardless of nationality, nearly half (seventeen out of thirty-six responses) agreed to both simultaneously, indicating that the affective and instrumental reasons for socialising are difficult to distinguish. However, Japanese sample suppliers tended to value personal networks as a basis for trust (Q.4I), while British sample suppliers tended to consider customers' general reputation as sufficient to come to trust it (Q.4K).[9]

In the PCB industry, the normal frequency of communication, both preferred by the suppliers and expected of them by their customers, is daily visits to the customer's site. The large suppliers with resources actually did have their salesmen go to the major customers daily, while smaller ones had to do with visits two or three times a week although, ideally, daily visits would be desirable.

As an example, J1210(PCB)'s eighty salesmen all visit their customers daily, sometimes more frequently. Each salesman is typically assigned to one customer, or one product division of a customer enterprise, and is said to understand the predisposition (*taishitsu*) of the specific customer inside out. Daily commuting to the customer's site is necessary, not only to see buyers but also to visit the design and development department to pick up early information on future orders. Because J1210(PCB) is competing against four or five other suppliers to obtain prototype drawings, it is essential to know when – not just on which day, but what time – a prototype drawing will be ready. If it is said to be out at 10 p.m. and the salesman is not there at the customer's to pick it up, another supplier's salesman would take it away. Because a prototype drawing is handed out to just one supplier, and securing a prototype order more or less ensures obtaining the subsequent mass-production order, the salesmen's lives are a daily battle, fighting to get their hands on the prototype drawings. As there are typically two or three prototype drawings which come out every day, there is indeed something to discuss with the customer every day. But even if there is no specific business to discuss, it is necessary to drop in at the customer's, to let one's face be known, to provide snippets of information useful to the customer, and on the off-chance that some new orders originally destined for other suppliers are lying around to be picked up by anyone to meet a very short leadtime. In stark contrast to some British customers' complaints about being pestered, Japanese customers could claim that the reason why a supplier is not given more orders is because its salesman does not show up often enough.

Although salesmen are expected to do a lot, quality and production personnel also visit the customers, as does the Managing Director. The latter would be the one to attend the annual meeting of top executives from core suppliers to discuss the overall level of business for the next year and longer term business strategies.

In the Japanese electronic assembly sector, less frequent visits than in the PCB industry – once a week or once a month – suffice as customers' straight commission pre-empts the need to solicit new orders. Top managers attend six monthly meetings at which customers disclose the future business plans to the trusted few. And by far the most concentrated period of communication occurs whenever a new assembly line or a new piece of equipment is installed, with much assistance from customers' engineers.

In conclusion, the intensity of communication is highest among some Japanese PCB suppliers whose livelihood depends on securing prototype board orders. The norm of daily contact was considered desirable by all Japanese PCB suppliers, while the British PCB suppliers' normal intensity was lower. In the electronic assembly industry, intense communication was considered necessary not on a continuous basis but whenever new major orders were placed. On the whole, Japanese electronic assembly sub-contractors met more frequently and regularly than their British counterparts in order to receive information on customers' future production plans. Moreover, meetings with a group of suppliers take place in Japan, but rarely in Britain. The openness which comes with frequent communication in OCR-type relationships does not lend itself easily to the use of information as a negotiating power base. The essential skill of a salesman is not in the ability to strike a hard bargain, as in ACR-type relations, but more in the ability to obtain vital pieces of information earlier than anyone else. Here, the informal personal networks, what rapport a salesman has established with a particular buyer or an engineer at a customer company, matters greatly.

Technical guidance by customers

One obvious occasion for communication between customers and suppliers, as noted above is, when sales engineers and other technical staff at the supplier's liaise with the customer's technical staff over product design and process technology. Such a liaison is always necessary when exchange involves customised components, and whenever a new product line is being set up. For instance, PCB suppliers may query the customer-specified design in the artwork and suggest an improvement so as to make it easier to manufacture, improving the yield. Similarly, customers may send in their engineers to the suppliers to make sure that all the equipment is used properly according to specification. Such exchange of technical expertise is self-motivated, but by its very nature returns to the transfer of expertise are never completely appropriable. Because of this appropriability problem, little pooling of technical expertise occurs in ACR, and if technical guidance does occur, it is always fully costed and paid for. By contrast, OCR-type relationships rely much on informal exchange of technical knowhow and, given long-time horizons, technical guidance is rarely costed and paid for in the short run.

British practices
In the PCB industry, little pooling of technical expertise has occurred, as the customer specified the drawings, which the supplier is expected to follow faithfully. Customers are said to take little interest in how PCBs are actually made; 'buyers in all honesty don't want to know . . . as long as the product turns out to look according to the specification', was the opinion of B410(PCB)'s sales director. The division of labour is thus clear cut: the customer specifies, and the supplier manufactures. When a supplier needed to query customers' design or artwork, some customers reacted badly, their engineers taking suggestions for improvement as a slur on their professional expertise. B50(PCB)'s Managing Director said that a typical customer reaction is to treat suppliers' queries on design as a pain in the neck as they concern a job which they have finished for good. Moreover, B50(PCB)'s artwork inspectors do not generally look for improvements on customers' design, as 'we are not in the business of telling them [customers] what they can or can't do'.

The greatest contrast to the above attitude is detected in the case of B500(PCB). At this supplier, there are four technical service engineers whose sole task is to act as advisors to customers. They spend most of their time with the major customers, making suggestions on how to improve design, and even on the correct processes for component assembly. Engineers from the customer companies often come and use the CAD system at this PCB supplier, B500(PCB), to develop prototype design and necessary tools for prototype production.

In the electronic assembly sector, the relationship most intensive in technology transfer is found at B700(EA). The sub-contractor prides itself on having advanced design and component testing facilities, but is also keen to learn from customers. Visits by customer engineers are quite common; they are even given an office space at B700(EA) from where they operate, working together with the sub-contractors' engineers on process technology, installing new equipment, and setting up statistical process control. One day, there were apparently as many as fourteen engineers visiting from various customers. In a similar vein, a couple of North American customers to B205(EA) not only send in their engineers, but also provide videos and training courses for B205(EA)'s and other sub-contractors' employees on the latest techniques in Total Quality Control or Statistical Process Control. These training sessions may last for a weekend, provided free of charge by the customer, while B205(EA) pays for travel and hotel expenses only.[10] B205(EA)'s Managing Director felt that large companies have the responsibility to keep smaller suppliers up to date with new production technology.

There was, however, less willingness to learn by a larger sub-contractor, B1100(EA), whose technical director said that there was no real technology transfer from its Japanese customers located in the UK. This perception was despite the fact that every time a new line is set up, a customer engineer spends two whole days at B1100 (EA). By contrast, the production director of the same company – a Japanese national – thought that there had been numerous small production technology improvements made as a result of Japanese customer engineers spending time on the shopfloor. If defects occur, 'they [customer engineers] are swarming all over the place' to offer 'constructive support' which, in the technical director's view, is better than some British customer companies which 'just shout and do not offer any support'.

Japanese practices

The metaphor of child rearing in Japanese customer–supplier relations is applied to point out the importance of technical nurture over time with much care and attention (see chapter 3). Receiving technical guidance (*gijutsu shido*) is, at least at the initial stages of a relationship, thought to be a normal and integral part of trading with small and medium-sized enterprises.

Technical guidance is more common in the electronic assembly industry than in the PCB industry, as customer companies are more likely to possess in-house technological expertise in the former than in the latter. This probably explains why the Japanese assembly sub-contractors were exceptional in feeling that they owe their customers for achieving their present technological capability.[11] As an example, J250(EA) represents the most OCR-like practice of much technical transfer without costing its worth. First, every time an assembly line is reset for a new model, which is on average once a month, between five and twenty engineers from the customer company are stationed at J250(EA), instructing the operators in a hands-on fashion. Second, assembly operators may experience working in the customer's factory for a week or so. Third, J250(EA)'s four technologists are on placement at two major customer companies as trainees for a period of a week up to two months; they are accepted upon passing written tests set by the customer company, whose section chief (*kacho*) comments on the daily progress report written by the trainee himself, which in turn is passed onto J250(EA)'s Managing Director.

J265(EA) also had a similar system of technical guidance. Every time a new product is to be assembled, which is roughly twice a year, around three J265(EA) employees, from the operator up to sub-section chief (*hancho* and *kakaricho*) levels, are sent to its largest customer for a period of between ten days and a month. They study the production technology, inspection procedures and standards, in order mainly to reach a precise understanding with the customer of how best to produce and inspect the new parts. Upon returning to J265(EA), the 'trained' workers are expected to teach the other workers what they have learnt. With a longer term perspective, J265(EA) has also started (some ten years ago) sending in graduate technologists – around three at a time – to the largest customer company for three-year training. These technologists gain valuable experience working alongside the customer technologists doing design and development work. It goes without saying that benefits from such long-term training are appropriable by the sub-contracting company only with the assurance of long-term service by its employees, and by the customer only through long-term commitment by the sub-contractor. No fees are paid by J265(EA) to the customer. J360(EA) also mentioned the opportunity to send its technologists to the largest customer's R&D centres several days at a time; in return, J360(EA) repays its debt of gratitude (*on gaeshi*) by meeting the customer's demanding requirements.

The more ACR-like sub-contractors, J160(EA) and J170(EA), said that they used to have daily intensive engineer visits from the customer company in the past, at the initial stages of trading, but no longer. Both appeared to feel proud of this achievement of independence. Still dependent and in the process of being nurtured was J71(EA) which had asked for and got a production engineer from a customer on a one-year secondment to instruct workers at the company.

In the PCB supplier sample, the only supplier which perceives its current technological capability to have been unattainable had it not been for the customer's help is J120(PCB). This company started out as a paint and metal-pressing workshop supplying exclusively to JJ Electric. In the early 1960s, JJ Electric's PCB division wished to sub-contract out some of the processes in PCB manufacturing, and asked whether J120(PCB) would be willing to diversify into PCB production, which required skills similar to what was involved in the pre-painting cleaning process. With consent, JJ Electric sent in its engineers and installed equipment initially owned by them at J120(PCB), to transfer in-house expertise process by process, until J120(PCB) was producing whole PCBs. JJ Electric's way of ensuring that the benefits of such intensive technical guidance were appropriated fully was to insist on exclusive supply (though not entirely successfully; see chapter 10).

The other PCB suppliers said that although advice is sometimes given by their customers on general production management, no customer knows the process technology specific to PCB manufacturing well enough. J65(PCB) and J1210(PCB), in particular, stated most strongly that it is they who have something to teach their customers, not the other way round. In fact, a handful of J1210(PCB)'s customer companies send their new technologist recruits to J1210(PCB) for a short period as part of their induction training. Moreover, both J65(PCB) and J1210(PCB) get involved at the prototype design stage, making suggestions for improvements.

In summary, the PCB suppliers generally felt that their process technology was acquired through their own effort over time, except in a few cases in Japan. The PCB supplier's contribution of suggestions for yield-improving design changes was taken for granted in Japan, but was disliked by some of the British suppliers' customers. In the electronic assembly industry, customer company engineers got involved in setting up the suppliers' process technology in both Britain and Japan, but it was more of an accepted norm in Japan than in Britain. In Japan, it had the effect of building up sub-contractors' feelings of indebtedness to their customers. By contrast, in Britain, where the predominant perception was that of technological independence from customers, sub-contractors' reactions ranged from discomfort with too much customer intrusion on the shopfloor to the willingness to acquire general technical information provided free of charge by customers.

Risk sharing

The last feature to be examined, the extent of risk sharing, focuses on mutual willingness to respond flexibly to unforeseen circumstances so that the burden of adjustment, as well as unexpected benefits, are shared in a fair way. In ACR relationships, this amounts to devising prior explicit agreements which stipulate each party's obligation in every foreseen eventuality so as to minimise the extent to which the fate of a company is affected by its trading partners. In OCR relationships, much risk sharing over time exists and contingencies are resolved case by case. Instances of risk sharing were already mentioned in the sections on contractualism and various types of trust, particularly with respect to rules of thumb in the event of unforeseen changes in ordered quantity. Here, the discussion focuses on sharing of risk associated with material price fluctuations.

The most ACR way of dealing with material price fluctuations was found at B750(EA) whose customers in effect bear 100 per cent of the risk. B750(EA)'s plant manager has negotiated as part of the written contract a clause which obligates its customers to settle the difference between the 'standard' material price at the time of contract signing and the actual price B750(EA) pays, whether the difference is due to foreign-exchange fluctuations or due simply to relative changes in supply and demand. B1100(EA) was attempting to negotiate a similar clause, but without success at the time of interview. No such written clauses were found among the Japanese suppliers. Most sub-contractors, both Japanese and British, had at least some part of their materials supplied ('free issued') by their customers, who in effect bear the risk of those material price fluctuations.

A more common practice in Britain was to have a rule, either written or tacitly agreed, that the supplier has the right to renegotiate prices if the material price fluctuates by more than x per cent. For example, B500(PCB) had a written rule of renegotiation for over 10 per cent fluctuation, while B300(PCB) had an unwritten rule of renegotiation for material price hikes in excess of 5 per cent in any 6-month period. However, whether the suppliers actually manage to pass on whole or part of the cost increases to their customers depends much on the state of the market, with a better chance of succeeding if the supplier industry's capacity is tight. The British PCB suppliers, at the time of interviewing them, mentioned the general difficulty in passing on cost increases to the customer.

In Japan, the idea of raising an initially agreed component price due to material cost increases within the product lifecycle is alien to both customer and supplier companies. Suppliers are expected to absorb such cost increases internally, unless the increase is extreme; one such case was a three-fold increase in the prices of certain memory chips in 1988, part of which was borne by J240(EA)'s customers. Prices are generally reviewed every six months, with the expectations of price reduction through learning-by-doing and 'rationalization' (*gorika*). Suppliers are expected to comply with cost reduction (*costu daun*) requests, while their customers appeal to the shared goal of increasing sales (see chapter 11).

Table 5.3. *The ACR–OCR scores*

(A) TRANSACTIONAL DEPENDENCE
1 = Less than 20 per cent
2 = 21–50 per cent
3 = 51–100 per cent
(B) PROCEDURE FOR OBTAINING ORDERS
1 = Price quotations always sought from more than one supplier for both new and repeat orders; less than 60 per cent chance of winning orders.
2 = Price quotations always sought from more than one supplier, but good idea (over 60 per cent) of winning orders.
3 = Price estimate generally sought only from one supplier.
(C) PROJECTED LENGTH OF TRADING
1 = Short-term commitment is both desired and the reality.
2 = Long-term commitment is desired, but short-term is the reality.
3 = Long-term commitment is both desired and the reality.
(D) DOCUMENTS FOR EXCHANGE
1 = Written, detailed and substantive documents.
2 = Some reliance on oral agreements.
3 = Heavy reliance on oral agreement and tacit understanding.
(E) CONTRACTUALISM
1 = Contingencies are written out and followed strictly.
2 = Contingencies, some written and others tacitly understood, are followed strictly.
3 = Case-by-case resolution with much appeal to the diffuse obligation of long-term relationships.
(F) CONTRACTUAL TRUST
1 = Supplier never starts production until a written purchase order form is received.
2 = Supplier sometimes starts production before a written purchase order form is received.
3 = Supplier quite often starts production before a written purchase order form is received.
(G) GOODWILL TRUST
1 = Low transactional dependence (less than 20 per cent) combined with multiple sourcing.
2 = Low transactional dependence with single-sourcing, or high transactional dependence with multiple sourcing.
3 = High transactional dependence combined with single-sourcing.
(H) COMPETENCE TRUST
1 = Thorough 100 per cent or sample checks for all part numbers by customer on delivery.
2 = Some no inspection on delivery.
3 = Over half of part numbers receive no inspection on delivery.
(I) COMMUNICATION CHANNELS AND INTENSITY
1 = Infrequent and strictly business communication through narrow formal channels.
2 = Multi-channelled, but socialising shunned.

Table 5.3 (*Cont.*)

---

3 = Multi-channelled, frequent communication, often extending beyond strict business.
(J) TECHNOLOGY TRANSFER
1 = Pooling of technical expertise between trading partners has rarely occurred.
2 = Some pooling of technical expertise.
3 = Much unilateral or bilateral technology transfer over time, without attempt at costing it.
(K) RISK SHARING
1 = Little sharing of risk over input cost fluctuations.
2 = Some risk sharing.
3 = Much risk sharing over time.

Summing up: an overall assessment

The sample suppliers will now be ranked along the ACR–OCR scale, by assigning numerical values to what essentially are qualitative differences in each of the eleven features of customer–supplier relationships analysed in this chapter. This is an invidious task, given the rich diversity in the trading practices identified, but is undertaken in order to provide a convenient summary. Table 5.3 explains what the 3 point scores mean for each of the 11 ACR–OCR features. In Table 5.4, the 36 sample suppliers are assigned a score for each feature and an overall score which is the sum of all the 11 scores. The possible overall scores range from 11, the most ACR-like practice, through to 33, the most OCR-like practice.

On the basis of these overall scores, it is evident that the range of practices in the electronic assembly sector (score range 17–31) is more OCR than the range of practices in the PCB sector (12–28). In each sector, the range of Japanese practices is more OCR than the range of British practices, with an overlap in Japanese and British practices in the assembly sector (see Figure 5.1). Beyond such generalisations, however, variations have been identified within each sector in each country, even on the basis of a small sample such as this. The following chapters (6–10) will provide explanations for inter-country, inter-sectoral and intra-sectoral differences in the trading patterns.

A few last words are warranted on how the empirical findings relate to my starting hypothesis discussed in chapter 1. In particular, it was posited that the ACR features are internally consistent, as are the OCR features. This led to the hypothesis that a company was more likely to have ACR or OCR scores in all the features than to have a mix of ACR and OCR

The analysis of supplier companies

Table 5.4. *ACR–OCR Ranking of Sample Suppliers*

	A	B	C	D	E	F	G	H	I	J	K	TOTAL
B38(PCB)	1	3	3	1	3	3	2	1	1	1	2	21~
B50(PCB)	1	2	1	2	3	3	2	2	1	1	1	19
B107(PCB)	1	2	2	2	2	3	2	1	2	1	1	19
B118(PCB)	1	1	1	2	2	2	1	1	2	1	2	16
B120(PCB)	1	1	2	1	1	2	1	2	2	1	1	15
B203(PCB)	1	1	1	1	1	1	1	2	1	1	1	12ʌ
B222(PCB)	1	1	2	2	2	2	1	2	2	2	3	20
B300(PCB)	1	2	2	1	2	2	2	2	2	2	2	20
B410(PCB)	2	2	2	2	3	2	1	2	2	1	1	20
B500(PCB)	2	2	3	1	2	1	3	1	2	2	2	21~
B10(EA)	2	2	1	2	2	1	2	1	2	1	1	17ʌ
B15(EA)	2	2	2	2	2	2	1	1	1	2	2	19
B90(EA)	2	2	3	2	3	1	2	1	2	3	2	23~
B205(EA)	1	2	3	1	2	2	2	1	2	3	2	21
B230(EA)	2	3	2	2	2	1	2	1	2	2	2	21
B350(EA)	2	2	3	2	2	2	2	1	2	2	1	21
B750(EA)	1	3	3	1	1	1	2	3	2	3	1	21
B1100(EA)	1	2	3	2	3	1	1	1	2	2	2	20
J17(PCB)	2	2	3	3	3	3	2	2	2	1	3	26
J65(PCB)	1	3	3	2	3	3	2	1	2	1	2	23
J120(PCB)	3	3	3	2	3	2	2	2	3	2	3	28~
J140(PCB)	2	2	3	2	2	2	2	1	3	1	2	22ʌ
J150(PCB)	2	2	3	2	2	1	2	3	3	1	2	23
J220(PCB)	2	3	3	2	1	3	2	3	2	1	2	24
J480(PCB)	1	3	3	2	2	3	2	3	2	1	1	23
J650(PCB)	3	2	3	2	3	1	3	1	3	3	3	27
J700(PCB)	2	1	3	2	2	2	1	3	3	1	3	23
J1210(PCB)	1	3	3	1	2	1	2	3	3	1	3	23
J30(EA)	3	3	3	2	3	1	3	1	2	3	1	25
J71(EA)	3	3	3	2	1	1	3	1	3	3	3	26
J160(EA)	3	3	3	1	3	1	2	2	1	2	1	22
J170(EA)	2	1	3	2	1	2	2	1	2	3	1	20ʌ
J240(EA)	2	2	2	1	1	3	2	3	2	1	3	22
J250(EA)	3	3	3	2	3	3	2	3	3	3	3	31~
J265(EA)	3	2	3	2	3	2	3	2	2	3	3	28
J360(EA)	3	3	3	2	3	1	3	3	2	2	1	27

N.B. ʌ: the most ACR in the sector
~: the most OCR in the sector

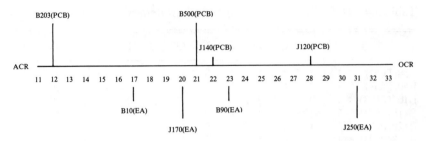

Figure 5.1 The ACR–OCR spectrum for sample suppliers.

scores. This is not borne out in practice; real-life situations deviate from the ideal-typical extremes *not* because the eleven features are equally intermediate (scoring two) but because of a combination of some ACR and some OCR scores. Given this fact, a simple summation of the eleven feature scores disguises some differences among suppliers with equal overall scores. For instance, B750(EA), scoring high on both contractualism and competence trust, must be distinguished from B205(EA), B230(EA) and B350(EA), low on both accounts, but all with an overall score of twenty-one.

A number of factors may account for the coexistence of ACR and OCR features within a company. One possibility is the fact that some aspects, but not others, of the supplier's trading practices are dictated largely by its customers which have different preferences from the supplier. Another possibility is that the supplier's trading pattern is undergoing a change from ACR to OCR (or vice versa), with differential rates of change for each feature. Lastly, it may be that each supplier differentiates between the core and periphery among the eleven ACR–OCR features, and that inconsistency (i.e. a mix of ACR and OCR) is not tolerated only among the core features. In fact, the correlation coefficient matrix of the eleven features indicates that reasonably strong correlations exist between transactional dependence and 'goodwill trust' (.566); between transactional dependence and technology transfer (.510); and between 'goodwill trust' and technology transfer (.509). The ordering procedure and 'goodwill trust' are correlated (.536), as are technology transfer and communication channels and intensity (.543), as one would expect. Lastly, if all eleven features are interpreted to be measuring the presence or absence of trust, the ACR–OCR scores are found to be moderately reliable (Chronbach's alpha = .66).

PART III

Explanations of variations

6

Economic and technological factors

What makes one company's relationship with another company more ACR (or more OCR) than another's? What explains the variations in the mode of customer–supplier relationships as discovered empirically and described in the previous chapters? This and the following four chapters provide a systematic analysis of factors underlying companies' choice of trading relationships along the ACR–OCR spectrum.

The present chapter concentrates on those factors which have traditionally preoccupied economists. In theory, the assessment of these factors must be carried out on a *ceteris paribus* basis, assuming that the surrounding national institutions, people's value preferences and social norms are the same for all. In reality, other things are not equal, while various factors may be subject to multiple and two-way links (see Figure 1.1). This chapter deals in the main with the direct effects of economic and technological factors on the ACR–OCR patterns, while being sensitive to two-way causation. The first section concentrates on technology. In particular, we will examine how inter-industry differences in various types of 'asset specificity' and product-development cycles affect the nature of customer–supplier relationships. We will then turn to the importance of market conditions, in particular market structures, the nature of competition, and the pace of economic growth which shape companies' expectations about the future of existing trading relationships. Five propositions are put forward in the course of the chapter.

Technology as a determinant?

It was shown in chapter 5 that in both countries of study, Britain and Japan, some industrial sectors were more prone to have ACR-type relationships than some others. In particular, regardless of country, electronic assembly sub-contractors' modal trading relationship was found to be more OCR than PCB suppliers'. Why should this be the case? Differences in technology constitute one explanation. In order to examine how various aspects of technology affect the ACR–OCR choice, this section distinguishes between *product* technology embodied in its design specification and *process* technology as reflected in the extent of customisation in tools and jigs (i.e. 'asset specificity').

Asset specificity

The first aspect to be examined is the nature of process technology. This aspect is captured by Williamson in his concept of asset specificity or idiosyncratic investment. Stated briefly, the greater the degree of specificity of investment to a particular customer company, the greater the scope for post-contractual opportunism by both trading partners. After the supplier undertakes such investment, it might refuse production and delivery unless higher prices are offered. The customer might equally threaten to cancel orders without compensation (leaving the supplier to bear the sunk cost) for the purpose of extracting lower prices. In order to remove such incentives for opportunism, there are said to be alternative 'governance structures', which may be: (a) complete financial vertical integration, if the degree of asset specificity is very high; (b) quasi-vertical integration, in which the buyer owns the specialised tools and machinery to be used by the supplier (Montverde and Teece, 1982; Klein et al., 1978); or (c) credible commitments, which may involve reciprocal trading (i.e. 'Company A agrees to buy Y from Company B as a condition for making the sale of X'), or simply a promise to pay compensation (equivalent to the unamortised cost of specialised investment made by the supplier) if orders are cancelled (Williamson 1985, chapters 7 and 8).

Credible commitments are more consistent with ACR than with OCR, as they reinforce contractualism. Whether credible commitments are entered into and remain credible depends on 'contractual trust' in the main. Quasi-vertical integration, by contrast, is consistent with either ACR or OCR. In ACR, the customer needs to rely on the credible threat to take away specialised tools if the supplier behaves intransigently. In OCR, such threat is not necessary because of the presence of 'goodwill trust'; the customer is willing to own specific assets because it is in its interest to increase the degree of asset specificity, particularly intangible know-how through technology transfer, to lock its supplier into the trading relationship. Thus, we can argue that the greater the preferred degree of asset specificity, the greater the need for long-term commitments on the part of both the buyer and the supplier, and therefore the more worthwhile it becomes for trading partners to invest in trust building. From this, the following proposition arises.

Proposition 1: The greater the preferred degree of asset specificity, the more likely OCR-type relations are to emerge.

We will examine this proposition with respect to our case-study supplier industries, namely PCBs and electronic assembly. Asset specificity includes specificity not only in physical assets but also in human assets, site specificity, and dedicated assets (Williamson 1985, pp. 95–6). Human asset specificity arises due to learning-by-doing, or in the process of R&D which may result in confidential innovation. Site specificity refers to assets which are immobile once installed, normally near the buyer's site so as to save on inventory and transportation costs. Lastly, investment in dedicated assets involves expanding existing generalised production capacity for a specific customer.

Manufacturing of PCBs involves a large number of processing stages, from design, artwork production, drilling, printing, plating, etching, to circuitry testing. Each process is subject to unavoidably lumpy investment, so that balancing the capacity throughout the processing line is a difficult task; hence the occasional use of sub-contractors. Physical asset specificity is minimal in the industry. The sum of specific investment in (a) artwork (i.e. photography or silk screens, and magnetic tapes for CNC drilling machines); (b) press punching moulds if required; and (c) circuitry testing jigs, may cost between a few hundred pounds to several thousand pounds. These customer specific assets are owned, and in theory paid for, by the customer in question. However, particularly if batch size is large, tooling costs may not be charged separately, but provided at a discount as a service. Such practice was observed more commonly in the Japanese PCB industry than in the British, consistent with the reasoning that it is more easily acceptable given OCR-maintaining than ACR-maintaining norms.

Compared to PCB industries, electronic assembly is an industry whose major process involves deceptively standardised, semi-skilled, operations. In terms of physical equipment, asset specificity is small as automatic insertion machines, surface mount machines, flow solder machines, etc. are all standardised machinery manufactured by large equipment suppliers. The only explicitly customer-specific physical assets are programming tapes for automatic machines and robots, and jigs for electrical circuitry testing.

There is, however, the proprietary firm-specific knowledge (i.e. 'specific human assets') of the exact speed at which bandoliered components ought to be fed into insertion machines, or the optimal temperature of

147

the flow solder. Frequent visits by customer technologists to sub-contractors' sites sometimes to instruct supplier operators in a hands-on fashion, as reported in chapter 5, may then be interpreted as for the purpose of ensuring a high degree of human asset specificity for efficient production.

Besides human assets, site specificity and dedicated assets abound in electronic assembly in both Britain and Japan. For instance, B230(EA) and B350(EA) in Britain and J30(EA) in Japan were all located near their respective major customer, which owned most of the expensive general equipment installed at the supplier. In particular, J30(EA)'s automatic insertion machines were all owned by its sole customer's HQ plant, while J30(EA) also built another assembly factory near the same customer's branch factory a few hundred miles away. More generally, due to the very nature of assembly, every manual assembly line tends to be dedicated at one time to a particular customer's order. Every line takes time to set up and once set up at a particular sub-contractor, it is costly to disassemble and transport it elsewhere.

The ultimate degree of asset specificity of all kinds depends much on the willingness of both customer and supplier companies to be locked into a relationship. Thus, the supplier would be more willing to make modifications to general purpose machinery to suit a particular customer's needs, so as to reduce production costs, the more commitment the customer shows in long-term trading. The customer, in turn, would be more willing to transfer its proprietary know-how to its sub-contractors, the greater the opportunity to reap benefits from such joint investment into human and physical assets. Expectations of long-term trading, as well as some customers' insistence on 100 per cent dependence by suppliers (e.g. in the case of J160(EA)), contribute towards greater asset specificity. Thus, the degree of asset specificity may be subject to choice, within the bounds allowed by the nature of technology, and the more OCR a relationship is, the greater the degree of asset specificity is likely to be.

The scope for choice may also be illustrated by the following. Micro-electronics technology has enabled machinery to become more general purpose and programmable for specific usage. For example, in the PCB industry, 'blank tools' for the old pressing technology cost several thousand pounds, while magnetic tapes for NC drilling machines cost only a few hundred pounds (although the NC machines themselves are expensive). The latter technology has been replacing the former as the PCB design becomes finer. This implies a reduction in physical asset specificity, and hence a possibility for more ACR-type relations. However, such logical possibilities are not always followed. A high degree of asset specificity may foreclose the choice of ACR, but a lowering in the degree of specificity does not necessarily lead to ACR but merely creates more scope for choice between ACR and OCR.

Lastly, when all types of asset specificity are taken into account, quasi-vertical integration may not lead to its presumed outcome that neither party loses anything if a customer moves the specific asset it owns from one supplier to another. In the plastic injection moulding industry, suppliers in both Japan and Britain are said to dislike using tools made by or for another supplier, as small details in specifications may not be to their liking. This indicates that assets are not only customer-specific but also supplier-specific. Moreover, asset specificity embodied in moulds cannot be totally attributable to physical features; some human asset elements exist, but more so for soft metal moulds which require careful handling than in Britain where 'idiot proof' tools are said to be made (see the case of TCP(UK) in chapter 4). When such human element is significant, the customer's ownership of physical assets does not remove the incentive for opportunistic behaviour in ACR relations.

To summarise, asset specificity provides a partial explanation for the variation between ACR and OCR. Electronic assembly sub-contractors tend to have more OCR links with their customers than PCB suppliers because of the greater degree of asset specificity (particularly in dedicated assets) in the former industry. But the degree of specificity of physical assets does not fully determine the choice between ACR and OCR. Human asset specificity due to learning-by-doing and tacit knowledge appears more important in inducing customers to place an order with the same supplier over the long run. Moreover, how much physical and human asset specificity is created is a matter of choice. The greater the trading partners' expectations to trade over the long term, the more willing they become to invest in specialised assets.

Product development and design

Next, coordination over product development and design necessarily involves greater exchange of information than coordination over production with fixed design specifications. Standardised components may be purchased 'off-the-shelf', whereas customised products may be made in a number of ways. Suppliers may manufacture according to drawings fully specified and supplied by the customer, or they may manufacture with their own design approved by the customer (Asanuma (1989) calls the former DS and the latter DA suppliers). Parts made using the latter method, with a greater supplier input into design, requires the customer

149

to trust the supplier's competence and goodwill. We may therefore assert:

Proposition 2: The most customised components are, and the more suppliers have an input into the development and design process, the more necessary OCR-type relations become.

At one extreme, standard memory chips are traded in the world market with much reference to prevailing prices which reflect the state of demand relative to supply. However, as semi-custom chips are projected to take up a growing proportion of the semiconductor market (from a quarter in 1988 to a third by 1992 according to Dataquest), greater coordination between the customer and the supplier in design is required. At the same time, the continuing inability of US semiconductor suppliers to penetrate into the Japanese market may indicate that Japanese semiconductor suppliers had already established OCR-type relations with their customers even in standard components, as a spill-over effect from normal practice in more customised goods.

In various contexts, if the customer and the supplier are found to have complementary expertise, joint development may be undertaken to share the risk associated with R&D and product innovation. In the automobile industry, for example, 'partnerships' between assemblers and component suppliers are increasing because of a greater reliance of assemblers on suppliers' specialist knowledge, especially in electronics technology which car assemblers do not possess in-house. OCR-type relations are likely to emerge if the specialist component supplier perceives a high degree of interdependence because its components can be sold only as part of the customer's final products.

The suppliers in the sectors which were studied in chapters 4 and 5 all produce customised components. However, an important difference among the sectors is the extent to which suppliers possess the design and manufacturing expertise which their customer companies may not have in-house. In the sample, almost all customers possess in-house expertise in electronic assembly, while not all customers do so in PCBs and plastic moulding. This affects the relative bargaining power at price negotiations in a different way under ACR and OCR.

In ACR relationships. customer companies with in-house design capability are reluctant to seek ideas or contributions on design and development from their suppliers. The reason for this is two-fold. First, design is proprietary, and customers in arm's-length relations wish to minimise the chance of confidentiality leaking to competitors via suppliers. Second, suppliers' design input gives them a stronger relative power when bargaining over prices. In contrast, in OCR relations which

150

presume long-term commitment, suppliers' contribution to design is encouraged, and their willingness to offer ideas for design improvements is seen by the customer as an indication of supplier commitment; the reward is in winning more higher profit margin orders in the future. Thus, OCR is more conducive to suppliers' contribution to design than ACR.

Evidence in chapter 4 suggests that, compared with GB Electronics, JJ Electric seeks more design and development inputs from its suppliers, including its PCB suppliers and assembly sub-contractors. They had formerly been given detailed specifications but are now entrusted with a portion of the development stage so as to save on JJ Electric's engineering hours. As described in chapter 5, Japanese PCB suppliers tended to become involved early in the prototype stage to be followed on by proper production orders, whereas in Britain, suppliers of prototype boards and production boards were more clearly delineated; their customers clearly saw the advantage in this separation for enhancing their bargaining power *vis-à-vis* suppliers of detailed specification PCBs.

The extent to which suppliers contribute to design and development therefore appears to be influenced in part by the prior choice of ACR or OCR trading norms. This reasoning is supported by Clark et al's (1987) research on the product development process in the car industry. By classifying parts into (a) supplier proprietary; (b) black box; and (c) detail controlled types, Clark et al. found that the a:b:c ratios were 8:62:30 in Japan, 3:16:81 in the USA and 7:39:54 in Europe. The Japanese car assemblers' extensive use of black box and supplier proprietary parts is indicative of their trust in suppliers' competence and goodwill.

Market conditions as a determinant?

This section deals with market structures, the nature of competition, the degree of uncertainty governing demand fluctuations, and actual and expected growth in demand, which may affect the choice between ACR and OCR.

Market structures

As was elaborated in chapter 1, the essence of the contrast between ACR and OCR is between a relationship in which the identity of trading partners does not matter and one in which it does matter due to a particularistic social structure. In an extreme situation in which there is

Table 6.1. *Printed circuit board industry structures in Britain and Japan*

	Britain	Japan
Total production (1987)	£286.7m	£3.141b (¥722.48 b)
Total employees	16,000	25,000
No. of companies	400	380
Average size of firm	40 workers	65 workers
Market concentration (1987) Market share of:		
the largest	9%	10%
the 5 largest	31%	38%

Sources: Printed Circuit Industry Federation and Business Monitor PQ3444 for the UK; Japan Printed Circuit Association for Japan.

only one buyer (a monopsonist) and one supplier (a monopolist), the distinction in practice between universalism and particularism becomes meaningless, as from either side of the market there is one and only one trading partner. Extending this line of argument, it is tempting to assert that the more alternative trading partners exist, the more scope there is for universalistic and hence ACR-type relationships to develop, and conversely that the smaller the number of alternative partners, the more scope there is for relationships to be of the OCR-type.

The fact that this is not necessarily the case can be gleaned from a cursory examination of the prevailing industry structures in Britain and Japan. In both automobile and electronic industries, the Japanese industry structure is less concentrated than the British structure. As a crude measure, in Japan, Toyota accounted for 34 per cent and Nissan 26 per cent of domestic car production in 1984 (Cusumano 1985, p. 99), while in Britain, the Rover Group accounted for 40 per cent, Ford for 34 per cent, and Vauxhall for 16 per cent of total British car production in 1986 (Rhys, 1988, p. 165). For the automotive sector as a whole, there were 28,100 establishments forming 11,116 enterprises in Japan in 1986, and 2028 establishments forming 1821 enterprises in Britain in 1985. Similarly, in the electrical and electronic engineering sector, 50,649 establishments (24,285 enterprises) existed in Japan in 1986, and 9527 establishments (8633 enterprises) in Britain in 1985. Moreover, if we focus on the PCB industry, the British industry structure is not significantly any more fragmented than the Japanese structure (see Table 6.1).

Thus, ACR is not necessarily more likely in atomistic market structures with many buyers and suppliers, and OCR in more concentrated markets. It appears to be largely a matter of choice whether companies are willing to enter into a committed relationship or not, regardless of whether there are potential alternative trading partners or not.

Competition through product differentiation

It has already been noted that when good quality, prompt delivery and continuous design improvements are regarded as essential to remain competitive, OCR-type relations may be preferred over ACR-type relations. This is because achieving those ends requires high trust of all types and much sharing of information.

Besides good quality, final goods producers also compete through product differentiation. Because product differentiation is effected over time by constantly launching new variants (models) of the same product range, the intensification of competition through product differentiation leads to shorter product lifecycles. Shorter cycles, in turn, require more intense coordination over design and development between customer and supplier companies, which OCR-type relations are better equipped than ACR-type relations to accommodate. Hence, we may put forward the following:

Proposition 3: The greater the perceived market advantages of product differentiation and diversification through the shortening of the product cycle, the more likely OCR-type relations are to emerge.

It is often asserted that there has been a secular trend away from mass consumption towards demand for differentiated products, due to changes in consumer tastes accompanying greater affluence (Piore and Sabel, 1984). Product differentiation may also be regarded as a consequence of producer-led attempts at creating new demand in the face of potential market saturation. Such mode of competition is more common in markets for consumer goods than for industrial goods.

The Japanese consumer electronics industry represents a typical case of intensified competition through product differentiation. For example, the largest 9 Japanese electronics companies are said to have announced 105 new models of colour television sets in 1985 and 155 in 1987, and 94 new VCR models in 1985 and 121 in 1987 (*Asahi Shinbun* 12 August 1988). The product cycles of TV sets, VCRs, and PCs are becoming shorter; annual model changes with six-monthly introduction of minor modifications are common. In the car industry, in which development costs are greater, Japanese manufacturers have developed a policy of full model changes once every four years, while the British producers have

Table 6.2. *Part numbers per supplier in the Japanese PCB industry (average per firm per month)*

Company size	1984	1985	1986
1–5	425	408	598
51–100	1030	1209	1125
101–150	792	753	1085
151–200	1261	1443	2225
201–300	3118	2836	2393
301+	2449	2820	2167
Total	1454	1649	1521

Source: JPCA (1987a) p. 58

used product cycles of between five and ten years (Cusumano, 1985, p. 108; Rhys, 1988, p. 177).

From the above logic, the modal trading pattern is more OCR in the Japanese PCB industry than in the British, partly because a greater proportion of the Japanese PCB suppliers trade with customers requiring short product cycles. In fact, in 1985, 37 per cent of total Japanese PCB output were for consumer electronics goods, while the corresponding figure was only 5 per cent in Britain. At the same time, Japanese PCB suppliers on average produce a large variety of PCBs (as measured by part numbers) (Table 6.2). No comparable statistics exist for the British PCB industry. But if we compare two large PCB suppliers, B410(PCB) produces 200 part numbers in a typical month, whereas 7000 part numbers go through J1210(PCB)'s production lines in a month. Even if we take account of the fact that J1210(PCB) trades with 4 times as many customers as B410(PCB), J1210(PCB)'s 17.5 part numbers per customer per month, as compared to only 2 part numbers per customer per month at B410(PCB), render the task of good coordination through daily contact essential.

Uncertainty in demand fluctuations

Related to shorter product cycles and large part numbers is the uncertainty in market demand, which multiplies potential problems in inter-firm coordination of production. Whether ACR or OCR is preferred under such circumstances is not clear cut. On the one hand, the customer company may prefer OCR-type relations so that existing

154

suppliers can change production scheduling flexibly at a short notice to satisfy difficult-to-predict market demand. On the other hand, OCR-type relations may create unwanted obligations for the customer to smooth the level of orders (at least the total order value) for a particular supplier; such a commitment is not necessary in ACR-type relations. Because of this freedom to chop and change suppliers as demand dictates, accorded in ACR but not in OCR, ACR may be preferred by some customers. This aspect accounts for the fact that Japanese electrical and electronic goods manufacturers retain a greater proportion of marginal suppliers than car manufacturers (Asanuma, 1989).

From the supplier's viewpoint, uncertainty in order fluctuations it faces may be decomposed into a behavioural element and an 'environmental' element (Williamson, 1985, p. 57). The former, behavioural uncertainty, is less in OCR as noted in chapters 4 and 5 due to (a) a greater exchange of information over the customer's future business plans and (b) the customer's consideration to give out smooth levels of orders. Customers' willingness to smooth out orders may be related to their being less risk averse than smaller suppliers (Kawasaki and Mac-Millan 1987). Behavioural uncertainty is greater in ACR relations because, for instance, customers may pretend to call off a large volume in order to extract low prices only to cancel part of the order later. Thus, much of the uncertainty in business is human-made, and can be treated as endogenous to the prevailing business norms concerning the strategic use of information. Consequently, suppliers facing ACR customers would be reluctant to make specific investment due to a high risk of customer quits, thus reducing the preferred degree of asset specificity and the willingness to enter into more OCR relationships.

From the above discussion, we may assert the following:

Proposition 4: The more uncertain the market demand facing the customer, the greater the proportion of suppliers with which it wishes to have ACR-type relations. At the same time, the supplier prefers to enter into ACR with customers who are associated with high behavioural uncertainty, and into OCR if customers are expected to reduce uncertainty associated with order fluctuations.

Growth in demand

Lastly, expectations about demand growth may be a factor affecting the ACR–OCR choice. In a static economy, companies may prepare for set-backs during recession by earning relatively high returns. Static market shares reinforce the view of a zero-sum game, in which one's gain in market share is another's loss, and the customer's gain is at the supplier's expense in price negotiations. Customer companies wish not to become committed to any suppliers, to reserve the freedom to change suppliers as prices dictate and to cancel or reduce order if need be. Such cancellations, even if contractually valid, undermine trust, particularly of the goodwill sort.

By contrast, in a rapidly growing economy or sector, creating 'goodwill trust' is relatively cheap because it generates general business confidence and a sense of shared goal in success between trading partners. 'Contractual trust' is also easily developed due to a reduced need to renege on contracts as long as growth is steady and predictable. Commitment is mutually beneficial as customer companies need to secure increasing capacity at suppliers, rather than to chop and change suppliers. When most customer companies are making such commitment, the supplier stands to lose much in future business if it is found to be cheating. Lastly, rapid growth renders a shortage of skills and good sub-contractors in markets more acute, thus biasing firms towards internal investment in 'competence trust' and hence the development of OCR.

Thus, again, though not definitive, there seem to be grounds for asserting that:

Proposition 5: The more rapid and steady the growth of demand, the more scope there is for OCR rather than ACR relations to develop.

The evidence which is consistent with this assertion exists both at the economy-wide level and at the industry level. At the economy level, in the post-war period, the Japanese economy grew faster than the British economy, by 174 per cent and 32 per cent in real terms respectively during 1960–70, and by 61 per cent and 20 per cent during 1970–80. At the industry level, the car production (in volume terms) in Japan grew spectacularly (165-fold) from 68,932 in 1955 to 11,464,920 in 1984, while in Britain, it grew from 898,000 in 1955 to a peak of 1,921,999 in 1972, then fell to 888,000 (below the 1955 level) before rising to 1,019,000 in 1986 (Cusumano, 1985, pp. 392–3; Rhys, 1988, p. 166). In the electronics industry, the diversity of products makes physical volume calculations impossible. But in nominal value terms, the Japanese industry grew steadily 15-fold from ¥198.5b in 1963 to ¥3157.3b in 1983, as contrasted to the British industry which grew 8-fold in the same 20-year period, from £1758m to £15,808m.

These different experiences in economic growth appear to have created quite different expectations and norms in business. In Japan, all transactions take place in the context of a shared dynamic-world assumption; steady productivity improvements of x per cent a year are built into

156

all calculations. In Britain, transactions tend to take place in the context of shared static-world assumptions; here, productivity increases tend not to be seen as continuous but one-off gains due to such exogenous factors as the installation of new equipment or the signing of a new collective agreement, which cause a shift to a new equilibrium.

These business assumptions change only slowly with a lag. Thus, Japanese customer–supplier relations remained largely more OCR than the British norm through the periods of 1973–5 (an oil price-induced recession) and 1985–7 (the yen appreciation) when OCR relations were put under much strain. Moreover, while national norms predominate, there are pockets of localised norms which may develop. For example, as already noted in chapter 4, the first 6 years of growth in colour TV production at a rate of 50 per cent per annum at TCP(UK) helped it to establish OCR relationships of 'goodwill trust' with some of its British suppliers.

In conclusion, economic and technological factors have some bearing on whether customer–supplier relations may be more ACR or OCR. A greater degree of asset specificity, suppliers' technical expertise and design input, shorten product cycles, competition based on product differentiation rather than price only, and expectations of steady demand growth all are favourable conditions for creating OCR- rather than ACR-type trading relationships. However, none of these factors are completely exogenous in the economy, and are influenced by such factors as business firms' objectives and businessmen's normative values and ideology, to which we turn in the next few chapters.

7
The legal framework

The time has come to look more directly at the underlying national institutions and social norms which predispose firms to enter into ACR-type or OCR-type trading relations. We begin, in this chapter, by examining the national legal framework. Our evidence in chapters 4 and 5 showed a considerable degree of similarity between British and Japanese practices with respect to contractualism, and the rationale behind those practices. Some supplier companies emphasised the importance of responding flexibly to customers' requirements for short leadtimes which may result in producing (and even delivering) before written contracts are received. A case-by-case resolution in the event of quality defects or late delivery was also said to be necessary because apportioning clear-cut responsibility on either side may not always be feasible.

There were, however, some major differences between British and Japanese practices. In Britain, the norm of short-term trading meant that a written agreement with a duration of up to five years was required to enforce long-term commitment. No such long-term written agreements were found in Japan; more common was a basic contract lasting twelve months, with automatic annual renewal if neither side notified to terminate the contract. In Britain, suppliers tended to have their own terms and conditions of sale, which might create a 'battle of forms' with their customers' terms. In Japan, no such terms and conditions of sale were found in the industries examined empirically.

This chapter provides explanations for the British–Japanese similarities and differences. A brief account of contract law traditions precedes the main sections on the legal provisions concerning customer–supplier relationships in Japan and Britain.

158

Contract law traditions and ACR–OCR

The principle of classical contracts, on which the mainstream legal scholarship has focused, according to Macneil (1974: 1985), starts from the basis of equality of contracting parties. once a contract is entered into voluntarily, parties aim to specify at present all relevant future contingencies. This serves to preserve contracting parties' independence and enhance the discreteness of exchange. A comprehensive contract in a formal written form becomes a perfect reference point for settling 'disputes'. In fact, as universalistic legal rules are applied to anyone regardless of the identity of the parties, litigation is resolved promptly, with little acrimony, in a well-oiled world of relative certainty. Parties to ACR-type relations would regard classical contract law as normative and ideal.

In reality, however, varying degrees of uncertainty and bounded rationality render all agreements incomplete; not all future contingencies can be anticipated, and appropriate adaptations may not be evident until the circumstances materialise. Thus, instead of attempting to plan rigidly, a contract drawn up in the neoclassical contract law tradition leaves scope for flexible 'adaptive, sequential decision making'. If disputes arise, trading partners may resort to third-party arbitration machinery either to verify the situation or to reach a compromise. Ultimately, however, the chances of reaching agreements depend largely on how much value trading partners place on continuous trading.

If continuous trading is the norm, and discrete exchange exceptional, relational contracts would result (Macneil 1974). In the extreme case, there is no formal written 'original agreement', because the reference point for effecting adaptations is the history of the trading relationship as it has evolved over time. Consequently, dependence and coercion are pervasive, and contracting partners accept that they may be bound in power-unequal (including hierarchical) relationships. In relational contracting, therefore, commencing a trading relationship is like gaining membership in 'a minisociety with a vast array of norms beyond those centred on the exchange and its immediate processes' (Macneil 1974, as quoted by Williamson (1979, p. 238)). Not adhering to these norms leads to refusal of further contracting, which is the ultimate sanction. And in a 'community' with established OCR trading norms, a firm which gets 'broken off' earns a bad reputation and would have difficulty finding other partners. Litigation is rare because it occurs only if the aggrieved party to a relation is no longer committed to salvaging it from breaking up. Partners to an OCR-type relation regard relational contracts as desirable.

The above framework of distinguishing among classical, neoclassical and relational contract law traditions is useful in gauging the assigned role of the state in settling disputes. In an ideal-typical classical contract law situation, there is no need for the state or any other third party, as parties to a contract are fully capable of making settlements. For example, Ramseyer and Nakazato argue apropos of traffic accidents (which are between strangers with no expectations of repetition) that the Japanese preference for out-of-court settlements is quite rational (Ramseyer 1988; Ramseyer and Nakazato 1989). This is because the rules judges apply in awarding damages are so much more clear and transparent in Japan than in the USA, partly because final judgments are unaffected by the jury system which does not exist in Japan. According to this argument, litigation in Japan is scarce not because of some cultural inclination for conflict avoidance (Smith 1983, p. 41), nor because the legal system is inefficient (as reflected in a shortage of lawyers, slow proceedings and high fees) (March 1988, p. 117), but because it effectively signals clear and predictable legal rules.

In a more relational context, litigation is also of marginal importance in settling disputes in practice (Gordon, 1985). For example, even in litigious North America, Macaulay (1963) found that businessmen often failed to use legal sanctions to adjust business relations or to settle disputes. Macaulay reasoned that non-legal sanctions, applied to those not honouring commitments, are effective in a stable business community; the sanctions take the form of blacklisting or poor reputation which may ultimately lead to not being able to continue conducting business in the area (Macaulay, 1963, pp. 62–5). As the game theoretic work on repeated games show (Axelrod 1984; Kreps 1990; Telser 1987), business firms may be conforming to communal norms not so much out of moral commitment as out of self-interest.

Japanese businessmen, more so than American or British counterparts for that matter, believe themselves to be relatively non-litigious and non-contractual, and that perception makes OCR- rather than ACR-type relations more likely. In general, the Japanese are said to tend towards a view that contracts are necessary only in cases where disputes are anticipated, or that the mere existence of contracts, by institutionalising the assumption of the need for suspicion and distrust, actually breeds them (Kawashima 1967). However, the Macaulay–Macneil perspective on relational contracts sheds a different light on why the Japanese are non-litigious, by highlighting the role of non-legal sanctions which may substitute for litigation. For example, nonconformist behaviour in Japan is deterred by boycotts, refusals to have further dealings, and ostracism

160

(*murahachibu*, the Japanese equivalent of sending someone to Coventry) by those abiding in the same community (Haley, 1982, pp. 276–81). Haley (1982) also refers to adverse publicity and the threat of damaged reputation, which are often evoked by governments to obtain compliance. These extra-legal substitutes developed in Japan, according to Haley, because the existing legal order lacked effective formal sanctions. It may well be, however, that such social sanctions did not just develop by default, but are positively preferred to legal sanctions for being more effective in areas where particularistic relationships of 'goodwill trust' are important. In fact, Upham (1987) goes so far as to argue that the Japanese state has actively encouraged informal conflict resolution by providing appropriate institutions.

The next section describes the legal provisions in Japan for regulating customer–supplier relationships. Is it indeed the case that formal legal sanctions are ineffective in this area? If so, what other mechanisms, such as arbitration machinery and non-legal sanctions, have been developed to regulate customer–supplier relations? Also, how divergent or convergent are the standards of conduct set out in law and the norms as developed in the Japanese business community?

Legal provisions concerning small firms and sub-contracting in Japan

The Japanese government's policy towards small firms has been about 'modernising' and 'rationalising' the industrial structure and inter-firm business practices. The thinking behind this developmental perspective is most comprehensively set out in the two laws enacted in 1963, namely the Basic Law on Small and Medium-sized Enterprises (*Chusho kigyo kihon ho*) and the Law on Promoting the Modernisation of SMEs (*Chusho kigyo kindaika sokushin ho*).

'Rationalisation' has meant structural improvement in industry to exploit scale economies. This may be achieved by encouraging small firms to grow over time, but more immediately by encouraging a group of small firms to organise into cooperative associations which may benefit from pooling together finance, and technical and managerial know-how. The 1949 Law on Cooperatives for SMEs (*Chusho kigyo to kyodo kumiai ho*) formalised this, and gave incentives for small firms to combine. An earlier example of policy, reflecting a similar thinking, but applied to sub-contracting relations rather than relations among small firms, is the Japanese government's rationalisation and consolidation programme, decreed in 1940 to concentrate resources for the war effort. The programme designated which sub-contractors were to receive technology

161

transfer from large companies; to make such transfer successful, it enforced stable sub-contracting relationships whereas previously trading relations were fluid and mediated by brokers (Minato 1987). The programme was abandoned in 1945 and has no direct link with the post-war policy on SMEs. However, it is generally understood that the wartime legacy of stable sub-contracting relations involving technology transfer stuck and became an accepted norm as firms attempted to enforce long-term relationships in the 1950s (Nakamura 1981, pp. 15–16). The subsequent governmental policy took this fact as given.

'Modernisation' involves not only structural improvement, but also strengthening the managerial and technological capabilities of individual small firms, in particular by encouraging firms to grow out of some 'pre-modern' business practices. Typifying the rotten core of such pre-modern practices is said to be the absence of written agreements which clarify the basic terms and conditions of trade. Without written agreements, so it is argued, there can be no recourse by the weaker party to redress the balance by resorting to law.

This tendency to identify modernisation with everything good and progressive came naturally to the government of a late developer nation, particularly as applied to what was considered a backward sector of the economy. However, this does not mean that all traditional Japanese practices are rejected as bad. And here lie certain tensions between conflicting ideological values, between tradition and modernity, between hierarchy and equality, between cooperation and individualism, and between equity and efficiency (Dore, 1986, pp. 226–30). First, there has been a tension, more in the past than today, between favouring concentration which allows maximal exploitation of scale economies on the one hand and ensuring that smaller and less efficient firms do not drop out of the programmes to improve productivity on the other. Given the government recognition that small firms constitute not only an economic but also a social problem, government policy has been pursuing the dual goals of efficiency and equity simultaneously. Fulfilling the equity goal may require that some protection, albeit temporary, be offered to the weak. But, as in any policy with a developmental perspective (like the infant industry argument), it is difficult to decide when the period of nurture, with the state offering a helping hand, ends, and when the period of independence and self-help starts.

More specifically in relation to customer–supplier relationships, there are conflicting perceptions about the virtue of traditional Japanese-style commercial custom and practice. On the one hand, hierarchical relationships on a long-term basis are considered good for promoting efficiency.

162

If this is the case, the more powerful party to the relationship may legitimately take responsibility to dictate the terms and conditions of trade unilaterally, while the role of the government would be to encourage the internalisation of normative values which lead to benevolent restraint in not exercising full market power. On the other hand, there exists the ideology of market individualism and freedom of contract, which the American Occupation Forces had a hand in implanting in the Japanese policy landscape. According to this ideological perspective, the law must ensure that each trading partner has the freedom to choose whether to enter into a contract or not, and to determine the content of the contract, including payment terms and prices (see All Japan Sub-contractors Promotion Association, 1987, p. 17). It appears that the series of legislation concerning sub-contracting in Japan has not quite resolved this issue of which one of the competing ideological perspectives ought to prevail.

Government regulations on sub-contracting relationships

It was the Anti-trust Sub-section of the Economic and Science Section in the US Occupation GHQ, which was entrusted with the responsibility for small business policy in immediate post-war Japan, and which formulated the Anti-Monopoly Law (*Dokusen kinshi ho*), enacted in April 1947. Having been modelled after the US anti-trust law, it comes as no surprise that the law presumes the transactions it intends to regulate to be discrete, not relational. The discovery of unfair trading practices as defined by the law depends totally on an aggrieved party notifying the Fair Trade Commission, which will then conduct an investigation and a court hearing. The US GHQ had a regulatory perspective, expecting the law only to fulfil the economic objective of ensuring a free market economy by preventing the concentration of economic power; the existence of independent small firms was then the barometer measuring the health of a liberal economy.

The Japanese government at the time – specifically the Ministry of Commerce and Industry and the Economic Stabilisation Board – did not share this perspective (Watanabe, 1987). They saw small firms as a social as well as an economic problem, and advocated government assistance in improving their technological and managerial capabilities as part of the programme for economic reconstruction. Even without this developmental perspective, the Anti-Monopoly Law looked inadequate for regulating sub-contracting relations between large and small firms. Because of unequal power between trading partners, *shitauke* (SME supplier) firms had rather not reveal their problems for fear of retaliation or ostracism which might easily put them into bankruptcy. The Fair Trade Commission therefore could not rely on them to notify it of the 'parental' (customer) firm's unfair practices.[1] Moreover, the FTC's investigative hearing proceedings are often lengthy (five-ten years from the time a violation is discovered to when a judgment is reached), which may lead to a loss of opportunity to resolve the problem before irreparable damages are inflicted on the continuous trading relationship. Lastly, the Law did not spell out exactly what constituted unfair practices in the context of *shitauke* relations.

The above inadequacies in the Anti-Monopoly Law led to a number of amendments, culminating in the enactment in 1956 of the Law to Prevent Delayed Subcontract Payment and Related Matters (*Shitauke daikin shiharai chiento boshi ho*; henceforth referred to as the Delayed Payment Prevention Law (DPPL)). The stated purpose of the 1956 Law was to prevent the 'parental' firm's abuse of its position of economic superiority, and to protect the *shitauke* firm's profitability. The Law defined *shitauke* relations as those in which manufacturing or repairing contracts exist (a) between a 'parental' firm with a paid-in capital of over ¥100 million and a sub-contractor with ¥100m or less; or (b) between a 'parental' firm with over ¥10m paid-in capital and a sub-contractor with ¥10m or less. Thus, power inequality was presumed to be the central feature which may cause unfair trading practices. In reality, the long-term continuity and the highly dependent nature of sub-contracting relationships are also essential features deterring small firms from voluntarily revealing their customers' malpractice.

The Delayed Payment Prevention Law, incorporating subsequent amendments, specifies both duties and forbidden acts. The duties include the requirement that the 'parental' firm draw up and exchange written contracts which clarify the basic terms and conditions of trade, and to preserve them for record; non-compliance with this duty leads to a fine not exceeding ¥30,000. Another duty is to mutually agree on the payment period from the time of delivery, which must not exceed 60 days; in the event of a payment being delayed beyond the agreed period, the 'parental' firm must pay an interest set at 14.6 per cent per annum.

As for forbidden acts which constitute unfair practices, the following are specified:

   (a) the refusal to receive delivery of commissioned goods;
   (b) delaying the payment to subcontractors beyond an agreed period;

(c) discounting sub-contract payment after prices have been agreed;
(d) returning delivered goods which have been commissioned without good reason;
(e) forced price reduction;
(f) compulsory purchase by sub-contractors of 'parental' firm's products;
(g) forcing sub-contractors to pay in advance for materials supplied by the 'parental' firm; and
(h) issuing bills which are difficult to discount.

The Fair Trade Commission (FTC) and the Small and Medium Enterprise Agency (SMEA) (established in 1948) are jointly responsible for administering the delayed Payment Prevention Law, although the ultimate power to enforce it lies with the FTC. The discovery of violations is pro-active, through regular annual investigations by postal surveys and on-the-spot inspections. Special investigations have also been carried out in selected industries which are considered to have a high incidence of violations (e.g. textile wholesaling), and to examine the effects of a specific event – most recently the post-1985 appreciation of the yen – on sub-contracting relations. Violations uncovered in this fashion are primarily dealt with by administrative measures, giving violating companies the opportunity to rectify unfair practices voluntarily. Only if companies do not comply with the administrative guidance are they subject to adverse publicity and formal judgment under the Anti-Monopoly Law.

The effectiveness of the Delayed Payment Prevention Law may be assessed by gauging what would have happened in its absence, by examining the extent of violations uncovered and how they were dealt with. The number of violations identified has been increasing over time, mainly because the sampling base of the annual postal survey has gradually been increased from the initial 300 customer establishments in 1956 to the whole population of all manufacturing establishments with a paid-in capital exceeding ¥10m. Since 1973, sub-contracting firms have also been surveyed to improve the chances of discovering violations. In 1987, half of the total manufacturing establishments with ¥10m or more capital, namely 30,187, and their 26,438 sub-contractors were surveyed by the SMEA. Of the 30,187 'parental' establishments, the SMEA conducted on-the-spot investigations at 3349 suspect cases; as a result, 2373 were found to have unfair practices, of which 2294 were rectified immediately, while 79 received guidance for a period of 3 to 6 months on how to improve their sub-contracting relations. By far the most common category of violations (90 per cent of the total) was the failure to exchange written contracts or to specify contractual terms clearly. The FTC conducted in the same year (1987) an identical survey for the other half, namely 18,954 'parental' establishments and 52,105 sub-contracting firms. Uncovered through this survey were 1242 violating 'parental' enterprises which received warnings (*keikoku*) from the FTC to rectify their practices immediately. As in the SMEA findings, the most common form of violation was the non-existence or incompleteness of written contracts.

Other forms of violations have been uncovered, but with varying frequency over time. In the late 1950s and early 1960s, delayed payments (beyond 60 days after delivery) were the most common form of violation. By the 1970s, the non-exchange and incompleteness of written contracts constituted half of total violations discovered, while the other half were mostly matters of delayed payments and unnecessarily long-term (over 120 days) bills. Since the second half of the 1970s, rationalisation demands due to oil shocks and the strong yen have led to a rapid increase in the incidence of unilateral reductions of sub-contract payments, although delayed payments still remained numerically more common. Over time, the FTC survey shows an improvement in the average payment period from just over a month in the early 1960s to just under 0.8 months (24 days) in 1985 (FTC, 1986). Even with such improvement, however, in 1986, 106 'parental' companies were made to repay a sum of ¥584,930,000 to 1185 sub-contractors who were subject to unfair reductions in their payments received, while 37 'parental' companies paid ¥24,890,000 to 215 sub-contractors as interest on delayed payments (Shoya, 1988, p. 198).

In a minority of cases in which the SMEA's guidance proves insufficient to induce compliance, the SMEA refers the cases to the FTC; the maximum number of such cases was 80 in 1978 (Table 7.1). Whenever warnings (*keikoku*) are considered inadequate, recommendations (*kankoku*) are issued by the FTC, which spell out exactly what has to be done by the violating company; 56 in 1971 was the largest number of such recommendations in any year. A decline in the number of recommendations in recent years may be interpreted as being in part a reflection of strengthened administrative guidance in the prevention of unfair practices. Such preventive measures range from (a) making available an annotated manual of the Delayed Payment Prevention Law written by trade associations (e.g. the Japan Electronic Industry Association, the Japan Department Stores Association) to their members; (b) sector-specific model basic contracts and purchase order forms made available

Table 7.1. *Investigations by FTC to enforce DPPL*

Year	Total surveyed violations discovered						Measures taken			
	Establish-ments	Enter-prises	Further investi-gations	Appeals from sub-contrac-tors	Referral from SMEA's director-general	Total	Recom-menda-tions	Warnings	Pass	Total
1956	304		61	20	0	81	0	19	46	65
1957	723		130	21	0	151	13	73	37	123
1958	769		161	21	0	182	5	110	39	154
1959	986		97	3	0	100	7	82	37	126
1960	1214		105	5	0	110	0	38	20	58
1961	1514		156	10	0	166	0	62	33	95
1962	1803		261	33	0	294	12	149	35	196
1963	1800		219	17	0	236	22	182	55	259
1964	2004		218	17	14	249	14	180	104	298
1965	2554		417	23	31	471	15	193	93	301
1966	2631		541	15	19	575	14	299	111	424
1967	5512		669	12	10	691	5	459	97	561
1968	6030		414	7	0	421	9	416	171	596
1969	6684		525	6	0	531	26	447	231	704
1970	7214		430	5	2	437	52	354	80	486
1971	8451		609	9	5	623	56	432	56	544
1972	8751		690	2	0	692	41	485	99	625
1973	10039	2915	707	2	0	709	17	569	130	716

Table 7.1. (Cont.)

Year	Total surveyed violations discovered						Measures taken			
	Establish-ments	Enter-prises	Further investi-gations	Appeals from sub-contrac-tors	Referral from SMEA's director-general	Total	Recom-menda-tions	Warnings	Pass	Total
1974	10045	3808	739	5	5	749	4	542	296	842
1975	12007	4861	1029	10	18	1057	6	686	269	961
1976	12171	6325	1220	15	18	1253	12	906	255	1173
1977	12315	7247	1391	38	59	1488	15	1097	191	1303
1978	10973	10663	1050	35	80	1165	7	916	406	1329
1979	12007	11546	1242	16	9	1267	2	746	146	894
1980	13490	21785	1126	20	35	1181	0	921	436	1357
1981	13668	18091	1158	9	8	1171	1	932	252	1185
1982	16026	20532	1131	19	4	1354	4	1014	271	1289
1983	16346	23138	1413	15	13	1441	0	1119	317	1436
1984	15959	66579	1458	24	0	1482	0	1224	693	1917
1985	16095	48031	3008			3039	1928	2243		
	(9574)		(1570)	(31)	(0)	(1601)	(0)	(1512)	(159)	(1671)
1986	18954	52105	2708			2759				
	(9559)		(1426)	(51)	(0)	(1477)	(0)	(1242)	(155)	(1397)

Note: Investigations and measures have been carried out at the establishment level until 1984, and at the enterprise level since 1985. This change was made in order to make companies deal more effectively with the FTC's warnings (*keikoku*) and recommendations (*kankoku*) at their headquarters, rather than at the level of the local establishment which does not necessarily let its local problems be known to the HQ. Figures in brackets refer to enterprises.

Source: Fair Trade Commission, Japan.

by the Sub-contractors Promotion Association to both sub-contractors and customer companies; (c) specifying November (since 1979) as the month for a campaign to promote fair sub-contract trading, during which the FTC and the SMEA organise lectures and workshops in all parts of Japan, as well as publicising in the media; and (d) notification (*tsudatsu*) in the name of the MITI Minister or the Chief Commissioner of the FTC, asking firms to observe the rules whenever it is anticipated that the burden of adjustment may be shifted unduly to sub-contractors, e.g. at times of oil-price hikes and yen appreciation.

Heightened awareness of the rules is one thing. It is another matter whether incentives exist to obey the rules or not. Thus far, no company has dared not to comply to an FTC recommendation. Nor has the final stage, under the DPPL, of publicising the company name and the nature of the violation, ever been invoked. Judging from this, one can conclude that the threat of adverse publicity and damaged reputation has been sufficient for companies to obey the law. As Haley (1982) noted, adverse publicity is a tool of law enforcement in various countries; and damaged reputation is an effective means of compulsion not only because it leads to 'loss of face', but also because it is likely to incur a tangible financial loss (Haley, 1982, pp. 275–6).

The threat of publicity, when it comes from a sub-contractor, is relatively ineffective because the counter-threat by the 'parental' firm to cease trading with the sub-contractor has serious consequences for dependent sub-contractors if the threat is carried out. There is no reliable evidence on how much relatively independent suppliers actually resort to such threat of publicity but, in my own sample, J65(PCB) once did. A customer made a demand for a large price reduction and duly withdrew it when J65(PCB) threatened to tell the world.

For the above reason, the FTC guarantees anonymity when investigating 'parental' firms as a result of sub-contractors filing direct appeals (*shinkoku*) to them. These appeals numbered only 2 during the boom of 1972–3, but rose to a peak of 38 in 1977 and more recently to 51 in 1986 (see Table 7.1). There appears to be some correlation between the number of direct appeals and the state of the economy, a recession being associated with an increase in the number. But the number remains generally low because the FTC's guarantee of anonymity is not foolproof; sub-contractors fear that their customers can easily work out which sub-contractor has initiated the investigation. Consequently, many of the appeals come from sub-contractors who are trading on a spot contract basis only, and therefore have little to lose if they are made known to their customers.[2]

Prices, quality and trust

The logical extreme of the above line of argument is to go for outright litigation only if there is nothing to lose. This was the case with a packaging material sub-contractor to Suzuki Motors, which had been declared bankrupt. It was suing Suzuki for forcing it to accept a 10 per cent reduction in total payment for work done, claiming that this was a violation of the Anti-Monopoly Law (reported in *Asahi Shinbun*, 26 September 1987). The case at the Shizuoka Local Court was reported to be the first of its kind, in which a sub-contractor resorted to law openly.

Newspaper reporting serves to spread adverse publicity, particularly in regions which depend heavily on a few identifiable large employers, such as Hitachi in Hitachi City or Toyota in Toyota City. For example, a local paper, *Ibaragi* (15 May 1971), reported the bankruptcy of a metal-pressing sub-contractor to Hitachi Sawa factory, attributing it to a drastic reduction in Hitachi's order. Only extreme cases, such as bankruptcies, however, are likely to be channelled via this route. With less sensational problems, adverse publicity is not an effective sanction which can be resorted to by most individual sub-contractors. This is so particularly for those which have traded with a small number of customers on a long-term basis, which captures the majority of SMEs in Japan; 68.2 per cent of all SME sub-contractors have apparently never changed their largest 'parental' company (according to the 1988 SME White Paper, p. 61). What alternative mechanisms exist for them, short of internalising the cost of unfair practices inflicted upon them by their customers?

Advisory and mediation services

One extra-legal mechanism for dispute settlement is through the advisory and mediation services offered by the All Japan Sub-contractors Promotion Association (*Zenkoku shitauke kigyo shinko kyokai*, established in 1978), and the 47 prefectural Sub-contractors Promotion Associations, some of which have existed since the 1960s. For example, the Osaka association was established in 1965, and the Tokyo association in 1966, which were both years of recession. Many of the prefectural associations were established with local initiative in order to strengthen their regional economies, by match-making registered customer and sub-contracting companies with complementary requirements, offering advisory services, and mediating disputes arising in sub-contracting relationships. The 1970 Law on Promoting Sub-contracting SMEs (*Shitauki chusho kigyo shinko ho*) subsequently formalised the pre-existing services by delegating responsibility for mediation to the dispute settlement committee at each association.

170

The legal framework

The dispute settlement committee typically meets once or twice a year. It consists of no more than 10 members, who are mostly not qualified lawyers, but academics, large or small company executives, and officials from trade or cooperative associations, who are considered neutral and capable of passing fair judgment. As every committee member has a full-time occupation elsewhere, the committee cannot be called upon every time a case is referred. Thus, in reality, much of the leg work and the administrative work are carried out by the Sub-contractors Promotion Association staff, known as 'advisors' (*adobaizaa* or *shidoin*). Only difficult cases are taken up by the committee. Throughout, confidentiality is maintained, and all mediation services are free of charge.

Many of the dispute settlement cases are between SMEs, commonly between primary and secondary or secondary and tertiary sub-contractors in such sectors as metal pressing and machining, garment making, plastic injection moulding, and consumer electronic assembly. Over half of the cases dealt with at the Tokyo association were disputes between companies both of which had a capitalisation of below ¥10 million; they do not constitute *shitauke* relations legally defined and are therefore not covered by the investigative surveys by the FTC and the SMEA. Thus, the mediation services fill in the vacuum, by dealing with sub-contracting relationships outside the bounds of the DPPL.

Complaints which are referred to the Sub-Contractors Promotion Associations are caused most commonly by the non-payment of bills for work done, followed by disagreements over how to deal with quality defects and in particular over the amount of compensation for which sub-contractors are liable. Of the total of 531 dispute cases the Osaka Sub-contractors Promotion Association had dealt with during 1971–86, 43 per cent concerned non-payment of bills and 15 per cent disputes over quality defects. Similarly, the Tokyo association dealt with 1849 dispute cases during 1971–86, of which 36 per cent were over payments, and 15 per cent over quality defects.

These categories of causes are often intertwined. For example, in one case recounted by an advisor at the All Japan Sub-contractors Promotion Association, a sub-contractor lodged a complaint against its customer for refusing to make payment for work done by using an excuse that the sub-contractor delivered a batch containing a high proportion of defective goods. The sub-contractor claimed that the materials supplied by the customer were responsible for the defects caused, but that the problem was put right when materials purchased directly by itself were used. Upon investigation, the quality problem was found not to be caused by materials supplied by either party, but by the sub-contractor's processing methods and the buyer's design specifications. It also emerged in due course that the sub-contractor was not paying its instalments regularly for a second-hand piece of machinery which was handed down from the buyer. The buyer thus felt more entitled not to make the payment. This case was resolved by the advisor calculating how much each party owed the other, and convincing the parties that on balance, the buyer had to make a small payment to the sub-contractor. The parties also exchanged a written record of agreement that in future the sub-contractor would pay the instalments regularly and that the buyer would not delay payments for work done.

In the absence of mediation, a vicious circle of mutual blame in this case might well have done irreparable damage to the trading relationship, possibly leading to its termination which neither party wanted. The mediation services therefore fulfill a useful function of restoring 'goodwill trust' between trading partners before it is too late.

Legal framework in Britain

Alternative Dispute Resolution (ADR)

The launch in November 1990 of the Centre for Dispute Resolution (CEDR), backed by the Confederation of British Industry (CBI), provides for the first time an alternative to litigation to settle commercial disputes in Britain (*Financial Times* 21 March 1991, 17 June 1991). The Centre is run as a non-profit-making organisation on a corporate membership basis, and offers a variety of alternative dispute resolution (ADR) techniques, including mediation and the mini-trial. They are private, voluntary and non-binding.

Modelled after the Centre for Public Resources in New York, CEDR is expected to bring benefits to business firms which have been so fearful of being bogged down by litigation that they dare not embark on the litigation process. Litigation has the demerits of the uncertainty of the outcome, the possibility of protracted legal battles caused by appeal, the drain on executive time and high legal charges. Perhaps the most serious is delay which renders the execution of a contract between disputing parties unrealistic (because either party may have found alternative trading partners). Mediation is cheaper, quicker and conducted in an atmosphere in which the parties' willingness to discuss settlement is not seen as a sign of weakness, thus pre-empting the need to adopt a war posture.

Alternative Dispute Resolution is said to have become popular in the

US largely because industry has rationally come to realise the high transaction costs associated with litigation, which reduces productivity by diverting managerial time, and destroys long-standing business relationships. Besides this reason which applies equally in Britain, the timing of the CEDR launch in Britain may be related to the 1990–1 recession, which has led to a sharp rise in commercial litigation, by 43 per cent among Central London law firms over the 12 months to mid-1991 (*Financial Times* 17 June 1991). However, unlike the mediation services offered to small firms in Japan, the major beneficiaries of the CEDR in Britain are large corporations, judging from the membership which includes BAT, Ford of Europe, Grand Metropolitan, ICI, Smiths Industries and Trafalgar House Construction.

Late payment of trade debts in Britain

For smaller firms in Britain, delayed payment has been recognised as a problem. Recently, according to a CBI survey of 400 small and medium-sized enterprises (SMEs), payment practice had become worse in 1990 than it was five years previously, reflecting the economic downturn and tightening cash flow position (CBI 1991). The same survey found that although standard payment terms specified by suppliers are overwhelmingly 30 days, they are obliged to agree to 60 days typically, while 20 per cent of respondents consider it normal for payment periods to exceed 75 days. At the same time, the majority of respondents (78 per cent) admit to paying their suppliers late. Another survey by Intrum Justitia, a credit management group, estimated that small companies in Britain were owed a total of £60 billion by their customers (*Financial Times* 11 February 1991).

High transaction costs are incurred as a result of delayed payment. The consequences of late payment, according to the CBI survey, were, in order of importance (a) the cost of financing shortfall in cash flow; (b) loss of management time; (c) cost of employing credit control management staff; (d) uncertainty in forward planning; (e) cost of legal fees in pursuing late payers; and (f) jeopardising relationships with financial providers (including banks). In an attempt to reduce late payment, respondents used the following methods, again in order of importance: (a) regular reminders of statements of account; (b) refusing to take any new orders from a customer who has not paid; (c) appointing an individual whose sole responsibility is for credit control; (d) using a debt-collection agency for one-off debts; and (f) using a factoring company for collecting outstanding monies.

173

Not all companies take these measures, however. As Macaulay (1963) noted, businessmen are often reluctant to insist on their terms due to the relational nature of contracts. The CBI survey found that 53 per cent of respondents felt inhibited from taking a strong line with overdue customers, so that a majority have had to pay the price of writing off a debt. Moreover, nearly three quarters of respondents do not have a contract clause entitling them to interest if payment is late. Of those, 58 per cent say enforcing such a clause would cause too much ill feeling, and 35 per cent do not even have written contracts.

A large majority (80 per cent) of small and medium-sized firm respondents apparently believe that a statutory right to interest on outstanding debts would make a real difference to the speed with which bills are paid. A majority also believe that standard payment periods for all business contracts should be legally prescribed. The Forum for Private Business has campaigned since the mid-1980s for a statutory right to interest, while another small firm group, the National Federation of Self-Employed and Small Businesses (NFSE), believes that the solution lies not in giving their members additional legal rights but in making court enforcement procedures more effective. Towards this end, NFSE wants court judgments to be followed by automatic enforcement hearings to ensure that claimants actually got their money, and a public notice to be published naming defaulters who have not paid their debts. Despite these pressures, the British government has favoured voluntary codes of practice, allowing contracting parties the freedom to agree upon terms as they choose. There is no move, therefore, towards legislating a bill which may correspond to the DPPL in Japan, particularly in the present policy climate in favour of greater deregulation.

Delayed payment is nevertheless regarded by the British government as enough of a problem to be taken up in a public information pamphlet, 'Prompt Payment Please!', issued by the Department of Employment's Small Firms Service (Central Office of Information, 1988). This contains advice on credit management, factoring and legal action for suppliers, and codes of practice for buyers. The pamphlet exhorts large buyer firms to recognise their special responsibility to deal fairly with small suppliers, and appeals to the long-term advantage in having trust, not mere contractualism, in business.

> Trade credit will only work if both buyers and suppliers
> understand their obligations and comply with them. This
> requires clear terms of contract which are understood and
> accepted by all concerned. It also requires *trust* [emphasis in

the original]. Trust can be abused. The purchaser can gain an advantage at the expense of the supplier by delaying payment beyond the agreed period. This is an unfair practice and in the long run it is bad business. If trust breaks down, business suffers. (Central Office of Information, 1988, p. 3)

The British government is appealing to the self-interest of individual businesses to invest in a reputation for 'contractual trust'. But when a majority of businesses are delaying payment beyond the agreed period, as in Britain, the payoff to one company of being exceptionally trustworthy (i.e. paying promptly) does not outweigh the payoff when following the convention. It may therefore require statutory powers to instigate a discrete change in the business norm.

Summary

To summarise, the Japanese legal framework has attempted to pre-empt unpalatable aspects of OCR-type relations between power-unequal trading partners (a) by insisting on the exchange of written contracts which, though ACR-like, are for the purpose of providing legal protection for weaker partners; (b) by appealing to the reputation effect and moral responsibility of stronger partners to prevent them from abusing their market power; and (c) by offering informal dispute resolution services so as to facilitate the sustenance of trust relations. In (b), a reliance on internalised normative values is as important as external sanctions of damaged reputation. (Dore (1986, p. 229) aptly described the former as 'the bureaucratization of benevolence and the moralization of hierarchy'.) However, the relative importance of moral and economic factors in this combination of moralised appeal and economic calculation of loss due to damaged reputation is difficult to assess.

In Britain, the legal framework is abstentionist. It therefore gives more scope for the powerful party to a relationship to go unchecked if it intends to delay payment to improve its own cash flow at the expense of weaker parties. The British government believes that the principle of equality of contracting parties, central to ACR-type relations, applies to all commercial transactions, whereas in reality it is no more than a polite fiction in some cases in which firms are reluctant to insist on their terms because of the relational nature of contracts. The government also apparently believes that appealing to the self-interest of individual firms is sufficient to eliminate delayed payments. In reality, the reputation effect does not work well because a significant majority is delaying payments, and because delayed payments do not lead to adverse publicity. In short, British firms have had a legal institution which tends to reinforce the ACR-ness of business relations, while Japanese firms have faced one which has facilitated the creation and maintenance of OCR-type relations.

8
Banks and financial links

One of the most pronounced differences between British and Japanese customer–supplier relationships is the norm concerning the projected length of trading. Chapter 6 discussed how sectors requiring greater asset specificity – electronic assembly more than PCB manufacturing – tended to have longer-term trading norms than those with less transaction-specific investments. However, such inter-sectoral differences do not wipe out the British–Japanese gap. Within the PCB sector, for instance, some suppliers in Britain preferred long-term trading but faced fickle, uncommitted customers. In Japan, the most ACR supplier now specialising in small-batch production felt obligated to take on low margin orders from a long-standing customer. From the Japanese customer company's viewpoint, slight price fluctuations do not normally constitute a sufficient reason for breaking off a trading relationship; as we saw in the case of JJ Electric, a strong norm works towards giving out as smooth and continuous a level of order as possible to its core suppliers and sub-contractors. What national institutions enable customer companies to make such commitment for long-term continuous trading? Both the bank-oriented financial system and the lifetime employment system in Japan appear to reinforce long-term trading in product markets (see Figure 1.1).

This chapter focuses on the financial system in Britain and Japan as a possible reason behind the difference between the British norm of short-term trading and the Japanese norm of long-term trading in customer–supplier relationships. In particular, how does the financial structure of each firm, be it a customer or a supplier company, influence the firm's ability to take a long-term view in inter-firm relations and investment decisions? Financial structure refers here not only to the debt-equity ratio, but also to different roles creditors and shareholders play in controlling the firm, and to 'financial links' between firms. These links may involve not only unilateral shareholding, but also mutual shareholding, and the customer company advancing a loan or acting as a guarantor for commercial loans. The first section explores the issue theoretically. The second section provides a general picture of the contemporary financial systems in Britain and Japan, and the third section presents case-study evidence.

Financial systems in Britain and Japan, and ACR–OCR[1]

In discussing the financial structure of a firm, it is normal to make a distinction between equity finance and debt finance. The extent to which shareholders and creditors exercise control in the firm they invest, as well as claim rights to return streams, differ from country to country. This empirical observation has led to theorising about corporate financial structures using the incomplete contracting theory (Aoki 1989, Berglof 1990). The starting point in this theory is to accept the general fact that contracts, including financial contracts (between owners and managers, and between creditors and debtors), are necessarily incomplete because of imperfect information and bounded rationality. Alternative responses are conceivable in this situation.

One is to attempt to stipulate the parties' obligations for every conceivable eventuality (Aoki (1989) calls the resulting contract A-type). A prior agreement may be made for the clear allocation of control, so that equity claims imply ownership and risk bearing, while debt claims confer no control over management but also bear less risk. Managers, as the appointed agents of shareholders, must maximise the market value of equity, or else they would face dismissal or takeover of the firm. This is the discipline imposed by the impersonal market forces in the securities market, underlying the control shareholders may exercise over the firm as residual claimants. Creditors have little role to play in this securities market-oriented system, other than as mere money lenders.

An alternative response would be to leave contracts incomplete and to rely on case-by-case resolution, which would result in a more diffuse allocation of residual rights (in J-type contracts (Aoki 1990)). According to one version, managers may be left alone to run the firm as they see fit, except when it is seen to be badly managed. When the firm is in financial distress, control may be transferred to a creditor who has the expertise to undertake an internal reorganisation of the firm. Because of this control creditors are permitted to exercise in this bank-oriented system, they are willing to carry greater risk, as reflected in high gearing ratios, than in the securities market-oriented system. Moreover, creditors may wish to hold shares of both debt and equity in the same firm to enhance their control.

178

A number of consequences which follow from the two ideal typical financial systems make ACR-type buyer-supplier relationships more likely in the securities market-oriented financial system, and OCR-type relationships more likely in the bank-oriented system. First, shareholders in the market-oriented system can spread their risk, and buy and sell shares in efficient securities markets. This renders 'exit' (i.e. selling shares) a feasible and preferred option when a firm is in decline. By contrast, shareholders in the bank-oriented system tend to be more concentrated, commonly in the hands of banks and other committed shareholders who are locked in to a firm, particularly if securities markets are underdeveloped. This makes the exercise of 'voice' (i.e. attempts at improving the firm) more likely. Thus, ownership changes are more common in the market-oriented than in the bank-oriented systems, and the stability provided in the latter system conduces to forming long-term continuous trading relationships.

Second, because banks are not in the business of providing risk capital in the securities market-oriented system, they require some form of collateral or security before advancing loans. Given a hands-off relationship between a bank and its client firm, the bank does not have access to accurate information about the firm's business potential and constraints. Banks therefore resort to a capital-gearing approach to loan evaluation, treating a firm's tangible assets as collateral (Binks 1991). By contrast, a close relationship between a creditor-cum-shareholder bank and its client firm in the bank-oriented system gives the bank superior access to the client firm's operations. The bank is therefore willing to evaluate loans on the basis of the income generating potential of the business. Particularly for smaller firms for which equity finance is not possible, the securities market-oriented system poses a more severe constraint on raising funds to finance investment than the bank-oriented system. Greater information sharing between banks and client firms make investment less costly, and enhances firms' willingness to enter into OCR-type relationships involving specific investment.

The financial systems of Britain and Japan

As is evident from the above theoretical discussion, the British financial system may approximate to the market-oriented ideal type, and the Japanese system to the bank-oriented ideal type. But some similarities between Britain and Japan, and country-specific peculiarities are also evident.

The simplest indicator of financial structure, the debt–equity ratio, has been higher on average in Japan than in Britain. In 1986, the book value gearing ratios in Japan were 0.81 in all industries and 0.72 in manufacturing, compared to 0.53 in all industries and 0.55 in manufacturing in Britain (OECD *Financial Statistics*). However, if adjustments are made to correct for the Japanese accounting convention of valuing assets at historic cost, the Japanese gearing ratio at market value may be as low as 0.56 in 1981 (an unofficial Bank of Japan estimate quoted by Corbett (1987, p. 34)). This figure, combined with the fact that gearing ratios are falling in Japan as large corporations have come to rely increasingly on equity finance, indicates that the British–Japanese gap may be closing in this respect.

Alongside this possible convergence in debt–equity ratios lies a similar pattern of evolution in share ownership in Britain and Japan in the post-war period, away from individual towards institutional ownership (see Table 8.1). By the late 1980s, Japan had 24 per cent (in 1986), and Britain 18 per cent (in 1989), of all shares in the hands of individuals. However, this similar trend away from individual ownership disguises a number of important institutional differences. First, a significant proportion of shares (20.5 per cent in 1986) are held by banks in Japan. Although shareholding by banks is not illegal in Britain, British banks have held a negligible and declining amount. Japanese banks are allowed to hold up to 5 per cent (up to 10 per cent until the 1977 amendment to the Anti-Monopoly Law) of shares in nonfinancial corporations. This has enabled main banks to hold shares in their client firms to reinforce the long-term nature of the bank–client relationship. They monitor their client firms' management closely through clients' frequent visits to the bank, their quarterly presentations, secondments of personnel between banks and their clients, and in some cases daily contact to exchange views on general matters of mutual interest (e.g. exchange-rate and interest-rate movements) (Corbett, 1987, p. 45). In turn, main banks accept risks in advancing long-term loans, and engage in restructuring client firms in financial crisis.[2]

Second, around a quarter of shares in Japan, compared to 4 per cent in Britain, are held by nonfinancial corporations. The original Anti-Monopoly Law in 1947, which effectively dissolved the pre-war Zaibatsu groups by making holding companies illegal, was relaxed in the 1949 and 1953 amendments. This facilitated horizontal mutual shareholding within the same corporate groupings, such as Mitsubishi and Mitsui. This practice spread, particularly in the 1960s when trade and capital liberalisation led to the fear of takeovers by foreign firms. Japanese firms responded by asking other firms which could be relied upon to be 'safe'

Table 8.1. *Distribution of Share Ownership in Britain and Japan*(%)

YEAR	Britain 1963	1969	1975	1981	1989	Japan 1949	1963	1969	1975	1981	1986
Individuals	54.0	47.4	37.5	28.2	18	69.1	46.7	41.1	33.5	28.4	23.9
Banks	1.3	1.7	0.7	0.3	0						20.5
Insurance companies	10.0	12.2	15.9	20.5	25	9.9	21.4	30.7	34.5	37.3	17.7
Pension funds	6.4	9.0	16.8	26.7	29						0.9
Investment & unit trusts, other financial companies	12.6	13.0	14.6	10.4	9	12.6	11.7	2.6	3.0	3.0	6.9
Industrial & commercial companies	5.1	5.4	3.0	5.1	4	5.6	17.9	22.0	26.3	26.3	24.5
Public sector	1.5	2.6	3.6	3.0	5	2.8	0.2	0.3	0.2	0.2	0.9
Overseas sector	7.0	6.6	5.6	3.6	8	–	2.1	3.3	2.6	4.6	4.7
Charities	2.1	2.1	2.3	2.2	2	–	–	–	–	–	–
TOTAL	100	100	100	100	100	100	100	100	100	100	100

(For Japan, the Banks, Insurance companies and Pension funds figures are combined for years 1949–1981, shown on the Insurance companies line.)

Source: Stock Exchange Fact Service (1984) *The Stock Exchange Survey of Share Ownership* Table 2.1b; London Stock Exchange (1990) *Quality of Markets Quarterly Review* October, Table 3.1; Zenkoku shoken torihikijo kyogikai (various years) *Kabushiki bunpu jokyo chosa* (Survey of share ownership distribution).

shareholders. They included not only industrial and commercial corporations with which a firm traded goods and services, but also main banks from which they borrowed, and insurance companies which insured their business. Thus, inter-firm shareholding patterns tend to be the expression of some other business relationship; in Dore's words, 'A high proportion of the holders of Japanese equity have more to gain from the other business they do with the companies whose shares they hold than from profits or capital gains on the shares themselves' (Dore, 1987, p. 113). Close to 70 per cent of shares in Japan are held in this manner, judging from Table 8.1. Even smaller unquoted firms have come to ask their customers and suppliers to have an equity stake, as we shall see later.

In Britain, the 4 per cent of shares held by nonfinancial corporations are mainly for the purpose of investment and exercising control. More significant are non-bank financial institutions which doubled their share ownership from 29 per cent in 1963 to 58 per cent in 1981. Institutional investment by pension funds in particular, and insurance companies and trust to a degree, grew in the 1970s due to the tax advantages given to indirect methods of investment as well as to the growth in occupational pension schemes in Britain. Institutional investors are generally uncommitted, and tend to diversify their portfolios among a great number of companies in order to obtain high returns with security. The rate at which investors turn over their portfolios has in fact increased in the 1980s. The availability of share capital in this form has facilitated industrial and holding companies to engage in the buying and selling of companies through takeover bids, sometimes for financial gains which have little to do with coordinating production. When companies are bought and sold for reasons other than to better serve the coordination of productive activities, customer–supplier relations may be disturbed due to changes in management personnel and in company strategy.

The qualitative, rather than the quantitative, differences in shareholding patterns in Britain and Japan have led to a notion of two types of capitalism, one financier-dominated as in Britain and the other producer-dominated as in Japan (Dore 1987). In the former, managers face a strong pressure to maximise the market value of shareholders' equity; their sensitivity to quarterly share prices inhibits productive investment with long-term payback periods and consequently damage the company's competitive position. In the latter, corporate shareholders take a back-seat role, leaving internally promoted managers to run the main business of the firm according to their long-term plan, and interfere only in the event of crisis or scandal.

It should be noted that the shareholding patterns in Table 8.1 are directly relevant to quoted companies only. The rest, limited but unquoted companies and unincorporated enterprises, play a significant role as suppliers and sub-contractors and depend largely on internally generated funds and bank loans. The difference in the role of banks therefore becomes more critical in making investment funds available to small rather than to large firms. At a superficial level, there is similarity between Britain and Japan in the maturity structure of bank loans: roughly 40 per cent of Japanese corporate borrowing is for maturities in excess of one year, while around 40 per cent of loans in Britain in 1980 were classified as being medium or long term (Corbett, 1987, p. 42). Thus, both Japanese and British companies rely much on short-term loans.

The differences between Britain and Japan are two-fold. First is the aforementioned main bank system in Japan and its absence in Britain. Just as for large quoted corporations, branches of major commercial banks act as main banks to smaller companies, which are closely monitored, and for which advice and expertise in management and accounting are offered, as part of a package in advancing loans.

The second difference concerns the availability of long-term loans with favourable repayment terms for SMEs in Japan, and the relative lack of such finance in Britain. In Japan, there are three government financial institutions as well as some private banks which specialise in advancing loans to SMEs. In 1987, total loans outstanding (excluding overdrafts) to SMEs stood at ¥212 trillion (£965b at £ = ¥230); of this sum, 35 per cent came from financial institutions specialising in SMEs. This proportion used to be as high as just over 50 percent in the late 1960s and 1970s, but is declining because major banks are more keen to lend to SMEs to compensate for the loss of business from their traditional clients, large companies. There are therefore no fund shortages for SMEs, particularly as customer companies may act as guarantors for such bank loans; or else, the mere fact that a small company is a core supplier to a reputable local customer may be sufficient for a bank to give good lending terms. This provision lowers the entry cost into the small firm sector, increasing competition.

In Britain, by contrast, partly because banking institutions have developed primarily as deposit protection services rather than to channel direct funds to industry, there are no government financial institutions nor significant provisions for SMEs. The small firm policy in the 1980s created a Loan Guarantee Scheme, but has been criticised for low take-up rates (NAO, 1988). The total cumulative sum of loans guaranteed amounted to only £579m by March 1987. Although difficult to estimate, aggregate lending by member banks of the Committee of London and Scottish bankers to firms with an annual turnover of up to £1 million was said to be £25–30 billion (NAO, 1988, p. 14). This is a non-negligible sum, but interest charged at the commercial rate must clearly be detrimental to small firms which wish to take a long-term view.

In conclusion, the committed role banks play and the practice of inter-corporate shareholding have contributed to a stable continuity of management in Japan, while hands-off banks and the predominance of institutional investors have facilitated ownership changes and short-termism in Britain. Our next task is to assess how different financial environments in Britain and Japan have affected case study firms' propensity to entertain OCR-type customer–supplier relations.

Case Study Evidence

GB Electronics and JJ Electric compared

GB Electronics' financial structure is typical of large British companies, in that its debt–equity ratio, on a rising trend from 55 per cent in 1982 to 64 per cent in 1987, is similar to the national averages. A great majority of the shareholders are trust companies, insurance companies and pension funds (Table 8.2). JJ Electric is also typical of the Japanese company in its financial structure. First, the debt–equity ratio of roughly 3:1 – falling from 80 per cent in 1980 to 71 per cent in 1987 – is close to the national average for the manufacturing sector. Second, just over half of all shares are held by financial institutions, the majority of which are banks and insurance companies, some belonging to the same *gurupu*. The ten largest shareholders held 35 per cent of total shares, and were all 'institutional' (a bank, 3 trust banks, 4 insurance companies, a trading company and an industrial firm). Lastly, mutual shareholding is significant; while 18 per cent of JJ Electric's shares are held by other non-financial companies, JJ Electric also holds shares in 191 non-affiliate companies, 13 of which are within the *gurupu*.

GB Electronics and JJ Electric are similar in at least two respects. First, top management's shareholding is very low in both companies, although GB Electronic's 16 directors hold shares whose proportion to total, at 0.2 per cent, is nearly four times as great as the proportion held by JJ Electric's 35 directors. Second, the maturity structure of bank loans and overdrafts is not so different either, although JJ Electric has made slightly more use of long-term loans (46 per cent of loans and overdrafts

Table 8.2. *Share Ownership at GB Electronics and JJ Electric (%)*

	GB Electronics	JJ Electric
	(1986)	(1987)
Financial institutions	n/a	52.7
Trust companies	25.6	n/a
Insurance companies	20.9	n/a
Pension funds	15.8	n/a
Unit trusts	1.4	n/a
Investment companies	1.3	n/a
Stockbroking companies	0	2.9
Nominee companies	21.9	n/a
Other companies	1.3	17.9
Foreign companies & individuals	n/a	10.0
Individuals	10.3	16.6
Dollar ordinary shares	1.5	n/a
TOTAL	100	100

Source: Company Report and Accounts for GB Electronics; *Yuka shoken hokoku sho* (Report to the Ministry of Finance) for JJ Electric.

to be repayable beyond one year) than GB Electronics has done (with 32 per cent repayable beyond one year).

By far the greatest difference in the financial environment between GB Electronics and JJ Electric is in the stability of its ownership identity at JJ Electric, as contrasted to a constant fear of being acquired by a competitor in recent years at GB Electronics. The takeover bids resulted firstly in forming a joint venture company which was studied in chapter 4, and more recently in a wholesale takeover finally approved by the Monopolies and Mergers Commission. Within a matter of 3 years (1987–9), therefore, the ownership structure of GB Electronics' Sites X and Y had changed twice. Although the company's resolve to implement its Preferred Supplier Policy was said to be unaffected, in practice, the rationalisation of production sites to consolidate two previously separate parts of the company has caused major disruptions in some supplier relations. This only contributed to undermining the credibility of long-term commitments central to PSP.

Before the takeover was approved, GB Electronics put up a consortium to mount a counter-bid to take over its competitor. The fact that the consortium bid was to be financed by a clearing bank which was also a main bank to the original bidding company, led to the resignation of the chairman from the clearing bank's board. In his judgment the clearing bank reduced itself to a mere moneylender by showing neither loyalty nor commercial acumen in supporting a counter-bid. Bank–client relationships which this clearing bank wishes to cultivate are evidently of the arm's-length type.

By contrast, JJ Electric has grown steadily during the whole of its history, with no instances of takeover bids. This is partly because of the stability and concentration of inter-corporate shareholding as described above (with 35 per cent of all shares held by the largest ten shareholders), but also because the lifetime internal promotion employment system makes mergers and takeovers less acceptable (Odagiri and Hase 1989).

Suppliers and sub-contractors

The viability of OCR-type relations, more commonly observed among Japanese than among British firms, depends on the capacity to ride out short-term adversities for long-term gains. How much of this capability is due to the financial structure of supplier companies?

All the sample suppliers and sub-contractors, as described in chapter 3, are limited companies, but only a handful are quoted publicly; they are B203(PCB), B410(PCB) and J1210(PCB). A number of British suppliers belong to a group headed by a holding company. For example, B120(PCB) is part of a group and was hived off from one of the group companies making mini-computers, of which it had been an internal division. In 1985, B120(PCB) experienced a complete overhaul as a whole new management team was brought in by the holding company which considered the old management team incompetent; worker morale and reputation with customers had to be restored. Such holding company structure is illegal in Japan; instead, a group of hive-off companies was found, of which J120(PCB) and J250(EA) are members (see chapter 10).

In Japan, a number of suppliers had part of their shares in the hands of their major customer company. For example, 30 per cent of J150(PCB) are held by its largest customer, a medical instrument manufacturer, which was a sole customer at the time shares were first acquired around 30 years ago. Similarly, J360(EA) was founded by a local entrepreneur; its managers subsequently asked the customer company in consumer electronics to take a 40 per cent equity stake in the company as a condition for making it its sole customer. J360(EA)'s Managing Director explained that this arrangement for firming up commitment was mutually beneficial; J360(EA) could prevent its customer from withdrawing at its

Table 8.3. *Share Ownership at J1210(PCB) and B400(PCB) 1987 (%
of total shares)*

	J1210(PCB)	B400(PCB)
Managing Director	18.5	15.9
Other directors	20.9	3.0
Other individuals	15.8	32.1
Financial institutions	17.7[*]	49.2[**]
Non-financial corporations	21.3	0
Foreigners	5.7	0
Stockbroking companies	0.1	0
TOTAL	100.0	100.0
TOTAL SHARES IN ISSUE	24,600,000	20,079,769

[*] They are banks and insurance companies.
[**] They are pension funds, unit trusts, trust companies and insurance companies.
Source: Respective company annual reports.

convenience, while the customer could make sure J360(EA) would not walk away having received training and technology transfer. This last is a good example of a case in which shareholding is the expression of some other business relationship, not so much a relation in itself.

As a direct comparison, the shareholding patterns of the only publicly quoted sample PCB firm in Japan, J1210(PCB), and a British firm, B410(PCB) are given in Table 8.3. The two companies are similar in that their Managing Directors are also founders of the respective companies, and held a significant proportion of total shares, together with their trusted directors. J1210(PCB) is, however, different from B410(PCB) in having two distinct types of shareholders whose equity stakes reflect the other business they do with the company. One is the main bank, which holds 1.9 per cent of shares. The other involves three major raw material suppliers, which each hold 4.6 or 4.7 per cent of total shares; the main business, of course, is the supply of laminates and other raw materials to J1210(PCB). Thus, while J1210(PCB) can rely on over half of its shares being in the hands of committed shareholders, B410(PCB) has no more than 30 per cent in that category.

The extent of reliance on bank loans between the two companies are not so different, with gearing ratios of 59 per cent for B410(PCB) and 53 per cent for J1210(PCB) in 1987, and the proportion of loans maturing beyond one year being 52 per cent for B410(PCB) and 55 per cent for

J1210(PCB). What is different is the close relationship J1210(PCB) has developed with its main bank. Not only does J1210(PCB)'s main bank hold shares in the company; the bank has also been seconding its management personnel, at the company's request, to upgrade its accounting system, in preparation for quotation in the first section of the Tokyo Stock Exchange (which was achieved in 1989).

Capital participation in the PCB industry

Contrasting developments in the British and Japanese PCB industries illustrate the fact that financial vertical integration or dis-integration takes place for varying reasons, including those other than to better coordinate production activities. One such consideration is the availability of internally generated funds.

In the late 1980s, the extent of financial vertical integration (i.e. equity ownership by a downstream company) in the PCB industry was quite similar in the two countries; around 40 per cent of total PCB output in Japan and 30–40 per cent in Britain were accounted for by in-house production. But this situation was arrived at in Britain from a greater degree of vertical integration, estimated to be as high as 50 per cent in the mid 1980s. Since then, major companies sold off their internal facilities, following a business strategy to concentrate on their so-called core business. B500(PCB) is one such company sold off by GB Electronics. Although GB Electronics sources from and remains satisfied with B500(PCB), it no longer has to reserve internal funds for investment in PCB manufacturing equipment.

In Japan, there is no tendency for large diversified electronics manufacturers to sell off their in-house PCB facilities; if anything, companies such as NEC and Fujitsu are investing to expand their in-house production capacity. Moreover, there are also new providers of share capital for the Japanese PCB industry, who wish to participate financially in, or form joint ventures with, existing independent PCB companies. A major type of corporate shareholders in PCB companies used to be material suppliers (as in the case of J1210(PCB)), which wanted to secure markets for their products. More recently, however, there are large corporations in maturing industries, such as steel and textiles, which wish to diversify in order to employ their excess lifetime employed workers. Joint ventures between newly privatised Japan Tobacco and CMK, and between Unichika (a spinning company) and Airex, are examples of a good match between one partner with financial clout but no technical expertise in PCBs and the other with technical expertise but insufficient funds for new investment.

The post-Plaza Accord yen appreciation in the mid-1980s drove many Japanese PCB suppliers to making losses (-1.2 per cent gross profit over sales on average in 1987 (JPCA 1987a)). The fact that many of these PCB suppliers survived is due to (i) the stability provided by their trading relationships with customer companies which nevertheless bargained to reduce prices drastically; and (ii) the availability of low-cost finance to continue investing in equipment. Funds came in the form of both debt and equity. First, long-term loans were advanced to small and medium-sized firms from government financial institutions under the Structural Improvement Programme (*Kozo kaizen keikaku*) and the Programme on Modernisation of Small and Medium Enterprises (*Chusho kigyo kindaika keikaku*), based on the 1963 Law to Promote the Modernisation of SMEs.[3] Second, major customers, raw material suppliers, or unrelated large companies as described above were a source of share capital. As a result, there were by early 1989 over 90 PCB companies in Japan, which were either joint ventures or existing companies with equity stakes by customers or raw material suppliers (*Densan Shinpo* 20 and 27 February 1989).

In conclusion, the provision of long-term bank loans has been just one contributory factor in ensuring equipment investment to take place even in the downturn. Long-term bank loans are helpful in creating OCR-type relations. But just as, if not more, important for committed interdependent relationships is the roles banks and customer companies play; both engage in a range of activities (e.g. a customer having an equity stake in the supplier for whom it acts as a guarantor for bank loans on top of placing orders for components) which make the relationship 'thick' and not easily breakable.

9

Employment system links

The next supporting national institution to be examined is the employment and industrial relations systems of Britain and Japan. It is argued in this chapter that (i) there is a close parallel between customer–supplier relations and employment relations in each country (a point noted by Dore (1983, p. 472) and Aoki (1988)); (ii) the similarities are due to logical links underlying parallel historical developments in the employment and subcontracting systems; and, more specifically, (iii) the functional flexibility and stability of the workforce at both supplier and customer companies in Japan have enabled the development of 'competence trust' and 'goodwill trust' which are indispensable in OCR-type customer–supplier relations.

Analogy between employment relations and supplier relations

At the risk of oversimplification, this section presents a stylised characterisation of the parallel between 'organisation-oriented' employment relations and OCR-type customer–supplier relations in Japan. In doing so, the contemporary Japanese situation is contrasted implicitly with a combination of 'market-oriented' employment relations and ACR-type customer–supplier relations which are the norm in Britain.[1]

Community and association

The Japanese enterprise is ideally a community whose members, both workers and managers, work towards a shared goal to make it prosper. Factors promoting a sense of community include the stability of the membership due to the practice of lifetime employment and internal promotion, the company assuming the responsibility for providing welfare for its employees, and the enterprise union which reinforces the idea that workers' primary affiliation is with the firm rather than with their occupational group.

190

Employment system links

A similar sense of community exists in a vertical *keiretsu*, a hierarchical network of core suppliers and sub-contractors, headed by a patron customer company. The pervading mood in each *keiretsu* is not that of unilateral control by the patron company of its smaller suppliers. Rather, it is sustained by the ideology of co-prosperity and co-existence (*kyoei kyozon*) which emphasises mutual dependence and common destiny among the member firms. The 'co-existence and co-prosperity' motto does not stop at the level of an ideology.

One tangible institution which promotes this sense of community is the suppliers' association (*kyoryoku kai*, literally translatable as 'cooperating association'), formed at the initiative of the patron company, and whose membership is controlled by it. The earliest of these associations came into existence immediately preceding and during the Second World War for the purpose of transferring technology to core sub-contractors *en masse*. For example, activities at Toyota Motors which led to the formation of Kyohokai in 1943 may be traced back to 1939 (Cusumano, 1985, p. 252). Interestingly, this period of organisational solidarity and the reinforcement of hierarchy also saw the development of the patriotic Sanpo movement which laid the foundation for enterprise unionism. In post-war Japan, suppliers' associations spread from the automobile industry to other sectors, including the electrical and electronics industry and even the apparel industry.

Today, the association facilitates intense communication between the patron company and its primary sub-contractors, providing a regular forum for technology transfer and disclosure of confidential business plans to the trusted few. Primary sub-contractors themselves may have their own associations of their suppliers. Much lateral communication which occurs among the association member suppliers, some of whom are direct competitors, is another facet of the association as community. Mutual help is offered in technical matters both because of a rational awareness of mutual dependence, that one supplier's defective components affect the reputation and sales of the final product which in turn rebounds on other suppliers' order levels, and because of affective sentiments developed through socialising amongst the suppliers' managers.[2] The suppliers' association is different from the enterprise union, however, in that (a) suppliers may have multiple membership in more than one customer company's associations (MIRI 1987), and (b) the association hardly functions as a negotiating body to collectively bargain over prices.[3]

Long-term commitment as a norm

Long-term commitments are made by large firms to their core suppliers and sub-contractors, in the same way that they implicitly guarantee lifetime employment to their regular employees. This enables companies to take a long-term view in investing in both human resources and capital equipment. Lifetime employment is an ideal and the norm upheld by a wider section of the Japanese economy than the large companies which actually put it into practice. Similarly, the long-term mutual commitment ideal is a powerful norm embraced by non-core suppliers and sub-contractors whose reality may differ substantially from the ideal. This is the reason why Williamsonian factors such as asset specificity do not fully capture the British–Japanese difference in the nature of customer–supplier relations.

The selection procedure and the core-periphery distinction

Selecting employees for lifetime employment requires more care than hiring temporary workers. In the same way, screening potential long-term sub-contractors before placing an order is a more serious affair than placing one-off orders. A factory visit to appraise a potential sub-contractor's performance in quality, cost, delivery and management is conducted thoroughly before taking on any sub-contractor.

A distinction between core suppliers and periphery suppliers exists in Japan, just as the core-periphery divide is a feature of the Japanese employment system. The periphery consists of (a) new sub-contractors who normally go through a probationary period before some are selected into the core of trustworthy suppliers, and (b) some old established suppliers which, for some reason, have consistently performed badly and are occupying the lowest position in the supplier ranking.

Continuous training, performance appraisal and internal promotion

Long-term commitments made by customer companies to their core suppliers have a similar historical origin to the lifetime employment system in Japan. A stable system of sub-contracting with long-term commitments proliferated during the high-growth period of the 1960s, although the wartime legacy of consolidation with large-to-small firm technology transfer contributed to developing this system (Nakamura 1981, p. 15). For Japanese customer companies, the option of purchasing existing competencies from suppliers was not readily available, just as they found it difficult to buy in skills in the early part of the twentieth century. Therefore, they were obliged to create competencies in their suppliers by their own investments. Having invested, they had an incentive to make those competencies of general application captive, to minimise spillovers to competitors. A common form of customer companies' attempts to appropriate full returns from their own investments was to insist on exclusive supply from their sub-contractors. The analogy with commonly accepted accounts of the origins of lifetime employment (e.g. by Dore, 1973; Gordon, 1985; Taira, 1970) – the motivation being the appropriation of returns from training for scarce skills – is evident.

Core workers are given continuous training for broad-based skills, and are regularly assessed on their performance; the results of such performance appraisal affect the rate at which individual workers are promoted. Similarly, suppliers are given technical guidance to be functionally flexible, and are regularly appraised on their performance (in quality, price and delivery). A ranking according to performance becomes a basis for determining the size and type of future orders.

Partial gift exchange

Just as better ways of doing things are constantly sought from employees through suggestion boxes and quality circles, sub-contractors are expected to make continuous improvements in their cost, quality and delivery performance. Sub-contractors are willing to perform in excess of the minimum standard, as set out in written contracts, because customer companies reciprocate, not by offering higher prices, but more through assuring a smooth level of orders, giving technical guidance and financial help whenever sub-contractors require such assistance. This may be interpreted as an inter-firm equivalent of what Akerlof called a 'partial gift exchange' in labour contracts (Akerlof, 1982).

Functional flexibility

In lifetime employment, workers are hired not for specific tasks but to carry out a variety of tasks as required by the company. Similarly, Japanese sub-contractors are willing to accede to customer companies' requests which may otherwise be regarded as outside their task demarcation. As demarcations are blurred, sub-contractors are willing to undertake extra new tasks as well as switch from one task to another. Just as there are multi-skilled workers, some specialist suppliers in Japan are developing into multi-tasked suppliers, diversifying, for example, into product development and design, to meet the demands of the existing customers. Of course, the achievement of such functional flexibility at the suppliers is likely to involve costs in training and technology transfer, which may be partially borne by customer companies.

Thus, in the Japanese context, the concept of functional flexibility is applicable to inter-firm relations, across the firm's boundary, as well as to the core workforce. This contrasts with the tendency to focus only on the numerical flexibility of sub-contractors, which are all in the periphery, in the British discussion of the flexible firm. If sub-contractors are resorted to for numerical flexibility's sake, then skill shortages would worsen as companies rely on the existing stock of sub-contractors without providing training in-house for the sort of skills they require (Atkinson and Meager 1986, pp. 10–11; Curson 1986, pp. 163–4).

Having spelt out the parallel between the ACR–OCR contrast in customer–supplier relations and the market- vs. organisation-oriented contrast in employment relations, the next issue is to examine if there is any logical consistency in the internal organisation of a firm and the mode of relationships it establishes with other firms. This issue will be tackled from the viewpoint of the supplier company as well as the customer company.

Consequences of the Japanese employment system

The conventional explanation of the use of suppliers and sub-contractors, consistent with the core-periphery framework, is in terms of (a) the use of low wage costs at the sub-contractors, and (b) the protection of the security of employment for the customer company's core workforce.

Table 9.1. *Pay differentials by establishment size 1985* (Manufacturing only)

Size	JAPAN (¥ thousand)	BRITAIN (£)
−99	2550 (52.6)	7232 (75.9)
100−999	3544 (73.1)	8069 (84.7)
1000+	4847 (100.0)	9528 (100.0)

N.B. Figures in brackets indicate differentials as percentage of the 1000+ size levels.
Sources: MITI *Kogyo Tokei Hyo* (Industrial Statistics); Business Monitor *Census of Production* PA1002.

Table 9.2. *Pay differentials by enterprise size and type of workers (Manufacturing only)*

Size	JAPAN (1986)		BRITAIN (1985)	
	Manual	Non-manual	Manual	Non-Manual
−99	78.7%	82.2%	82.1%	89.9%
100−999	84.0%	86.7%	84.6%	93.0%
1000+	¥290,800	¥345,400	£8,136.8	£10,622.4

N.B. Percentages are as a proportion of the 1000+ size pay level. Japanese figures are monthly take home pay for male regular workers only. The differentials are narrower than in Table 9.1 due to the exclusion of (i) female workers and (ii) bonus payments. British figures refer to annual wage costs.
Sources: Business Monitor *Census of Production*; *Rodo Tokei Yoran* (Handbook of Labour Statistics) 1988, pp. 116–21.

Wage differential by firm size

Pay differentials by firm size are greater in Japan than in Britain (see Table 9.1) due to the history of Japanese industrialisation as a late developer (Broadbridge 1966). Differentials among manual workers are greater than among non-manual workers in both Britain and Japan (Table 9.2). It is also among the Japanese manual workforce that wage differentials by firm size become more pronounced with age. Given that smaller firms tend to have more older workers, differentials in Table 9.1 contain this age effect as well as other factors, such as length of service, educational level and gender. However, even if all relevant factors are controlled, pay differentials still remain particularly for older workers (Figure 9.1).

The advantage for large firms of using smaller suppliers to save on labour costs was greatest in the decade following the end of the Second World War. Pay differentials by firm size were much greater then than now (see Figure 9.2). However, the only way such pay differentials could be exploited was to organise smaller suppliers as separate companies. A determining factor was the enterprise union in large Japanese corporations, which insisted on the same terms and conditions of employment (including pay) for regular employees of all establishments within a company. Moreover, an egalitarian ethic, upheld by ensuring a homogeneous workforce within a company, may have been a driving force behind a greater degree of vertical dis-integration in Japanese industry (Smitka, 1989, chapter 4). Other contributory factors were the shortage of capital and the abundance of small firms.

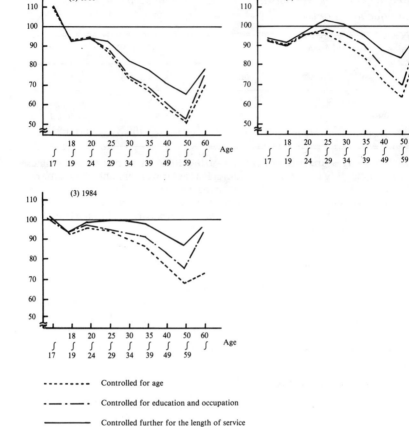

Figure 9.1 Male wage differentials by firm size, controlled for age, length of service and education in Japan (manual workers, manufacturing only).
Note: Wage differentials are the ratios of wage in 10–99 employee firms to wage in 1000+ firms.
Source: SMEA 1986, p. 22.

Over time, particularly in the 1960s, this advantage in saving on labour costs was eroded because of rapid growth and labour shortages made worse by a rising school leaving age. But by the time the low-cost reason for sub-contracting became less significant, large customer companies had already invested in creating 'competence trust' at their suppliers; once the skills, attitudes and institutions (e.g. suppliers' associations) necessary to manage a system of 'governance by trust' (Smitka 1989)

196

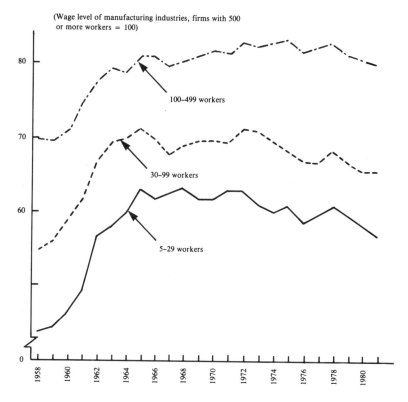

(Wage level of manufacturing industries, firms with 500
or more workers = 100)

Figure 9.2 Trends in wage differentials by size of enterprise.
Source: Ministry of Labour, Japan *Maigetsu Kinro Tokei Chosa*
(Monthly Labour Statistics Survey).

were in place due to past investments, the benefits of vertical integration
were correspondingly reduced.

There is, however, a mechanism through which the differential is likely
to be sustained, namely the Spring Offensive wage rounds. Because of
the custom of large firms settling their negotiations before smaller firms,
suppliers take account of wage settlements at their major customer
companies as well as such factors as local area comparability. Suppliers,
particularly if they belong to a *keiretsu*, tend to settle at or below their
customer's rate of increase, so as not to elicit a demand for price
reduction in the next round of commercial negotiations. The logic
followed is thus: if a supplier can grant a large wage increase to its
workers, it must be doing well in terms of profit; if so, why not pass on
some of the earnings to customer companies? This reasoning is in stark

197

contrast to the logic often followed in Britain: if a supplier has to grant a wage increase to its workers, its profit is being squeezed; the customer must expect it as inevitable that the supplier wishes to pass on at least part of its wage cost increase to the customer.

As an example, J650(PCB)'s average wage was said to be around 80 per cent of JJ Electric's, its largest customer (although the starting salaries were not so different). Every year, J650(PCB) studies the percentage wage rise at JJ Electric, which becomes the benchmark against which J650(PCB) determines its own increase. The actual percentage rise is slightly lower than that at JJ Electric, naturally at bad times, but even at good times – apparently as a matter of courtesy to JJ Electric.

Employment security, job rotation and secondments

Besides pay, employment security also declines with firm size. The advantage of stability in the Japanese employment system at large customer companies lies in the fact that job rotation and on-the-job learning among managers, engineers and workers facilitate greater communication within the firm. For example, new graduate recruits in engineering may work for six months in the sales office and then the quality assurance department before being assigned to the post of development engineer. With a broad-based knowledge of the company, a closer marketing–development–manufacturing link is forged within the firm. This helps shorten leadtime in product development, and the flexibility and information sharing which close links engender are an internal prerequisite for establishing OCR-type relations with suppliers.

The viability of the Japanese employment system at large companies has depended so far in part on the numerical flexibility provided by the existence of temporary, part-time and sub-contract workers working for the same companies. More recently, however, with less rapid growth and the aging population creating promotion blockages, companies are extending the frontier of the 'lifetime employment zone' to loosely defined corporate groupings (Inagami 1988, p. 10; Inagami 1989, chapter 1). In other words, while much of the lifetime employment career has hitherto been spent within one company, there are increasing instances of seconding or permanently transferring those hired for lifetime to group companies, affiliates, and sub-contractors within the *keiretsu* grouping.

At the aggregate level, secondment (*shukko*) can be classified into temporary secondment (*ichiji shukko*) and pre-retirement secondment (*taishoku shukko*). There is evidence that both types of secondment are on the increase (Inagami, 1989, p. 16). According to the Employment Management Survey (*Koyo kanri chosa*) conducted by the Japanese Ministry of Labour, there were in total 567,705 temporary secondees (338,906 being in the manufacturing sector) as of 1 January 1987. The duration of secondment varied, but two to three years were the modal periods, while shorter one-year secondment was more popular the smaller the firm size. Of the total of 148,680 whose period of temporary secondment started within the year 1986, 30.4 per cent were aged 45 or over, and 63.2 per cent were dispached to *keiretsu* firms. The pattern was similar for pre-retirement secondees; there were 25,746 in 1986, of whom 57.3 per cent were aged 45 or over, and 66.2 per cent placed within *keiretsu* firms.

Some systematic differences by firm size are also evident (Table 9.3). First, secondment of both types is more common the larger the firm size. Second, pre-retirement secondment is most common among the 50 year olds at larger firms. Third, temporary secondment is geared to young employees at small firms and for mid-career 40 year olds at larger firms. This indicates that temporary secondment conflates the movement of workers of various types across the firm's boundary for different reasons, including technology transfer, on-the-job training, and more general career development.

A specific case may shed some light on this matter. J650(PCB), which is effectively part of JJ Electric *keiretsu* – supplying 85 per cent of its output to JJ Electric, although there are no shareholding links – had 30 employees on secondment in 1987 from three companies. These were JJ Electric, another major customer and a textile company with which J650(PCB) had recently started a joint venture in PCB manufacturing. There were said to be three types of secondment. First, in order to achieve a 'soft landing' in retirement, JJ Electric has dispatched over the years a few 50-year-old employees from time to time who, after 2 to 3 years, become employees of J650(PCB), taking a 20 per cent cut in salary. They work until the J650(PCB) retirement age of 60 to 65. J650(PCB)'s willingness to bear the burden of its major customer's wish to ease the retirement process of unwanted employees may be interpreted as a process of give and take, to repay the accumulated obligation of receiving ever-expanding orders and invaluable technical and management advice from JJ Electric. Secondly, 10 of the 30 secondees were young technologists in their late 20s from the textile company, who would spend up to 5 years at J650(PCB) to learn about PCB manufacturing technology, before working for the joint venture PCB company. Lastly, there are a handful of older technologists, who were 'scouted' for

Table 9.3. *Secondment of workers in Japan 1986 (% of firms)*

Size	% firms*	AGE** −29	30–39	40–49	50–59	60+	n.a.***
Temporary secondment							
5000+	91.6	7.6	24.4	26.8	19.6	0	21.6
1000–4999	77.0	12.9	21.0	29.3	20.5	0.2	16.3
300–999	49.4	18.4	27.4	23.9	15.7	1.6	13.0
100–299	19.4	26.9	27.8	20.5	12.4	0.3	12.1
30–99	7.8	29.7	29.9	12.3	10.5	0	17.6
All sizes	14.2	24.4	27.8	19.0	13.4	0.4	15.0
Permanent secondment							
5000+	34.2	0	4.2	5.9	66.1	1.7	22.1
1000–4999	23.1	6.9	5.0	9.1	60.0	6.9	12.1
300–999	10.4	11.0	11.7	18.0	45.0	2.1	12.2
100–299	4.7	13.4	3.7	18.6	32.3	1.0	31.0
30–99	1.5	2.6	6.0	0	49.4	17.7	24.3
All sizes	3.2	8.1	6.2	10.7	45.2	7.4	22.4

* Proportion of firms which seconded workers during 1986.
** Refers to the most common age range of workers seconded by respondent firms. The age range percentages add up to 100; the total corresponds to the firms which seconded workers in the first column.
*** Not available, or an even distribution of ages.

Source: Rodo Tokei Yoran (Handbook of Labour Statistics) Tokyo: Okurasho insatsukyoku, 1988, p. 52. Original source is Japanese Ministry of Labour *Koyo Kanri Chosa* (Employment Management Survey) 1986.

by J650(PCB) from another major customer, and who hoped to extend their temporary stay to join J650(PCB) as regular mid-career recruits. J650(PCB), like most other firms of its size, is keenly aware of the inadequacy of relying solely on in-house training to accumulate the necessary amount of technical expertise, and is willing to obtain any outside help it can to rectify the shortcomings. Thus, recipients of secondees are not always acting out of returning obligations only.

In Britain also, both pre-retirement and mid-career secondments occur (although no survey evidence is to be found about its numerical significance). However, the major difference from the Japanese use of secondment is that secondment is regarded more as a service to the community in general, thus making charitable and other community organisations a more likely placement than commercial organisations ('Secondment – a two-way process' *Financial Times*, 26 August 1988). Moreover, secondees are all volunteers, who are to apply for placements, rather than nominated by the company. Thus, secondment in Britain may be for 'high fliers' who are generous enough to give their precious time for community work as part of the process of broadening one's mind and accumulating an enriching experience. But it has little to do with inter-firm relations in general.

Flexibility of workers at supplier companies

This section turns to the employment system of the SME sector which tends to remain an ill-defined receptacle for numerically flexible workers. What features of the supplier company's employment system are prerequisites for entertaining OCR-type relationships with customer companies?

A degree of numerical flexibility is evident in both Japan and Britain. Classifying the labour force into core and periphery in an internationally consistent fashion is not easy. But as an indication, in 1988, 76.4 per cent of the total 44.22 million employees in Japan were full-timers with a regular status, while the rest were either part-timers (10 per cent of total employees), student temporary (*arubaito*) workers (3.5 per cent) or other types of temporary workers (JIL, 1989, p. 25). Another indication is given by an OECD comparison (OECD 1987; see Table 9.4), which shows that while part-time working is more widely spread in Britain than in Japan (21.6 per cent in Britain, 11.7 per cent in Japan of total workers in 1986), a greater proportion of part-timers have a temporary status in Japan than in Britain.

Another possible source of numerical flexibility is the actual work hours which are longer the smaller the firm size in Japan. The longer

Table 9.4. *Employees in permanent and temporary jobs, by full-time and part-time status 1985* (All non-agricultural industries)

	JAPAN	BRITAIN
Full time	37,460,000	16,483,900
Of whom: Permanent	93.8%	97.0%
Temporary	6.2%	3.0%
Part Time	4,710,000	4,565,200
Of whom: Permanent	57.7%	84.0%
Temporary	42.3%	16.0%

N.B. Temporary workers are persons employed for a specific period of no more than a year.
Source: OECD *Employment Outlook* 1987, p. 38.

hours give more scope for adjusting work levels by varying hours. Denki Roren's surveys (1985) on shorter work hours indicate that one of the major reasons why Japanese companies in the electrical and electronic machinery industry are finding it difficult to implement the five-day working week is because of work demands put upon them by their larger customer companies.[4] Entrepreneurs and managers of supplier companies are resigned to the fact that customers, who themselves benefit from a five-day working week, may place an order on Friday afternoon, and expect delivery on the following Monday morning.

Next, more specifically with reference to the sample supplier companies, there is evidence of numerical flexibility in both Britain and Japan but to a varying degree. Supplier companies reported that they generally had to cope with some order fluctuations, with a magnitude ranging from very little to more than 100:40 between peak and trough months at some companies (including B38(PCB), B107(PCB), B205(EA), B750(EA)).

The major method of varying work levels in both Britain and Japan is to switch between one to three shift systems. Certain processes, such as plating and drilling in the PCB industry and automatic insertion in assembly, tended to be worked on a 24-hour shift system throughout the year, while other processes were subject to overtime, an extra shift, or a half shift such as the 'back shift' between 6 p.m. and 10 p.m. at B205(EA), worked by up to 50 temporary female workers, mostly housewives who are trained specifically to do this shift.

Another method of varying work levels, or of being covered for drastic changes in workload, is to employ full-time workers with a temporary status. One British company which has taken this advantage to its extreme is B700(EA), 40 per cent of whose employees work full-time but on a rolling monthly contract. The cost B700(EA) has to pay, however, in its practice of retaining numerical flexibility is that labour turnover among temporary workers is as high as 30 per cent; once they acquire skills at the company, there is nothing stopping them from getting a regular job. Partly in defence of this numerical flexibility strategy, B700(EA)'s plant manager also said that 'the day there is a union, that's the day we close the plant'.

A lower rate of unionisation generally applies the smaller the firm size in both Britain and Japan. Although the presence of a union does not necessarily imply job demarcation and hence lack of flexibility in Japan, the desire to keep small and medium-sized firms union-free reflects some managers' fear of work disruption through disputes, which leads to loss of business. As an example, J1210(PCB) faced an organising drive in the mid-1970s by the radical Zenkin and Zenkoku Ippan unions. It took three months to quash the attempt by establishing a house union. During the few months of strife, however, J1210(PCB)'s customers, particularly those who themselves experienced problems with unions in the past, promptly curtailed their orders, with the consequence for J1210(PCB) of having to survive on half its normal level of business.

So, are workers at Japanese suppliers' primarily unorganised, unskilled, numerically flexible workers? The answer is no. There is firstly considerable stability in the regular workforce for firms of all sizes. The average length of service in manufacturing was 14.8 years for firms employing 1000 or more workers, and 9.5 years for firms employing less than 100 in 1985 (according to the Wage Structure Survey (*Chingin kozo kihon tokei chosa*)). There has also been a secular long-term trend towards average job tenures becoming longer in Japan (Dore et al., 1989, pp. 56–7). Comparing Britain and Japan directly, employees with job tenures of over ten years accounted for 57.2 per cent of male (28.8 per cent of female) employees in Japanese manufacturing, as compared to 39.3 per cent of male (22.5 per cent of female) employees in the British manufacturing sector in the mid-1980s (OECD *Employment Outlook* 1989, p. 187). Without such relative stability in Japan, the type of long-term investment some Japanese supplier companies undertake in training workers, especially technologists to be seconded to customer companies over 3–5 years as described in chapters 4 and 5, would not be worthwhile.

There is also greater-than-expected stability of so-called non-regular workforce at Japanese suppliers and sub-contractors, which can minimise wastage in repeatedly training new personnel for the same skills (as

Prices, quality and trust

at B750(EA)). Particularly in rural areas, the same women who want to help out nearest to home are said to come back at peak periods. Thus, temporary contract (*paato*) working in rural areas is more stable than that in metropolitan areas, typically for supermarkets and personal service sectors.

Lastly, some Japanese PCB companies actively buy in skills – both managerial and technological – by headhunting (or 'scouting' (*sukauto*) as it is more commonly called). The case of J650(PCB), which asked for secondment first rather than attempt direct poaching, was already described. Instead of such 'institutionalised poaching', J1210(PCB) engages in more outright scouting of managers and technologists from its material suppliers and larger competitors. There appears to be social acceptability in Japan of the weak poaching from the strong, but not vice versa, within an established relationship.

Where no such hierarchical order of acceptability exists, in Britain, it is a free-for-all world in which anyone can poach from any other. Complaints of poaching engineers and technicians were encountered among British PCB companies (to such an extent that poaching was a subject of panel discussion at the 1989 trade association (PCIF) annual conference). There is very little individual companies can do, as complaints of poaching co-exist with own attempts at poaching and employees' desire to move on from company to company. Discontinuity of personnel at all levels in British suppliers was given by Japanese companies located in the UK as one reason why their attempts at training supplier operators and at communicating new ways of organising or inspecting to supervisors are often in vain. They are often back to square one with change of personnel; 'skills belong to individuals, and never seem to stick to the organisation', said a Japanese manager at a UK-based Japanese plant.

In sum, the practice of the customer company's loaning of its engineers, and its provision of training for supplier employees, emerge as the central OCR-sustaining mechanism. The stability of employment at suppliers upholds the customer's incentive to provide technology transfer and training. At the same time, Japanese supplier companies do not passively rely on technology transfer from their customer companies but also actively recruit mid-career technologists to increase 'competence trust' in the eyes of their customers. Such trust is required, as it is the basis on which orders are won, and also because it is essential in responding flexibly to customer companies' demands, including last-minute changes in delivery dates. The market-oriented employment system at the supplier company, with greater labour turnover, is not favourable to a successful implementation of OCR-type relationships.

10

Entrepreneurship and the dynamics of small-firm creation

Conventional discussions on why sub-contracting is more extensive in Japan than in Britain concentrate on such factors as greater wage differentials by firm size in Japan than in Britain as discussed in the previous chapter, and the abundance of small establishments in Japan relative to Britain (see Table 10.1).[1] But our interest is not just in why sub-contracting is extensive, but why a particular type of sub-contracting relationship – namely the obligational contracting type – is widespread in

Table 10.1. *Distribution of Establishments and Employment by Firm Size 1985 (%; Manufacturing only)*

	JAPAN		BRITAIN	
Size	Establishments	Employment	Establishments	Employment
1–9	57.8*	13.9*	69.0	6.5
10– 19	19.3	10.7	12.9	5.1
20– 99	19.4	30.2	12.3	15.7
100–999	3.3	31.2	5.4	41.7
1000+	0.2	14.1	0.4	30.9
Total	100.0	100.0	100.0	100.0
Number	438,518	10,890,000	142,681	4,976,000

N.B. Due to rounding, percentages may not add up to 100.0
* These figures refer to the 4–9 size group only. According to another official survey, *Jigyosho Tokei Chosa* (Establishment Survey) by the Management and Coordination Agency, Japan, the proportions of establishments in the 1–4 and 5–9 size groups were 51.2 per cent and 22.2 per cent respectively, and employment proportions 8.0 per cent and 9.6 per cent respectively, for the manufacturing sector in 1986.
Source: MITI *Kogyo Tokei Hyo* (Industrial Statistics); Business Monitor *Census of Production* PA1002.

Japanese manufacturing. To answer this question, we must go further, and enquire into the nature of entrepreneurship in Japan. Where do small firm entrepreneurs come from? How do their outlook, attitudes and ideology affect their business strategy and the nature of relationship with their customer companies?

This chapter is structured as follows. The first section examines the use of sub-contractors by the sample suppliers described in chapter 5. Next, the dynamics of small-firm creation in Japan is analysed on the basis of evidence from government and academic surveys on entrepreneurship as well as the supplier sample. Lastly, conclusions are drawn on how particular types of entrepreneurship predispose firms to enter into OCR-rather than ACR-type relations with other firms.

Use of sub-subcontractors: evidence from the sample suppliers

The questions to be addressed in this section are: (a) the extent of use of sub-contractors by the sample suppliers; (b) reasons behind the use or non-use of sub-contractors; and (c) how they were identified or created.

Electronic assembly

The British–Japanese contrast is most pronounced in the electronic assembly industry. The sample of eight Japanese assembly sub-contractors all had their own sub-contractors, while the counterpart sample of British sub-contractors did not (see Table 10.2). This difference reflects the presence in Japan of a vertical *keiretsu* structure with a multi-layer of suppliers and sub-contractors. In the absence of such an institution in Britain, British sub-contractors generally dislike contracting out their work further because of the lack of control, particularly over quality.

Diversity within each country's sector ought not to be ignored. A single exception to the uniform non-use of sub-contractors in the British sample was the case of B1100(EA), 60 per cent of whose business is with Japanese companies located in the UK. It has created four assembly sub-contractors, each employing 30 to 40 workers and all 100 per cent dependent on B1100(EA). All four are located nearby. Three of the four had been set up by ex-employees of B1100(EA) – one was a production supervisor – and the other by a local businessman. B1100(EA) had shifted whole production lines from its factory to the sub-contractors' sheds, where '110 per cent technical assistance and backing is provided by us', according to the production manager, who is Japanese. The

Table 10.2. *Use of sub-contractors by sample suppliers*

Company	Number	Payment	Company	Number	Payment
Printed circuit board industry					
B38(PCB)	4	<1%	J17(PCB)	10	55%
B50(PCB)	1	0.6%	J65(PCB)	10	20%
B107(PCB)	6	5%	J120(PCB)	20	10%
B118(PCB)	0	0%	J140(PCB)	15	36%
B120(PCB)	2	1%	J150(PCB)	25	22%
B203(PCB)	1	0.3%	J220(PCB)	20	8%
B222(PCB)	3	0.2%	J480(PCB)	15	15%
B300(PCB)	3	2.6%	J650(PCB)	30	7%
B410(PCB)	5	3%	J700(PCB)	2	7%
B500(PCB)	0	0%	J1210(PCB)	10+	1%

Electronic assembly industry			
Company	Number	Company	Number
B10(EA)	0	J30(EA)	0
B15(EA)	0	J71(EA)	1
B90(EA)	0	J160(EA)	2
B205(EA)	0	J170(EA)	0
B230(EA)	0	J240(EA)	6
B350(EA)	0	J250(EA)	16
B750(EA)	0	J265(EA)	19
B1100(EA)	4	J360(EA)	6

N.B. Number = Total number of sub-contractors used (excludes homeworkers)
Payment = Total annual payment to all sub-contractors as a percentage of annual
sales turnover

source of inspiration for this organisational innovation in Britain is
obvious. With a ten-fold growth between 1985–8 and a further doubling
of sales in 1988–9, B1100(EA) has also faced an environment similar to
that of 1960s' Japan which gave rise to the sub-contracting system as we
know it today.

There is also diversity within the Japanese electronic assembly industry. At one extreme, J170(EA), the most ACR in the Japanese sectoral
sample, has a handful of homeworkers in the neighbourhood and five
design houses which are resorted to whenever it is busy, but has no
assembly sub-contractors at all. At the other extreme, J250(EA) and
J265(EA), the two most OCR in the sample, both make extensive uses of
sub-contractors. In the case of J265(EA), there were in total 19 assembly
sub-contractors, each employing 10 or 20 on average, all 100 per cent

dependent on J265(EA). Sub-contractors' costs were said to be 60 per cent of J265(EA)'s. Similarly, J250(EA) used 16 sub-contractors in 1987, each employing between 30 and 80, and all 100 per cent dependent on J250(EA). Locational proximity is important for frequent communication, and therefore all are within a 50 km radius of J250(EA). Four out of the 16 were set up by ex-employees of J250(EA) who wished to become independent, just as in the 1940s and 50s large companies, including JJ Electric, as noted in chapter 5, had their ex-employees hive off as sub-contractors.[2] 'It's natural to want independence, if you are a man', according to J250(EA)'s Managing Director, who willingly gives financial backing as well as moral encouragement to hived-off operations. He went on to note that such acts are not out of pure altruism or charity, for his self-interest lies in 'ploughing the field' (*hateke zukuri*) for future eventuality: 'Even if I retire, there will always be others who can continue work (as sub-contractors) for J250(EA). And also you never know when you have to become indebted to others (*osewa ni naru*).'

The other twelve sub-contractors were identified by the MD. He drove through the neighbouring mountainous terrain in search of good (i.e. cheap but competent) potential factory hands and/or existing small workshops whose owners invariably have ambitious dreams (often signified by rebuilding their shabby and rusty shed into a neat, whitewashed concrete building, made attractive for women to come and work). In such attempts to identify untapped sources of entrepreneurship and labour, the MD often found himself beaten to it by large consumer electronics companies who were also in intensive search of cheap and competent labour.

As of spring 1989, J250(EA) reduced the number of sub-contractors from 16 to 10, with a further plan to concentrate on 6 in the near future. The choice of which sub-contractors to retain has been made by preferring those which are locationally near, whose top management has a good attitude, and which essentially are willing to remain 100 per cent dependent on J250(EA) and to do as they are told. Between two months' and a year's warning was given to those sub-contractors with whom trading stopped. The core group of six sub-contractors belong to J250(EA)'s study group. Its activity involves a social gathering of the six MDs every two to three months, and once-a-month visit to one of their factories to learn from, and offer constructive criticisms to, each other.

The PCB industry

According to an annual survey by the Japan Printed Circuit Association, Japanese PCB manufacturers use on average twenty-four sub-contractors each; and the production stages most frequently sub-contracted out are the production of whole PCBs, followed by drilling and plating (JPCA, 1987). No corresponding industry-wide statistics exist for the British PCB industry, but Table 10.1 indicates a less common use of sub-contractors, numbering between zero and six per supplier, accounting for a total subcontract cost of no more than a few per cent of total sales. Those who were adamant in never resorting to sub-contractors, B118(PCB) and B500(PCB), based their conviction on the need to directly control quality and the lack of trustworthy sub-contractors. The processes sub-contracted out by the British suppliers were restricted to drilling, maslamination (i.e. bonding of inner layers of multi-layered PCBs), gold-plating, hot-air solder levelling, and bare-board testing. All usages of sub-contractors were sporadic and not continuous.

Who are these sub-contractors to the British PCB industry? In the field of drilling, a handful of companies, whose main line of business is in selling NC drilling machines, offer a sub-contract drilling service. Similarly, maslamination service may be offered by manufacturers of laminates or of maslamination materials. In all other processes, the companies acting as sub-contractors are themselves whole PCB manufacturers with spare capacity in certain processes which they attempt to fill by sub-contract work. Such unevenness in capacity utilisation among different processes in PCB manufacturing is due to most processes requiring lump-sum investments.

The situation is rather different in Japan. There, drilling sub-contractors are no appendages to sales of NC drilling machinery makers, but specialise in drilling only. Hitachi would not dream of offering sub-contract services, as Excellon of the USA has done in the UK, as there are too many small entrepreneurs who can do it more cheaply. Just as there are sub-contractors which do nothing but drilling, there are those specialising in gold plating only or in copper plating only. In fact, sub-contractors specialising in one process of PCB manufacturing exist in virtually all processes except in the technically most difficult process of etching. These sub-contractors are relatively small, but vary in size from ones resembling homeworking to those employing over 100 in the case of plating operations. An overwhelming majority of sub-contractors used by the sample Japanese PCB suppliers did work for more than one customer.

Many sub-contractors in Japan are used to coping with spill-over tasks, but there is also much continuous usage. One extreme example of the latter is J17(PCB), which uses five drilling sub-contractors, two plating sub-contractors and three solder levelling sub-contractors, simply because there are no in-house facilities in these three processes. Even if in-house facilities exist, they may not be enough to cope with all orders; more or less continuous usage of sub-contractors was made by most other Japanese sample PCB suppliers for this reason. The unplanned nature of coping with growth by resorting to sub-contractors is seen at J650(PCB), which grew ten-fold in sales during 1975–85, and has grown 20 per cent per annum since then. Its thirty sub-contractors are nominally to be used as buffers, but in actual fact are resorted to constantly and continuously. Of those, four make whole PCBs, 10 per cent or so more cheaply than in-house due to the sub-contractors' rural location. By contrast, J1210(PCB) tends not to use sub-contractors, as it has been able to make sufficient capital investments.

Unlike in electronic assembly, none of the sub-contractors was a hive-off from the Japanese PCB supplier sample. The closest to a hive-off was the case of two drilling sub-contractors supplying exclusively to J700(PCB), which were started by personal acquaintances of J700(PCB)'s Managing Director. Having spent six months training at J700(PCB), the two entrepreneurs bought NC drilling machines and now employ fifteen and seven people respectively twenty-four hours a day, six days a week. More commonly, sub-contractors are identified by asking around for companies with a spare capacity and a good reputation. J220(PCB) mentioned the role of the trading company which, in its capacity as a supplier of raw materials to both sub-contractors and PCB manufacturers, may act as a broker, match-making trading partners. Traditional skills, such as plating and drilling, exist in abundance at small workshops (*machi koba*) in urban areas, such as around Osaka and Tokyo. This may partly explain the relative lack of need for PCB suppliers to create their own hive-off sub-contractors. However, the following study of J140(PCB) illustrates that much sub-contracting exists even in rural areas.

Inside sub-contractors and a cooperative association

J140(PCB) is located in Chino, Nagano Prefecture, a two-hour train journey from Tokyo. It is a rural area, renowned for its concentration of electronic and precision machinery workshops – Seiko in Suwa is nearby – due to its clean air and water. The company was established as a joint venture between a plating company and a power supply unit company in 1961. The latter's major customer, Oki Electric, transferred much of its in-house technical know-how in PCB manufacturing to J140(PCB).

J140(PCB) is unusual in using inside sub-contractors, of which there were 8, which in total employed 60 workers in 1987. Each sub-contractors is responsible for a particular processing line, but does not generally own the machinery and equipment with which they work (except in resist printing and drilling). Sub-contractors are therefore supplying labour only and receive the rate for the job which is negotiated bilaterally twice a year. Most inside sub-contract workers are old or female, and are paid much less than J140(PCB) workers.

Although low wage costs are one consideration, the full reason for the use of inside sub-contractors must be understood in the context of union militancy in the past. The enterprise union at J140(PCB) belongs to Zenkoku kinzoku (the metal industry federation of enterprise unions), owing to the fact that one of the original joint venture partners forming J140(PCB) was in metal plating. Around 1970–1, this union staged a series of strikes and an overtime ban. The company was already facing difficulty recruiting enough workers in the area to keep up with growing orders, and decided to make more use of outside contractors in order to meet delivery deadlines. But when the union quietened down, some sub-contractors were gradually brought in-house, as closer communication and supervision were considered more conducive to better quality.

Besides labour-only inside sub-contractors, there are also more conventional outside sub-contractors, such as the two NC drilling companies. J140(PCB) has neither the space nor the money to purchase drilling machines, and therefore sub-contracts out 100 per cent of its drilling operations. One sub-contractor, Koyo, was set up by a son of one of J140(PCB)'s directors; the other, Yahata, was set up by a J140(PCB) director who also holds shares in J140(PCB). In fact, Yahata is also an inside sub-contractor, operating three NC machines on J140(PCB)'s site attended by Yahata employees. Both drilling sub-contractors are around 60 per cent dependent on J140(PCB) business, the rest of their work being with other PCB manufacturers in the area.

Also notable are two whole PCB manufacturers which act as regular sub-contractors to J140(PCB). One, Sanze, was originally founded in 1968 as a plating company which traded with J140(PCB). It converted to PCB manufacturing at J140(PCB)'s request. Ever since, J140(PCB) has held 34 per cent of Sanze's shares, while Sanze's and J140(PCB)'s Managing Directors are on both companies' boards of directors. In the past, J140(PCB) gave technological guidance by seconding its technologists to Sanze. Today, most of Sanze's business is in PCBs requiring the TAF additive process, a facility which J140(PCB) does not have.

Prices, quality and trust

Table 10.3. *The Nagano PCB Cooperative Association 1987*

Company	Established	Process	Employees
J140(PCB)	1961	whole PCBs	219*
Ain	1970	whole PCBs	67
Aruga Kako	1975	small PCBs	30
Sanze Kogyo	1968	whole PCBs	90
Shinatoku	1972	whole PCBs	70
Nihon Mikuron	1975	whole PCBs	42
Sanyo Kogyo	1980	whole PCBs	58
Koyo	1979	drilling	50
Ooshan	1924	plating	56
Yahata Seiko	1974	drilling	25
TOTAL			707

* The employee number includes those in the power supply division.
Source: Japan Printed Circuit Association Membership List.

Thus, Sanze does not compete directly with J140(PCB). The other whole PCB sub-contractor, Shinatoku, is dependent on J140(PCB) for no more than 10 per cent of its business, and is used due to cheaper costs for simple work. Another non-competing sub-contractor is Ooshan, which undertakes gold plating for J140(PCB), another process it does not have in-house.

In 1981, J140(PCB) decided to register a group of local companies with which it had some linkages, past or present, as a cooperative association. This consists of J140(PCB), the five outside sub-contractors described above, plus four others (see Table 10.3 for a list of member companies). One of the four, Ain, was set up by an ex-employee of J140(PCB), who quit as he wanted to become independent. Another, Aruga, used to be a metal pressing company, which became a sub-contractor to J140(PCB) but eventually ceased to get any of its orders. Aruga has subsequently found its market niche in very small-sized single-sided PCBs. The cooperative association provides a forum for communication even among companies which no longer have direct trading links with each other.

At one level, the existence of a cooperative association has an instrumental basis. First, the members cooperate to take advantage of government financial incentives provided with a view to encouraging small firms to combine and exploit scale economies; they include low-interest loans from government financial institutions, and subsidies

212

for joint research. Second, members cooperate because irrespective of the government, benefits (e.g. access to information, joint purchase of materials, joint marketing, and the joint use of machinery) clearly outweigh costs of being a member. Each entrepreneur is individualistic and head-strong, determined to run the company as he sees fit through self-help. Ultimately, no company would be willing to join an association unless there is some tangible benefit to itself. The self-interest here is a broadly defined one, based on a recognition of a state of inter-dependence. As there is tacit understanding that a member might call on any other to complete a customer's order on time, it is thought to be of mutual benefit to equalise technical standards. For this reason, free and open exchange of information on production techniques and management among member companies is forthcoming. Moreover, there has been a conscious strategy on the part of each entrepreneur to find his own market niche to avoid direct competition.

However, association activities cannot be understood fully in rational-calculative terms. There is a definite communitarian sub-culture among this regionally concentrated group of companies. Hive-offs and joint directorships in some cases, and regular meetings and much socialising among directors, form the basis of informal personal networks. Cooperation from a sense of friendship predisposes members to a looser reciprocity than recognised in strict cost-benefit calculations. Moreover, there is an expectation that J140(PCB), as the largest and the initiator of the association, takes on a leadership role in looking after other member firms, although here, there is no explicit hierarchy as in the case of a larger company organising its suppliers' association.

To summarise, this case has illustrated a number of points. First, the use of inside sub-contractors – labour only or otherwise – may be preferred over outside sub-contractors whenever closer communication and supervision are important. Second, hiving off is a major mechanism through which sub-contractors are newly created particularly in electronic assembly but also in the PCB industry. Third, the cooperative association companies, by virtue of serving the same market, are competitors, but have chosen to avoid direct competition by each finding its own market niche. Lastly, the fine balancing between such competition and cooperation is feasible because of a communitarian sub-culture.

Entrepreneurship in Japan and Britain

The previous section described how hive-offs are created amongst SMEs in Japan. Is this indeed the major form of entrepreneurship in Japanese

213

manufacturing? What about in Britain? Why do people set themselves up as independent firms rather than become employees? How does the way they are set up affect whether their customer–supplier relations are more OCR or ACR? This section addresses these questions. An entrepreneur in the present context refers to a small-scale owner-manager who makes incremental technological or organisational innovation, not to a more grand Schumpetarian notion of an agent of radical or novel changes. Thus, entrepreneurs encompass a broad group of 'opportunity fillers' (Leibenstein, 1987, p. 199) who may more appropriately be referred to as 'enterprisers' (Ronen, 1987), as the Japanese term, *kigyoka*, conveys. Because of the unfamiliarity of this label, the term 'entrepreneur' is used throughout.[3]

Some British–Japanese differences and divergence are evident in the official statistics. In Britain, there has been an upsurge of self-employment from 1.9 million in 1979 (7.7 per cent of total employment) to 3.4 million in 1989 (12 per cent of total employment) (Hakim 1989). This rising trend is reflected not only in the number of self-employed (from 2.0 m in 1980 to 3.4 m in 1989) but also companies (from 1.3 m in 1980 to 1.7 m in 1989) registered for Value Added Tax (Curran and Blackburn (eds.) 1991, p. 163). By contrast, the self-employed in the non-agricultural sector in Japan has increased very gradually from 6 million to 7 million in the last two decades, which constitutes a fall in proportionate terms from 14.6 per cent of total employment in 1969 to 13 per cent in 1984 (OECD 1986, p. 44). In both countries, self-employment grew more rapidly in services than in manufacturing during the 1970s and 1980s. But, in the mid-1980s, Japan still had 23 per cent of non-agricultural self-employment in manufacturing, while Britain had only 2 per cent; only 3 per cent of those engaged in manufacturing were self-employed in Britain, while 11 per cent were in Japan (OECD, 1986, p. 49–51).

How can these Japanese–British differences be explained? In Britain, the re-emergence of small firms may be ascribed to a number of factors including a greater use by large firms of manpower flexibility, the diffusion of microprocessor-based information technology, and the impact of recession in the early 1980s. These factors coincided with the British government's ideological commitment to encourage an enterprise culture through its small-firm service bureaux. However, barriers to entry into the small-firm sector in Britain have remained relatively high, not least because of the high cost of raising finance, as mentioned in chapter 8.

Moreover, the opportunity factor of great importance in Japan, namely the encouragement of former employers, is largely missing in Britain. Employers, especially in large firms, are more likely to fear the loss of business through direct competition. British employers entertain expectations of a zero-sum game in a static market – in which the limited good premise which the anthropologist, Foster, developed for Mexican villages applies (Foster, 1969, pp. 82–4) – as contrasted to the predominant assumption in Japan of ever-expanding markets. Because of this premise, it is common for British companies to ask their employees (particularly professional and managerial) to sign an employment contract which forbids them from setting up business within so many miles radius for so many years after quitting.

Thus, some sample suppliers, such as B40(PCB) and B410(PCB), were set up by technologists with work experience in large companies, but their contacts with ex-employers ceased the day they voluntarily quit the company. More recently, a major mechanism through which small firms are set up is through redundancies and subsequent unemployment of large firm employees. For example, owner-managers of both B10(EA) and B15(EA) had set up their firms after being made redundant. Sometimes former employers help those who have been made redundant to start up, but not in their own industry. The founder and chairman of B222(PCB), who has a social concern for high unemployment in his area, is involved in the local county council's employment creation activities, and has himself assisted a handful of his employees to set up their own businesses, some with financial assistance. This appears to be a rare case in Britain, though the idea that such help could only be pure charity is not so rare ('It's nice to help others', said B222(PCB)'s chairman). In Japan, there seems to be less pure public-spirited altruism in business, but more enhanced self-interest instead.

In Japanese manufacturing, small firms are regenerated mainly within the SME sector. Various survey evidence indicates that a great majority of small manufacturing firms are set up by former blue-collar employees of small firms, typically in their 20s and 30s. For example, Kiyonari (1970) demonstrated that close to 70 per cent of all SME manufacturing enterprises were run by former blue-collar employees of small firms; he also estimated that as many as 50 per cent of Japanese small-firm blue-collar workers would become independent during their careers.[4] Subsequently, Koike showed that in the late 1960s and early 1970s, manufacturing startups were greatest in the smallest 1–9 employee firms, at 45 per cent of workers, as compared to 20 per cent at firms employing 30–99 (Koike, 1981, p. 89).[5] The Japanese SME Agency has also been conducting a series of longitudinal surveys, which indicate that within manufacturing, the proportion of SME founders who had been SME employers has been around 40 per cent (and former SME managers around 30 per cent), while the proportion who had been large-firm managers, technologists or workers was only just over 10 per cent. Moreover, startups by those coming from the primary sector have dwindled over time as one would expect given the shrinking farming and fishing population (SMEA 1986, pp. 53–8).

The SMEA survey also shows that 50 per cent of SMEs were founded by people 35 years old or younger. Similarly, a 1986 survey by Inagami et al. (Inagami, 1989) indicates that 80 per cent of all entrepreneurs set up their business before they were 40, and as many as 37 per cent before they were 30. The SME White Paper (1986, p. 56) notes that the modal age for startups, between 25–35, is when SME employees have just acquired a broad-based range of skills which make them able to become independent. But the mid-thirties is also when small-firm blue-collar workers begin to experience a wage gap relative to blue-collar workers in larger firms (see Figure 9.1), which is one economic reason why they may wish to seek their fortune elsewhere by becoming entrepreneurs or white-collar workers in hive-off companies (Friedman, 1988, pp. 144–5).

But that is not all. Becoming independent is part of a way of life and a life-plan for many small-firm blue-collar workers, whose ideology, based on individualism and self-help, differs much from that of lifetime employed workers at large companies. A strong determination and wish for independence are indicated by Inagami et al's (1989) survey. They found that over a third of entrepreneurs had the wish to become self-employed even before they entered the world of work at all.

That they often got help from, and subsequently retained relations with, their ex-employers, is not seen as compromising their independence. Typically, although new startups became direct competitors to ex-employers' operations, they commonly received sub-contract orders from ex-employers, or else were passed on some of the ex-employer's customers to look after (SMEA White Paper, 1986, p. 57). It is reasonable to suppose that these practices derive from, or at least are legitimised by the historical tradition of helping out the most able employees in merchant houses to set up branch business (*noren wake*). This was the normal preferred pattern of enterprise expansion. It was not restricted to family members but was extended to trusted employees. Here lies the difference between the Japanese system of hive-offs and hive-offs within the extended family, such as in China or in the 1850's Systeme Motte (Sabel and Zeitlin, 1985, pp. 151–2.) As already indicated in the J250(EA)'s MD's analogy with ploughing the field (*hatake zukuri*), giving blessing to start-ups by ex-employees is equivalent to planting seeds of indebtedness, which grow into branches of goodwill trust.

From the point of view of the ex-employer, new start-ups can also be a way of circumnavigating his own ties of dependent indebtedness. When a customer insists on 100 per cent exclusive supply, he may spawn a separate hive-off as the only avenue to obtain orders from another customer company. In other words, customer diversification occurs not within the firm, but across a group of firms. The following account illustrates the organisational innovation devised by an independently minded entrepreneur who had to act under a constraint imposed by its sole customer company.

Taiyo Kogyo Group and the process of hiving off (Bunsha)

Taiyo Kogyo (J120(PCB)) was founded by a 19-year-old Mr Sakai as a painting workshop in Tokyo in 1947. His initial capital consisted of the family machinery factory which his father ran, and loans from a government financial institution. He and his partner worked hard long hours, picking up orders of all types and delivering goods themselves on mopeds and hand-pulled carts. By the early 1960s, orders from one customer expanded so rapidly that Taiyo Kogyo, like many other small firms at the time, found itself being a sub-contractor to a sole customer, JJ Electric.

Mr Sakai, with a strong sense of independence, intensely disliked the slavelike position of being bound to one large company. But JJ Electric forbade Taiyo Kogyo to do business with other firms at any time, but particularly after much of JJ Electric's technical know-how in PCB manufacturing was transferred to Taiyo Kogyo in the mid-1960s.

The only alternative – riskier than relying on (but also obeying) JJ Electric – was to establish an entirely new company manufacturing PCBs for other customers. This he did in 1968, much to JJ Electric's dissatisfaction. Thus Mr Sakai's scheme to diversify customer outlets predated JJ Electric's change of heart after 1973 when it found that the moral obligation of giving out stable orders became too onerous.

Taiyo Group found this a successful strategy, and continued to expand by hive-offs, spawning 35 divided companies (*bunsha*) by 1989. Four of them are PCB companies with a joint market share of 11 per cent in the Japanese PCB market (Sakai and Sekiyama, 1985, p. 46). Others are in electronic assembly (J240(EA) is one such company), precision machinery, design and development, and real estate. The ownership of these divided companies is totally institutional; existing group companies become shareholders of every newly created company.

There is a fine balance between competition and cooperation within the group. Independence of each entity is encouraged by the rule that any group company ought not to do more than 30 per cent of its business with other group companies. Although they are not true entrepreneurs, the executive managers who are appointed to run a new hive-off are given total autonomy in recruiting their own workers and seeking new customers. Moreover, group companies in the same line of business compete with each other in obtaining orders from the same customers. Despite such competition, the cohesion of the group is maintained by the fact that managers in different companies may have once worked together in the same company. There is also a club of Managing Directors of group companies, Kisshokai, which meets once or twice a year.

To conclude, a particular type of entrepreneurship predisposes firms to enter into OCR rather than ACR relationships with customer companies. It was shown above that the system of hiving off businesses with the blessing of ex-employers, rather than without (quit, and compete), contributes to the general stock of 'goodwill trust', thus diffusing OCR-type relations. A sense of give and take develops more if entrepreneurs live with an accumulated obligation to ex-employers (some of whom remain as customers) for training, providing financial help and opportunities for new business, than if new businesses do not owe anything to anyone for their viability.

PART IV

Outcomes and implications

11

Implications of ACR–OCR patterns for competitiveness

As stated at the beginning of this book, one major task of this study was to examine various factors which explain why ACR-type or OCR-type transactions occur between an industrial buyer and a supplier. This was done and results systematically presented in chapters 6–10.

This chapter turns to the second major task, which involves examining the consequences of the ACR–OCR choice for the performance of enterprises, industries and national economies. It is tempting to conclude from a cursory look at the relative industrial competitiveness of Britain and Japan that there is some direct linkage between ACR–OCR patterns and industrial performance. OCR-type relations and superior performance coexist in Japan.

But that loose correlation could only be accepted as having some causal significance if one can hypothesise, and find empirical evidence for, the micro-mechanisms which can account for that significance. Theoretically, there are no conclusive causal links between ACR–OCR patterns and organisational efficiency (as defined in chapter 2). One may argue, for instance, that ACR traders achieve allocative efficiency by reserving the right to switch their partners as prices dictate. But there are not sufficient grounds for thinking that ACR-type relations lead to X-efficiency also. Similarly there is no theoretical basis for asserting that the existence of 'goodwill trust' in OCR-type relations constitutes a sufficient condition for generating incentives to maintain efficient practices over time. It is quite possible that such trust, by diminishing the expectation of trading partners quitting, reduces the incentive to make an effort and hence coexists with X-inefficient practices.

If this is the case, what mechanisms in Japanese customer–supplier relationships ensure relative organisational efficiency? This chapter concentrates in the main on studying the *processes* of improving organisational efficiency at case study firms, and not on measuring outcome variables which reflect organisational efficiency, such as productivity levels and growth. In doing so, this study contributes towards the accumulation of case study evidence of micro-mechanisms which provide causal hypotheses, which may some day be subjected to a broader econometric study.

This chapter is structured as follows. Section 1 summarises what we already know about the impact of ACR–OCR on transaction costs in the light of case study evidence in chapters 4 and 5. Section 2, the core of the chapter, examines empirical evidence and supporting theoretical insights on the micro-mechanisms for achieving total organisational efficiency. The last section draws conclusions about the circumstances under which ACR and OCR enhance organisational efficiency respectively.

Superiority of OCR over ACR in saving on current transaction costs

Transaction costs, as outlined in chapter 2, consist of a variety of components, which may be itemised as follows:

(a) SEARCH COSTS associated with finding new trading partners;
(b) NEGOTIATION COSTS involved in arriving at agreements over prices, quality, delivery and other terms and conditions of trade;
(c) INVENTORY COSTS associated with managing the product flow from the supplier to the buyer;
(d) MONITORING COSTS associated with inducing compliance and mutual observation of contractual terms;
(e) TRUST BUILDING COSTS which are for investment into creating convergent expectations about mutual competence, ethical codes and business norms; and
(f) ADJUSTMENT COSTS associated with changing design, market conditions, etc.

It is clear, both *a priori* and from the evidence in chapters 4 and 5, that OCR-type relations incur lower current transaction costs ((a) – (d)) overall than ACR-type relations. For instance, OCR traders' search costs are incurred initially to choose trading partners carefully. But once they are chosen, OCR traders engage in search activity – e.g. advertising in trade journals – less frequently than ACR traders. OCR traders may also benefit from the introduction of new trading partners in particularistic settings, for example through recommendation by existing trading partners.

Overall negotiation costs incurred by OCR traders are also less than those for ACR traders. The former make savings in the process of allocating orders by relying on straight commission; in the process of price fixing (see the next section for more details); and in the process of drawing up written agreements, if any, as much can be left to tacit understanding and oral promises.

Costs associated with managing the product flow from the supplier to the buyer company are also lower for OCR than for ACR transactions. In particular, more inventories have to be held by ACR traders who generally do not benefit from flexible responses to last-minute changes in delivery dates which are not feasible were it not for the existence of 'goodwill trust' and frequent and intense communication between OCR traders.

Lastly, monitoring costs are lower for OCR traders who can rely on a combination of 'competence trust' and 'goodwill trust' to do away with quality inspection on delivery. The principle of *caveat emptor* in ACR transactions necessitates monitoring in order to be on one's guard, not so much to offer constructive feedback on badly performing suppliers as to deter opportunistic behaviour.

If the above analysis were all there is to the assessment of performance, we might conclude that OCR performs better than ACR, and must focus our attention to asking why more firms do not adopt the OCR pattern of trading. The answer to this question lies in the risk involved in entering into OCR relationships, particularly if the expected level of trust is generally low. From the customer's viewpoint, entering into OCR is risky because large costs must be incurred to transfer technology and offer training to their suppliers to build up 'competence trust' in return for open-ended and difficult-to-appropriate benefits. From the supplier's viewpoint, being locked into a small number of customers exposes itself to the risk of the latter's abuse of trust, especially if customers are not constrained by the fear of damaging their reputation. 'Goodwill trust' can only in part be created intentionally through frequent and intense communication, which sometimes extend beyond that required by immediate business to golfing, wining and dining. Only if such investment costs are expended can current transaction costs be lowered under OCR.

Moreover, in order to assess total organisational efficiency, the cost-benefit analysis involving current and investment transaction costs is not the whole story. For this, one needs to examine whether incentives exist to enhance X-efficiency, which may be generated within the firm or as a result of inter-firm transactions. An alternative way of posing the same question is: what conditions or institutional arrangements exist which contribute towards enhancing organisational efficiency?

Another unknown magnitude, *a priori*, is the cost of adjustment to changing circumstances. In theory, the ACR pattern of trading has the advantage in flexibly chopping and changing trading partners as prices dictate, whenever contracts expire, while the OCR pattern has the complementary disadvantage of rigidity. It is not possible to change order levels or trading partners, because of moral obligations which sustain the relationship. From this reasoning, allocative efficiency is more easily achievable under ACR than under OCR. But are there any mechanisms under OCR which effectively translate the market stimulus pressures into incentives for suppliers to make continuous productivity-enhancing improvements? The next section examines this issue among other things.

The micro-mechanisms for achieving organisational efficiency

This section examines in turn (a) how prices are determined; (b) what incentives exist for making cost-reducing innovation; and (c) the nature of inter-supplier rivalry which may encourage continuous improvement.

Initial price determination

Pricing is partly a matter of norms which may be industry-specific or country-specific and partly a matter of relative bargaining power between the buyer and the supplier. The norm is found to differ between industrial sectors, but also between Britain and Japan in the same industrial sector.

In the PCB industry, prices are negotiated for each part number on the basis of quotations made out by suppliers. In both Britain and Japan, there are two broad methods of costing utilised by PCB suppliers. The first, much criticised and declining, practice is to rely on a rough rule-of-thumb calculation used most often for simple single-sided PCBs, related to the area of boards. The second more scientific method is to calculate the standard processing time for each process, multiplying overall processing time by a labour rate, then adding an element of overhead and a target profit margin. The latter method has the advantage of greater accuracy, but also a complementary disadvantage of greater resources required in the estimation exercise.

The price quotation which becomes the basis for negotiations is more often than not an overall price without any cost breakdown, while showing design costs and tooling charges separately. British PCB suppliers tend to be asked to quote against varying quantities and leadtimes, whereas such practice is absent in the Japanese sample. The general reluctance on the part of both British and Japanese PCB suppliers to reveal their internal cost calculations to their customers indicates that withholding such cost breakdown information from customers is seen as strengthening their relative bargaining power. Only in a minority of cases are customers given a breakdown into material costs, labour costs, overhead and profit (in the case of B222(PCB) and B300(PCB), although 'the trick here is how to show that profit is not large', according to B300(PCB)'s Managing Director. In the Japanese sample J150(PCB) is the only one whose two major customers ask for and get a detailed breakdown into processing time, material costs, labour costs, overheads and profit.

In electronic assembly, the sub-contractors and their customers base their costing on (a) the per minute (or per hour) processing rate which includes not only labour costs but also elements of overhead and profit; (b) the total processing time; (c) material costs and (d) other (e.g. packaging and transport) cost. In Britain, the prevailing convention is for the supplier to undertake an in-house calculation of the processing rate and time, but to quote only the overall price to the customer. Only the major (typically non-British) customer companies to B205(EA), B230(EA), B350(EA) and B750(EA) ask for more details and are given a breakdown into material costs, a mark-up on materials, total labour costs, and other costs. Material costs are often fully known to their customers which may specify the material suppliers with whom they may have preferential pricing agreements for bulk-buying. It may even 'free issue' (i.e. purchase direct and deliver) materials to the supplier. B205(EA) and B750(EA) were exceptional in also revealing the processing time and processing rate information to a North American data-processing company.

This exception is the norm in the Japanese electronic assembly industry, in which negotiations over the processing rate are separated from negotiations over processing time specific to each part number. Just like wage negotiations, the processing rate is in principle reviewed every year, although J30(EA), J71(EA), J160(EA) and J360(EA) said that the rate, once fixed, hardly ever changes, and if altered only gets reduced. The processing time is negotiated or unilaterally fixed by the customer for every new model, and is subject to a review every six months (see the next subsection for details).

Thus, the pricing conventions in the PCB and electronic assembly industries differ. Consequently, the amount of knowledge customer companies have about their suppliers' cost structure is greater in electronic assembly than in the PCB industry. According to the suppliers' questionnaire, more electronic assembly sub-contractors (14 out of 16) than PCB suppliers (6 out of 20) think that their customers know their costs almost as well as they know themselves. (Q.1(ii)).[1] However, even in the case of Japanese PCB suppliers which are just as reluctant as their British counterparts to submit such costing, customers are said to have a good idea of their suppliers' cost structure. This is because large Japanese customer companies, including JJ Electric, require SME suppliers to submit annual financial statements. Such submission is often made a precondition for trading at all. The Japanese practice is therefore to be explained by a combination of the customer's power over suppliers in setting a norm for the disclosure of information, and open communication in OCR-type trading.

From the customer's viewpoint, exercising its power in this way to obtain greater access to information has its rationale in reducing time (part of transaction costs) wasted in price negotiations. Japanese customer companies also often specify their own format for price quotations rather than leaving it to the suppliers to estimate in the format which suits them. In doing so, Japanese customers have attempted to diminish the scope for disagreement.

Whether such practice is found to be acceptable and fair depends on the view one takes about the potential use of information disclosed. For instance, when requested to make price quotations by Japanese customer companies located in the UK, British suppliers are said to be willing to provide some cost breakdowns as an atmosphere of open communication is preferred over that of secrecy. But they show resistance to itemising overheads and profit margin separately, because they fear that the major focus of price negotiation would then be to chisel the profit margin away. Although some British sample suppliers thought that the British business norm had been shifting towards greater openness in the exchange of cost information, Japanese companies located in the UK, including TCP(UK), have not managed to extract as much financial information from their British suppliers as from their Japanese counterparts.

This comes as no surprise as the British business norm has been to regard information asymmetry as being mutually advantageous for the customer and the supplier. From the customer's viewpoint playing a supplier off against another enables it to drive the negotiated price below cost if the state of the market allows such a price level, whereas knowing suppliers' costs would tend to result in a higher cost-plus price; hence 'buyers in all honesty do not want to know our costs', according to B410(PCB)'s sales manager. From the supplier's viewpoint, withholding cost information from customers is believed to result in securing its target profit margin. As a piece of evidence of this perception, British sample suppliers tended to agree more than Japanese ones with the statement in the questionnaire 'we obtain the best price by revealing the minimal information which is necessary during negotiation' (Q.4C).[2]

There is also evidence that the codes of ethics in commercial negotiation differ between Britain and Japan. To a hypothetical situation posed in the questionnaire (Q.3B):

> When you are negotiating a new order, the customer talks about other favourable offers he is getting, implying that if you don't put the price down, he will switch to sourcing from your competitors instead of you. By this time you have become quite dependent on this customer for business, and agree to lower the price. Subsequently, you discover that the story of other offers was entirely fictitious.

The majority of the sample suppliers, whether British or Japanese, responded that it was not quite acceptable behaviour, while a minority of British, but no Japanese, companies found it quite acceptable. At the same time, more Japanese than British suppliers responded that such a situation was unlikely to arise. Upon being asked why, more suppliers in Japan than in Britain cited customers' trustworthiness as the sole reason for their refraining from opportunism only a minority in both countries thought that they could rely on sanctions through monitoring customer behaviour alone. A significant number in fact found it difficult to distinguish between trust and sanctions.[3] A common reasoning in Japan was that most of the time, customers were trustworthy, but even if they were not, they could easily check who the other competing suppliers were, as they were most likely to be regular suppliers in the same suppliers' association.

To summarise, a lesser degree of information asymmetry between the customer and the supplier was found in electronic assembly than in the PCB industry in both countries. However, even within the PCB sector with greater information asymmetry, the modal trading norm of OCR in Japan has enabled customers to have good information about suppliers through frequent and intense communication. However, this is also a reflection of the power of large Japanese customer companies over their suppliers, which is applied not only at price negotiations but also over other aspects of trading.

This power inequality between trading partners is fully consistent with the characteristics of OCR trading. In ACR, negotiations take place without the buyer knowing its supplier's cost; here the argument is over what price the market dictates, given the alternative sources of supply. In contrast, in OCR, negotiations take place with the buyer's knowledge of suppliers' costs; the argument then becomes a discussion of what is a 'fair' division of profit. The former involves a non-normative mode of negotiation in which opportunism is acceptable, while the latter mode of negotiation is partly normative. At the same time, there is a greater possibility of unresolvable clash between different concepts of fairness than between different perceptions of objective market conditions (Elster 1989, pp. 215, 244–7). In OCR, potential conflict over concepts of fairness is at least lessened in explicitly hierarchical relations because the 'superior' customer can dictate the definition of fairness.

Lastly, a lesser degree of information asymmetry between the buyer and the supplier in OCR than in ACR potentially leads to pricing which is more allocatively efficient (i.e. prices which reflect costs more accurately). Price negotiations in ACR take on an air of hard commercial bargain with importance attached to tactics and strategy, while OCR negotiations tend to centre more around engineering effort to lower costs. This contrast in approach becomes starker when prices are reviewed and renegotiated.

Price reviews: frequency and methods

Once prices are determined, they are subject to renegotiation at varying intervals. Generally, the frequency of price review is greater in Japan than in Britain, and price reviews tend to focus on engineering efforts to reduce costs in Japan and on making references to prevailing market prices in Britain.

In Britain, an annual price review is common though the interval can be shorter if material prices fluctuate by more than a pre-agreed percentage. In the 1970s, when inflation was running at double digit figures, suppliers often invoked their reserved right to renegotiate prices every 3 to 4 months in order to pass on their material cost increases. Past inflation has undoubtedly created a built-in expectation and norm in British business of suppliers passing on costs to their customers.

In the 1980s, there has been a shift from a more cost-plus towards a fixed-price arrangement particularly for customers, such as GB Electronics, which give out annual or longer contracts. However, with a high degree of information asymmetry between trading partners, the supplier can incorporate in its price an insurance premium against material price increases which would have to be absorbed in-house as part of the guarantee to fix prices for a year. This tallies with a statement by the purchasing manager of GB Electronics Site X that negotiated prices are maximum prices, and therefore 'you won't find us reviewing prices during the year typically, so a supplier knows that he can live with a certain price for the whole year'. By extension, the less frequent the price review, the more incentive there is for a supplier to build in a mark-up to cover for the contingency of unforeseen cost increases beyond its control.

Building such a cushion into the initial price is not as easy in Japan where customer companies know their suppliers' cost structures better. The incentive for suppliers to quote prices with built-in contingencies is also less as six-monthly price reviews are the norm in Japanese manufacturing. But even before six months are up, customer companies may respond to reviewing prices if suppliers find that their realised costs are far above the estimated costs. J265(EA) and J250(EA), the two most OCR sample suppliers, both mentioned occasions (albeit not too frequent) when their requests to raise prices were granted by their customers who recognized major miscalculations in the initial cost estimates. Both these sub-contractors face benevolent customers who pay according to need, but also take cost reductions due to learning-by-doing for granted and are willing to offer help in technical guidance if cost reductions are not achieved. The most formalised system of incorporating learning-by-doing into the pricing formula is found at J265(EA), whose major customer, JJ Electric, negotiates the processing time which ought to be attainable after three months of full production. JJ Electric then agrees to pay for a 75 per cent premium in processing time in the first month, 50 per cent in the second month, 25 per cent in the third month, and zero thereafter.

The expectations of continuous cost reduction due to learning-by-doing and rationalisation lie behind the Japanese practice of bi-annual *cosuto daun* (cost reduction) requests by customers. This is a well-entrenched practice in the Japanese automobile and electronics industries. For example, a customer company may set a uniform semiannual cost reduction target for all its suppliers, publicising it as an all-out campaign through the suppliers' association. The major reason behind the need to regularly reduce costs is the fierce competition in the final product markets. Consumer goods prices have continuously come down, and it is up to the customer and supplier companies to jointly manufacture within the bounds of ever-declining final prices. The targets become severe in crises such as after the first oil shock (1973) and during the post-1985 yen appreciation period. In the Japanese electronic assembly sample, J265(EA) had received from its major customer a regular six

Table 11.1. *PCB prices and profitability in the Japanese PCB industry*

	Types of PCBs				
Year	Single-sided price (¥)	% Change	Double-sided price (¥)	% Change	Profit*
1972	5265	-	58043	-	
1973	6662	26.5	68691	18.3	
1974	8074	21.1	77876	13.4	
1975	8985	11.2	64447	−17.2	
1976	9036	0.6	62998	−2.2	1.5
1977	6455	−28.6	64589	2.5	4.0
1978	6381	−1.1	61151	−5.3	3.0
1979	6342	−0.6	59052	−3.4	3.6
1980	6667	5.1	55220	−6.5	4.5
1981	6780	1.7	52710	−4.5	6.0
1982	6228	−8.1	45895	−12.9	2.8
1983	6135	−1.5	43440	−5.3	1.5
1984	5738	−6.5	39842	−8.3	3.3
1985	5611	−2.2	36056	−9.5	2.4
1986	5373	−4.2	31738	−12.0	−0.2
1987	4487	−16.5	29380	−5.6	−1.2

Note: N.B. Prices are calculated from the total value of boards sold divided by total area of board (in square metres) sold during December each year.
* Pre-tax profit as percentage of total sales.
Source: Japan Printed Circuit Association survey, various years.

monthly cost-reduction request of 5 per cent, which jumped to 15 per cent in 1985. J240(EA) mentioned up to 20 per cent and J71(EA) up to 30 per cent reduction to be achieved in six months in 1985–6.[4]

The data collected by the Japanese trade association, JPCA, shows that there has been a general downward trend in PCB prices in the 1970s and 1980s (see Table 11.1).[5] A fall in the price of raw materials, in particular oil-based products, contributed to a price decline in the early 1980s. However, by 1985 the most pressing problem in Japan was the strong yen, which appreciated 42 per cent in 1985 and 15 per cent in 1986 against the US dollar. This meant that although yen-denominated prices fell considerably during 1985–8, by 20 per cent for single-sided boards, 40 per cent for PTH boards and 30 per cent for multilayer boards, they were not sufficient to circumvent dollar-denominated prices from rising by on average 50 percent. In the meantime, a virtual standstill in the output value of PCBs at ¥605 billion in 1984, ¥613 billion in 1985 and ¥638 billion in 1986, but an increase to ¥722 billion in 1987, indicate that the physical volume of PCB production had been increasing during this period.

How were the price reductions achieved in Japan? Evidently not by customers merely relying on switching, or threatening to switch, to alternative suppliers, as such 'exist' strategy (preferred by ACR traders) works well only in recession when the resulting excess capacity in the suppliers' industry induces them to undercut each other. Suppliers are not motivated to make cost-cutting effort as they perceive the state of excess capacity to be temporary. This was probably what happened in Britain when PCB prices fell sharply in response to the 1985 slump in the data-processing market, leading to a 10 per cent decline in the total PCB output value from £298 million in 1985 to £268 million in 1986. In the case of Japan, as noted above, price reductions were accompanied, not by a fall, but an increase, in production volumes. This price-quantity combination is consistent with a shift in the supply curve ascribed to increased efficiency outweighing a contraction in demand due to the strong yen.

Japanese customer companies in both automobile and electronics industries have faced less cyclical fluctuations in their production levels than their US and European counterparts (see Womack et al. 1990, pp. 247–51 for US–Japanese comparisons in cars). In a situation of steadily growing demand, suppliers' capacity is always tight so that customers' 'exit' strategy is vacuous and would only lead to bidding up prices. A more effective strategy is to exercise 'voice' in existing relationships, to ensure that costs are reduced over the long run. The aforementioned expected decline in final consumer prices was a prime motive for customer companies wishing to devise a mechanism for cost reduction, which was perceived to be fair and hence relatively free of disputes.

The established mechanism relies on two inter-related techniques. One is specifying price-reduction targets, or a time path of price-reduction targets which remain unchanged whether suppliers enhance their efficiency or not. Suppliers then have a strong incentive to innovate as they can capture 100 per cent of the gain (McMillan 1990, p. 47). The other is the joint analysis of costs using the value analysis (VA) and value engineering (VE) techniques, with arrangements for sharing benefits (Asanuma 1985).

VA and VE are often used interchangeably to refer to an activity to obtain the best value for a component by analysing its function. It may result in cost savings by changing component design, production processes, or raw materials used without altering the function the component fulfills. As with quality control, value analysis was developed (by L. D. Miles of GE) mainly as an intra-firm exercise in the USA immediately after the Second World War. The rapid diffusion of VA techniques in the automobile, electrical and shipbuilding industries in Japan in the 1960s was triggered off not so much by a 1955 Japan Productivity Centre delegation visit to the USA, but by a series of public seminars given in Japan in 1960 by S. F. Heinlitz who was invited jointly by the JPC, the Centre for Japanese Management and the Japanese Materials Control Association. The practice of involving suppliers and sub-contractors in this industrial engineering exercise was a Japanese innovation (Mito 1987).

Japanese customer companies may require their suppliers to come up with a target number of VA.VE suggestions', which is the inter-company equivalent of individual suggestion schemes within a company. For example, JJ Electric's Site C has set a target for one monthly suggestion per supplier. These suggestions, in reality between 50 and 100 per month, are examined by JJ Electric's VA Department which decides whether the ideas are worth implementing. If so, the resulting cost saving is typically retained by the supplier who made the suggestion until the next occasion for *cosuto daun*, after which the benefits are shared between the supplier and the customer company. This arrangement provides an incentive for suppliers. (In the absence of a sharing arrangement in the VA.VE suggestion scheme, suppliers may well pocket the whole of the benefits without revealing them to their customers. J360(EA) said that as its major customer kept all the discovered savings to itself, it revealed only obvious VA ideas or understated the extent of cost reduction achieved, just enough to keep the customer happy.) Moreover, JJ Electric instructs suppliers in the value analysis techniques both as part of the suppliers' association study group activities and separately also for non-association member suppliers. Residential courses in VA techniques are offered at JJ Electric's expense for suppliers' technologists.

It is also possible that the sheer fact that targets exist creates a motivation for suppliers to meet them. Goal setting has recently become a focus of attention among some industrial psychologists (for e.g. Latham and Locke (1979)). They have empirical evidence that whether goals are set unilaterally by the supervisor or with the involvement of employees, the mere fact that goals (normally about output levels) are set significantly increases the level of production. It is possible that a similar motivational mechanism is at work when suppliers are asked to meet the goal of so many VE suggestions per month, or x per cent reduction in the next six months.

232

In order to meet the cost-reduction schedules, suppliers may also make their own efforts at rationalising their companies. These range from (i) saving on material costs by bargaining harder with existing materials suppliers or by finding cheaper alternatives; (ii) increasing capacity utilisation by increasing shifts; and (iii) internal cost cutting and quality and productivity improvement exercises through individual suggestion schemes and small group (including QC and TQC) activities. Suppliers which cannot meet the target cost reduction through these rationalisation methods find their profits squeezed, while those which overachieve the target can enjoy increases in profit margins. On balance, in the Japanese PCB industry, average pre-tax profits were squeezed from 6.0 per cent of sales in 1981 to 2.4 per cent in 1985 and −1.2 per cent in 1987 (see Table 11.1), while well-performing companies retained their profit, for example J1210(PCB) with 8.3 per cent in 1987. In the meantime, the average of 18 Japanese electrical and electronic customer companies' profitability also declined but to a lesser degree, from 6.2 per cent in 1981 to 4.6 per cent in 1985 and 2.7 per cent in 1987.[6] This put to test the tacit agreement over limits to what would be a fair distribution of joint profit (or loss).

Even with declining profitability, however, investment was maintained by PCB suppliers at an average of 8.4 per cent of output value in 1985, 5.5 per cent in 1986, 5.6 per cent in 1987 and 7.8 per cent in 1988, in order to meet cost-reduction targets and to ensure future orders. With hindsight, some sample suppliers reflected that their need to concentrate their minds due to the yen appreciation was good for them, and has strengthened their competitive position. The result is an industry with an average high productivity (value added per worker) of £34,000 (£ = ¥230) in the late 1980s. In the absence of aggregated value-added figures for Britain, sales turnover per worker of £42,000 for 1989 (which is the average of the top 40 UK companies) may be compared with that of £83,500 (an average for industrial PCB manufacturers surveyed by JPCA) in 1987. Even if value added in Britain were, say 60 per cent of sales (rather than 41 per cent as in Japan, allowing for the greater use of sub-contractors in Japan), that would still produce a figure of only £25,000 per worker, well below the Japanese £34,000.

In Britain, there was no institutionalised arrangement for suppliers to make VA suggestions. As noted in chapter 5, some customers did not expect to have, or disliked having, their suppliers interfere with already approved designs. But a few sample suppliers such as B300(PCB) said that suggesting design improvements to the customer was good for both parties. For them, it led to improved yield and hence increased retained profit until price renegotiation. As a *quid pro quo*, its customers got a better service as a result of less processing hiccups and quality defects.

More typically in Britain, customer companies appeal to prevailing market prices, even for customised parts like PCBs, in order to exert pressure for price reductions. For example, GB Electronics Site X has an internal cost reduction target of up to 20 per cent per annum, and an 11 per cent reduction p.a. on average has been achieved in the last 5 years. In the main, price reductions are achieved at the annual negotiations, when much reference is made to the lowest market prices. Thus, according to B300(PCB), as far as GB Electronics is concerned, the going market price is the lowest price quotation obtained – often from Far Eastern suppliers. The advantage of soliciting many price quotations lies in using them as a source of bargaining power vis-à-vis current suppliers.

GB Electronics also has a 'most favoured customer clause' in its contract document, as noted in chapter 4. It states that a supplier has the obligation to offer a similar price for a similar product with a similar quantity as between customers. There is a serious potential for opportunism in this clause as no incentive is built in for suppliers to reveal occasions when another customer is treated more preferentially than GB Electronics. Thus, the onus of discovery of such instances rests solely on GB Electronics which relies on various expensive sources of information. One is the in-house component pricing data; another is market-trend information by Dataquest. GB Electronics is also one of the thirteen members of an electronics companies' club which meets twenty times a year to share commercial and technical information, including prices of standardised components. According to Site X's purchasing manager, 'if we find through this forum that a particular vendor is offering a lower price to another member, then we approach that company to ask for a lower price . . . We try to say as little as possible about the source of our information, but sometimes it has to come out.' It seems that the major source of cost reduction is seen to be from lowering of standard component prices, rather than better design and processing of the final product and its customised components.

The relative lack of an engineering and cost analysis oriented approach to achieving price reductions in Britain is due to both (a) a belief by both parties that their bargaining power is enhanced if the arm's length nature of the relationship is maintained by minimum information exchange and (b) a low level of expectations concerning the ability of the majority of suppliers to contribute to design changes. TCP(UK) has broken from the British norm to set a target for a cost reduction of 10 per cent during

1988–90, by reviewing prices every 6 to 8 months. A reduction of 9 per cent was said to be achieved, but not without difficulty, because most suppliers do not contribute to the design process. Whether a new norm will emerge in British industry is not yet certain.

To summarise, a preference for great information asymmetry by ACR traders accounts for their choosing a 'commercial bargaining' approach, and a preference for open information disclosure by OCR traders facilitates their choice of an 'engineering problem-solving' approach. However, beyond this generalisation, historically conditioned country-specific norms enter into the picture. In Britain, much unproductive haggling in the commercial bargaining approach may have tempted trading partners to renegotiate prices less frequently. However, this trend towards longer fixed-price contracts contains the disadvantage that the initial negotiated price may include an insurance premium against unforeseen material cost increases; past inflationary expectations still influence the British norm in this way. At the same time, fixed-price contracts between British traders may potentially enhance efficiency, as suppliers may be motivated to innovate to capture 100 per cent of the gain. The ACR customer's not wanting to know the supplier's costs may provide a greater incentive for suppliers to innovate than an OCR customer wishing to know their cost breakdowns. Theoretically, an OCR customer could retain suppliers' incentive to innovate by devising sharing arrangements, as in Japan. But it could also dampen their incentive if cost-plus contracts are used, as in some defence and other public procurement. In the latter case, the supplier may tactically reveal all cost details to appeal to the customer's moral obligation not to ask for the impossible. The Japanese price-setting method is therefore not dictated, but facilitated, by the prevalence of OCR-type relations; it is the combination of OCR and the norm of cost reduction which accounts for efficient outcomes.

Inter-supplier competition

The last micro-mechanism to be examined is competition between potential and actual suppliers. This is the central process in ACR-type relationships which, through frequent bidding and multiple sourcing, is believed to ensure that suppliers have incentives to offer prices conforming to the going market rate. It is often presumed that such inter-supplier rivalry is reduced in OCR-type relations. But observe the following practices which have become the norm in Japan, to see how incentives for continuous improvement are maintained.

Vendor performance reviews and ranking of suppliers

For Japanese suppliers' association members, there is a mechanism for institutionalised competition, which operates on the basis of ranking according to quality and delivery performance of each supplier. The customer company typically publicises the monthly assessed ranking list, for instance by displaying it on a purchasing department notice board frequented by the suppliers, who may all see red circles around particularly bad scores. Some sample suppliers commented that this system of public display is just like what happens in the exam-centred Japanese education system. (Price and cost information is not displayed as it is considered confidential). Here, competition is for places in a ranking system based on scores for which the criteria are usually promptness of delivery and the maintenance of quality. Suppliers which climb up the ladder are assured an increasing level of desirable orders, while those which slide down the scale face diminishing levels of order. This incentive structure gives another momentum for continuous improvements by suppliers who may also feel a sense of shame in the public display of their not-so-good performance.

In Britain also, vendor performance reviews are undertaken for preferred suppliers by some customer companies, including GB Electronics. Each supplier is given a score, which depends on its performance in quality, delivery and service. However, the vendor rating is disclosed and discussed bilaterally only, presumably because in the absence of a suppliers' association which may promote a sense of community, multilateral disclosure to other suppliers goes beyond British suppliers' and customers' sense of what is acceptable and fair. According to GB Electronics Site X's manager: 'we won't tell them [suppliers] who the other people are below them or above them. We will tell them where they rank, first, fifth or seventh; and we also compare them sometimes with the average performance of all of the other vendors. That's as far as we've gone so far. Further than that, we'd like to go in small steps really because it becomes quite emotive.'

In theory, then, customer companies may rely on inter-supplier competition in the external market or rivalry among core suppliers in the 'internal market' (as it were) as an incentive structure. The latter may best be understood in terms of the theories of ranking hierarchy (Aoki 1988, pp. 69–86) and rank-order tournaments (Lazear and Rosen, 1981; Malcolmson, 1984) developed in the context of employment contracts and labour markets. Customer companies may rely on inter-supplier rivalry in order to elicit X-efficiency enhancing effort. Both mechanisms have the dual purpose of reducing moral hazard ('shirking') on the part of suppliers, and of enhancing reputation on the part of customers.

In the ranking hierarchy, all suppliers start out from the bottom of the ranking. As they realise their potential by achieving good performance records (in price, quality and delivery, and in some cases in making cost-cutting suggestions), they are promoted to higher ranks. Promotion depends on reaching prescribed absolute standards. Thus, as already noted in chapter 4, each core supplier to JJ Electric must earn its place by climbing up the ranking relatively slowly.

In the rank-order tournament, the reward – in terms of a greater level of orders with higher profit margins in the next contract period – is based not on achieving absolute standards but simply on the relative rank order of contestants. Suppliers, then, have an incentive to make continuous improvements, lest they fall behind in the ranking and lose out in the next round of contracts.

The viability of both the ranking hierarchy and the rank-order tournament depends on the buyer company being able to monitor its suppliers over time with a certain degree of accuracy and objectivity. The ranking and rules of promotion must be made explicit and considered fair and acceptable by all participants. Suppliers' incentives to make X-efficiency enhancing effort derive in part from inter-supplier rivalry, but also from the customer company's reputation for integrity in keeping its promise to reward those suppliers making greater effort. The suppliers' association reinforces the customer's need to keep up this reputation.

Lateral information disclosure among core suppliers in Japan
One mechanism which ensures that the reputation effect works well is lateral communication among core suppliers, more intense in Japan than in Britain due to the existence of the suppliers' association (*kyoryoku-kai*). As part of the association activity, there are study groups in which new production techniques can be learnt, such as Statistical Process Control, Just-in-Time delivery and Value Analysis techniques.

What may be most puzzling about the operation of suppliers' associations is that the process of learning for member suppliers does not merely depend on unilateral technology transfer from the customer company to its suppliers, but also on mutual teaching among member suppliers. This might be through mutual factory visits, to offer constructive criticisms and suggestions on factory layout, process technology, or quality control procedures. This is undoubtedly another source of inducing greater X-efficiency.

As an example, JJ Electric Site C's suppliers' association is subdivided into four specialist study groups, of which one consists of eleven electronic assembly sub-contractors which are potentially direct competitors to each other. As part of the study group activity, the top managers of the eleven companies decided to visit each others' factories with the overall objective of improving quality control performance. The results of the visits were reported back at one of the monthly meetings, at which JJ Electric managers were present, together with proposals for future measures to be taken by all. They included standardisation of the eleven companies' quality-control documentation format, more QC guidance to secondary sub-contractors, and education and training on quality control for both top managers and quality inspection personnel.

What motivates such cooperation, through lateral information disclosure, between suppliers who are direct competitors? According to JJ Electric, a judicious choice of a good theme for discussion is important, so that every group member feels there is something to learn. JJ Electric must also make sure not to let any supplier feel that orders have been taken away from one supplier and given to another; keeping all the suppliers busy with full capacity utilisation helps achieve this end. From the suppliers' viewpoint, there is a perceived shared interest and mutual interdependence among them, as improved quality performance of individual suppliers is thought to lead eventually to growth of orders for all. There is also a certain attitude towards information, first that much of the information about production techniques and new machinery would become public quickly anyway, and second that given that there is generally a plethora of information, there is an 'equality of opportunity' situation; it is up to individual top managers' capability how many good ideas they pick up, analyse and apply during a factory visit.

Summary: ACR–OCR and organisational efficiency

In theory, the ACR and OCR patterns of trading have the following advantages and disadvantages in adjusting to changing needs and circumstances. Enhancing competitiveness under each pattern amounts to creating conditions which heighten advantages and diminish the importance of disadvantages.

A major advantage of arm's-length (ACR) transactions is that each trader is free to pursue its own interest and to change the definition of its interest as circumstances change. ACR traders are not at the mercy of other traders to fulfill their objectives. For such an individualistic approach to succeed, however, there must exist a strong universalistic ethical code about keeping promises. In areas where no explicit promises

238

	ACR pattern	OCR pattern
Advantages	Flexibility to chop and change trading partners as prices dictate, whenever contracts expire	Intense communication, based on trust, enabling good quality and prompt delivery
Disadvantages	Minimal information exchange, potential for misunderstanding in design or quality specifications	Rigidity in changing order levels and trading partners. Potential lack of market stimulus

are made, individual traders are free to improve their own position, regardless of the implication for others. The major source of competitive stimulus lies directly in the availability of alternative traders in markets for final products and components. The market structure must therefore be reasonably atomistic. The incentive for ACR traders to make X-efficiency improving changes, then, derives from their fear of losing out in the market, if enough trading partners carry out the threat to switch away. The nature of competition is therefore by 'exit', with a bias towards the short run (Odagiri 1992).[7] Given a clear perception of independence, the outcome of bargaining over prices and quantities reflects the relative power of the trading partners. For this reason, there is no force which counters a dominant powerful trader to become more dominant if opportunities arise. Thus, at a minimum, conditions which are likely to render ACR transactions X-efficient are:

(i) a universalistic ethical code to keep promises;
(ii) a clear perception of autonomy and independence by the firm;
(iii) a perception that the untempered exercise of bargaining power in commercial negotiation is fair;
(iv) not so unequal relative bargaining power between the buyer and the supplier, and the ability of suppliers independently to finance necessary investments of a risky kind; and
(v) atomistic market structures to give scope for multiple sourcing and potential alternatives to existing trading partners.

A rather different set of conditions are required to bring about X-efficient outcomes in OCR-type relationships. To start with a clear perception of dependence, either mutual or unilateral, must exist between trading partners. Specifically in the case of unilateral dependence between power-unequal partners, there must exist shared norms about the limits to which the strong partner can fairly push the dependent one into compliance. Without such shared sense of fairness, unilateral specifications of prices, which save on transaction costs, may lead to accusations of exploitation, which are hardly conducive to harmonious cooperative relations as a prerequisite for enhancing organisational efficiency. As for the sources of incentives to create X-efficiency and reduce the cost of rigidities in adjustment which may come from lack of market stimulus, there is, first, rivalry in the final product market, which creates a perception of a shared interest in increasing efficiency. Besides such a perceived common goal between trading partners, a mechanism of inter-supplier rivalry by ranking suppliers according to observed performance creates an extra incentive for enhancing X-efficiency. Competition in OCR is therefore characterised by particularistic rivalry, effected through the exercise of 'voice' in the long run (Odagiri 1992). The conditions which render OCR X-efficient are:

(i) convergent expectations of trading partners, concerning acceptable levels of competence, intensity of communication, etc.;
(ii) a clear perception of dependence, mutual or unilateral;
(iii) a shared sense of fairness concerning the conduct of the stronger partner towards the weaker in hierarchical contracts;
(iv) rivalry of customer companies in the final product market, to give a perception of shared interest in increasing efficiency; and
(v) ranking hierarchy and/or rank-order tournament among core suppliers.

12
Conclusions

Summary

'What accounts for the competitiveness of the Japanese manufacturing industry?' has been an underlying question throughout this study, and is one which continues to receive much attention internationally. The contribution this book makes towards answering that question is through the examination of customer–supplier relationships in Britain and Japan. The present study, though limited in its scope and coverage, makes clear that buyer–supplier relationships have a strong effect on the industrial outcomes of prices, quantities and quality. And there seem to be good grounds for thinking that what has been called obligational contractual relation (OCR) can contribute to achieving superior performance. Prior to addressing the performance issue, the preceding chapters have also focused on (i) delineating types of buyer–supplier relations and identifying their empirical variations, and (ii) examining the factors – economic, institutional, moral and cultural – which affect the choice between different types of trading relations.

As a tool of analysis, a theoretical framework was developed to capture the range of possible buyer–supplier relations, the two extremes of which were called the Arm's-length Contractual Relation (ACR) and the Obligational Contractual Relation (OCR). The characterisation of the ACR–OCR spectrum were in terms of eleven empirically verifiable features. Thus, OCR, as compared to ACR, was characterised by a greater transactional dependence on trading partners, a longer projected length of trading, a greater willingness to accept or offer orders before prices were negotiated and fixed, less contractualism, a greater degree of uncosted sharing of technological know-how and risks associated with business fluctuations. The operation of OCR relates closely with that of networks and other intermediate modes of coordination which lie between 'market' and 'hierarchy'.

The essential normative value which underlies the ACR–OCR behavioural manifestations is the presence or absence of trust of varying types. In this study, three types of trust were conceptualised (in chapter 2). Both 'contractual trust' (the mutual expectation that promises made are kept) and 'competence trust' (confidence in a trading partner's competence to carry out a specific task) exist to a greater or lesser extent in ACR and OCR. It is 'goodwill trust' – mutual expectations of commitment to the relationship resulting in much give and take – which is present in OCR but not in ACR. The three types of trust are inter-linked and mutually reinforcing, but 'goodwill trust' can only be sustained if the other two types of trust also exist.

In order to compare the extent of ACR–OCR variation in British and Japanese customer–supplier relations, this study undertook case studies of a British customer company (GB Electronics), a Japanese customer company (JJ Electric) and a Japanese-owned customer in Britain (TCP(UK)), all in the electronics industry. Another set of evidence was collected, of eighteen supplier companies in each country, ten in the PCB industry and eight in the electronic assembly industry. A careful observation of a small number of companies through visits and semi-structured interviews became the basis for identifying variations of the eleven OCR–ACR features.

As expected, JJ Electric was found to have more OCR features than GB Electronics which was attempting to make a partial move towards OCR. TCP(UK), as a third dimension in the British–Japanese comparison, gave some insight into the factors which might promote or hinder the adoption of OCR-type relations in British industry. Among the suppliers, there were considerable variations from company to company. But of the two major supplier industries compared, the modal trading pattern in the electronic assembly industry in both Britain and Japan was found to be more OCR than in the printed circuit board industry. Moreover, the range of Japanese trading relations were found to be more OCR than the range of British relations.

Reasons behind these observed differences in trading patterns were then explored. First, inter-country differences are due to country-specific institutions and cultural dispositions (see chapters 7–10). Here, the historical development of institutions cannot be ignored, as buyer–supplier relationships have developed in the context of a number of supporting institutions, such as the legal framework, the financial structures, the employment system, and the form of entrepreneurship through hive-offs. Second, inter-sectoral differences are accounted for mainly by technological and economic factors (see chapter 6). For instance, the greater asset specificity in electronic assembly than in printed circuit board production accounts in part for the greater OCR-ness of the former industry. Third, inter-company variations within a sector ultimately result from differences in the objectives and attitudes of individual entrepreneurs and managers. The willingness to enter into dependent relations, or to invest in trust-building through friendly face-to-face communication, both conducive to OCR, exists to a varying degree within Japan and Britain.

Lastly, the study examined some micro-mechanisms in price and cost determination, which conduce ACR or OCR to good performance (in chapter 11). ACR-type relations are found to contain a high degree of asymmetry in information between the trading partners. Non-disclosure of information is preferred by both parties in order to increase their respective bargaining power during price negotiations. This commercial bargaining approach is to be contrasted with the engineering problem solving approach in OCR. A preference for openness in communication in OCR predisposes trading partners to arrive at competitive prices through the industrial engineering method of Value Analysis. Ultimately, the incentive for maintaining competitiveness derives from competition in the final markets for the customer company. But the way this works back to suppliers depends on whether they are in ACR or OCR relations. Inter-supplier rivalry is the essence in keeping suppliers on their toes. But in ACR, this is done in the marketplace by the customer changing suppliers as prices dictate. In OCR, the mechanism for competition is more particularistic, through the ranking of core suppliers through regular performance reviews accompanied by only marginal shifts in sourcing.

Implications for policy and business strategy

Although prescription has not been an integral part of this book's core aims, a question arises naturally as to whether ACR or OCR would be more effective in achieving competitive success in the future. In Britain, there have been moves in industry towards developing longer-term closer relationships between buyers and suppliers. GB Electronics is by no means an exception in developing a Preferred Supplier Policy. For instance, all major car assemblers have been reducing the number of suppliers with whom they sign long-term contracts. Although this phenomenon is given a label such as Japanisation (Oliver and Wilkinson, 1988), the major driving force behind it lies not only in competition from Japan but also in factors common to both British and Japanese firms.

These include features on which global competition is increasingly won or lost, namely cost-effective quality and shorter product development cycles, and the accompanying need to engage in technological innovation. To cope with these trends, OCR appears superior over ACR.

Given differences in the historical development of industry, financial structures, employment relations and culture, it would be neither feasible nor desirable to adopt OCR-type supplier relations in Britain. However, the process of learning is rarely wholesale, but commonly selective in borrowing, and adaptive so as to build on existing institutions. One can find many examples of this innovative imitation in the Japanese experience of industrial development. What the present study has shown is that ACR and OCR are based on fundamentally different values and attitudes in business, and that they are each supported by different national institutions. The awareness of these distinct approaches would hopefully contribute towards enabling business managers to assess not only the possibility of adopting popularised techniques such as just-in-time (JIT) production and delivery, but also other aspects of OCR trading which enable JIT to result in corporate success.

For example, an essential aspect of OCR trading is the existence of trust of various types. If OCR is deemed desirable as well as necessary, how to create trust where there is little foundation becomes a question of central importance. The decomposition of trust into three types, as in this book, could be an aid to prescription. In Britain today, 'contractual trust' already exists to some extent in most British business relations, but the relative lack of the other two types of trust is conspicuous.

First, establishing 'competence trust' depends in part on better training and retraining of the British workforce, which for the moment must be undertaken at the initiative of individual employers rather than across the firm's boundary as in Japan. Of course, it would help in building competence if industry can attract the best and the brightest in society to manufacturing, both in its management and engineering functions. Competence requires investment not just in human resources but also in new machinery and equipment, and raising investment may require not only lowering interest rates but making changes in the prevailing corporate financial structures.

Second, 'goodwill trust' may at first sight look as though it is founded solely on national culture. Indeed, the willingness to be indebted to someone and to recognise high mutual dependence in action appears to come about more easily in less individualistic Japan than in Britain. But this study has demonstrated that 'goodwill trust' between individuals can be deliberately cultivated to some extent by choosing trading partners carefully, and by frequent and intense communication required increasingly to achieve 'competence trust'.

Of course, building business relations based on trust may be necessary but not sufficient to achieve competitiveness. For corporate success, there must also be built-in incentives for competition. Consistently high quality with competitive costs is achieved in Japan, only by combining OCR-type trust relations with rivalry among known core suppliers who are made to compete in a ranking according to their performance. When good quality as well as low costs are part of the manufacturing concern, there may be benefit in replacing faceless competition in the marketplace which may breed low trust by particularistic rivalry which preserves high trust of all types.

Appendix

Buyer–supplier relations: a questionnaire survey of suppliers

This is part of a study which examines the nature of trading relationships between suppliers and their customer companies. If you would be kind enough to take a quarter of an hour to fill it in, I would be grateful.

1. **Tick the statement which reflects your company's situation most accurately.**

   (i).   A.   'We are one of the few companies which can manufacture and supply the component(s) we produce.'

        B.   'There are many competitors who can supply similar components to ours.'

   (ii).   A.   'The customer knows the details of our costs almost as well as we know our own.'

        B.   'Naturally the customer knows far less about our costs than we do.'

   (iii).   A.   'The markets we face are volatile and future demand difficult to predict.'

        B.   'The markets we face are stable and future demand easy to forecast fairly accurately.'

   (iv).   A.   'Our customers give consideration to the placing of continuous, stable orders.'

        B.   'Our customers change their order levels as it suits them.'

   (v).   A.   'We would not have achieved our current technological capability had it not been for our customers' assistance.'

        B.   'We have achieved our current technological capability on our own without customers' help.'

   (vi).   A.   'Our customers always let us know in advance their future production plans.'

        B.   'Our customers tend not to let us know their future plans.'

246

Appendix

2.   About your company
(i).   Nature of business————————————————————————————

(ii).   Total sales turnover (1988) £————————————————————————

(iii). Total employees (1988): regular——————————————————————

                              temporary——————————————————————

(iv).   Total number of customers supplied (1988)—————————————————

3.   Possible behaviour on the part of customers

Part I

Would you please, in the column below, right, indicate the degree of acceptability of the behaviour described below.
The scale is:
1.   Quite acceptable. I could see myself doing the same if I were in his or her shoes.
2.   I'd think rather badly of anybody who did that, but not to the extent of never dealing with him or her anymore.
3.   Unacceptable. *I would not deal with anyone who did that.*

Part II

Now please go through the same situations, this time assessing how frequently you encounter such behaviour from your customers.
1.   Quite often.
2.   Occasionally from some; rarely from others.
2.   Hardly ever.

Part III

Lastly, ONLY if you replied to 2 or 3 in *Part II* i.e. if you think some or all of your customers rarely behave as described, please indicate why.
1.   Because they are worthy of trust.
2.   A mixture of 1 & 2.
3.   They might well do that if they could get away with it. But we have the power to check that no such thing happens.

A.   A customer has made a commitment to you to purchase a   1 2 3
     large volume of component type. You have decided to make
     a significant investment to meet this order. Having made the
     investment, *the customer reduces the order to a fifth of the*
     original level. The customer pleads that as his own demand
     reduction was unforeseen and beyond his control, he should
     be let off without paying any compensation on this occasion.

B.   When you are negotiating a new order, the customer talks   1 2 3
     about other favourable offers he is getting, implying that if
     you don't put the price down, he will switch to sourcing from
     your competitors instead of from you. By this time you have
     become quite dependent on this customer for business, and
     agree to lower the price. Subsequently, *you discover that the*
     story of other offers was entirely fictitious.

Appendix

C. The price of one of your raw materials drops. The customer   1   2   3
    asks you to drop your price by the full amount of the saving.
    He promises to pass it on in a reduction of the final price of
    the product. That way, he claims, you should both benefit
    from higher volumes. *But he doesn't. He keeps all the
    savings for himself.*

4. **Below are a number of statements. Indicate whether you agree or
    disagree with each.**

		Strongly agree	Agree	Hard to say	Disagree	Strongly disagree
A.	'We may misrepresent our costs to our customers during price negotiation, if it is advantageous for us to do so.'	1	2	3	4	5
B.	'It is best to inform our customers of future business plans rather than keep them in the dark.'	1	2	3	4	5
C.	'We obtain the best price by revealing the minimal information necessary during negotiation.'	1	2	3	4	5
D.	'Most people in business respond to candour with candour. It pays to be open and honest.'	1	2	3	4	5
E.	'We only accept terms of trade we know for certain we can meet.'	1	2	3	4	5
F.	'We sometimes exaggerate our problems in order to obtain better terms.'	1	2	3	4	5
G.	'Ideally it would be nice to do business on the basis of complete candour. But, given the way the world is, you would just be taken advantage of if you tried it.'	1	2	3	4	5
H.	'We sometimes accept terms we are not sure we can meet at the time of agreement.'	1	2	3	4	5

248

Appendix

I.	'In order to do business with a customer on the basis of mutual trust, you need some fairly deep personal acquaintance.'	1	2	3	4	5
J.	'In commercial negotiations, our gain is their (customers') loss, and vice versa.'	1	2	3	4	5
K.	'The customer company's reputation is normally sufficient to come to trust it as a trading partner.'	1	2	3	4	5
L.	'We work with our customers towards the common goal of making good quality products for our ultimate customers.'	1	2	3	4	5
M.	'Socialising (golf, dinners) with the customer helps to deepen relations and establish an atmosphere of trust.'	1	2	3	4	5
N.	'Socialising is a good way of getting information about competitors, supply and demand etc.'	1	2	3	4	5
O.	'We start trading with a customer always in the hope of establishing a long-term relationship.'	1	2	3	4	5

Many thanks!

Notes

Introduction

1 Of the 2241 large company respondents (sampled from all industrial sectors except financial services), 60.7 per cent said 'almost all transactions are long-term and continuous' over at least the last 5 years, and a further 37.1 per cent said 'a significant majority of transactions are' with respect to their purchase of production materials. Among the multiple reasons given for maintaining long-term continuous trading, 'stable supply' (88.4 per cent) and 'good quality' (73.3 per cent) were the first and second most frequently cited, followed by 'competitive price (50.0 per cent). The fourth prominent reason cited by 47.7 per cent of respondents was 'trust relations accompanying long-term trading'. 'Belonging to the same corporate grouping' was a minor but significant reason (cited by 5.8 per cent with respect to vertical *Keiretsu* groups, and 2.3 per cent with respect to horizontal *Kigyo shudan* groupings) (EPA 1990, pp. 197–201).

2 In Dertouzos et al. (1989) chapter 7, similarly, the failure of firms to cooperate with each other is seen as a significant factor in the decline of US competitiveness.

1 A spectrum of transactional patterns: from ACR to OCR

1 The phrase 'contractual relation' is used advisedly. While the term 'contract' is prone to a narrowly legalistic interpretation, 'contractual relations' denote both explicitly contractual and some non-contractual but normative elements in all economic transactions.

2 ACR may be thought of as having some characteristics of futures trading contracts. Although both ACR and futures contracts involve agreements to deliver goods at a specified date in future, ACR applies to relations coordinating both productive and trading activities, while futures contracts are largely concerned with exchange, as the majority of traders are non-producing speculators.

3 OCR may be thought of as containing the anthropological characterisation of gift exchange. The difference is, however, that in OCR economic transactions are the primary purpose of forging and continuing trading relationships.

4 The view that economic activity can exist only within a matrix of non-economic, and especially sociological, factors, was already endorsed by Parsons in his assessment of Marshall's thought (Parsons, 1932).

250

2 Trust and organisational efficiency

1 The earlier discourse in calculative cost-benefit terms – maximising utility given one's preference for work and leisure (Leibenstein 1966, p. 413) – is disclaimed later for having little psychological foundation (Frantz 1988, p. xvii).
2 The exploration into the meaning of trust here is confined to the aspect of mutual trust between firms or individuals rather than trust in the persistence of the moral or social order (Barber, 1983, chapter 2) or in institutions such as a political system or the market.
3 McKean (1975) defines trust in this narrow way only.
4 Such trust in professional competence is noted by Barber, 1983, chapter 2. Also Dore (1985a) views managerial competence as responsible for infusing trust into Japanese worker–management relations.
5 The Japanese term for trust, *shinrai*, corresponds closely to the concept of 'goodwill trust', as the Chinese characters used convey the sense of a willingness to lean on a trustworthy person. This is to be contrasted with another term for trust, *shinyo*, which refers to credit. 'Goodwill trust' is also similar to what Fox called 'discretionary trust' (Fox 1973, p. 69–70).
6 This is analogous to the distinction Buckley and Casson make between forbearance and weak cheating. 'Typically, a minimal set of obligations will have been codified in a formal agreement, whilst a fuller set of obligations has been made informally. Failure to honour minimal obligations represents strong cheating, honouring only minimal obligations represents weak cheating, whilst honouring the full obligations represents forbearance' (Buckley and Casson 1988, p. 34).

3 Setting the scene

1 See Gerlach (1989) and Okumara (1987) for accounts of Japanese corporate groupings (*gurupu* or *kigyo shudan*).
2 An exclusive supply situation was predominant in the 1960s. Since then, the proportion of suppliers which trade exclusively with one customer has declined. The average number of customers per SME sub-contractor increased from 3 in 1976 to 4 in 1981 to 5 in 1987 (EPA 1990, p. 205). By 1987, 17.3 per cent of SME sub-contractors traded with a sole customer, 20.3 per cent with two, 26.4 per cent with between 3 and 5, and 14.1 per cent with between 6 and 9, leaving only 22.1 per cent having 10 or more customer outlets (SMEA 1988, p. 61).
3 A vertical *keiretsu* should be distinguished from corporate groupings (*gurupu*) which are also mistakenly referred to as *keiretsu* in some English language accounts. A vertical *keiretsu* also differs from a vertically integrated firm in that shareholding is not a major form of control over suppliers.
4 But see chapter 7 for an account of conflicting ideologies behind the Japanese government policy towards SMEs.
5 There is evidence in the European automobile industry that car manufacturers reduced the number of suppliers they trade with directly by at least a third in the 1980s; for example Austin Rover from 1200 to 700, Ford of Europe from 2500 to 900 and Renault from 1415 to 900 (see 'World Automotive Components' Survey in *Financial Times* 8 June 1989).

6 'Partnership', a fashionable term in both Japan and Britain, signifies an ideal towards which respective countries' relationships are said to be moving, but from different current positions, in particular from unequal to equal partnerships in Japan, and from adversarial towards cooperative partnerships in Britain.

7 Given that: Total sales = Material costs + wage costs + overheads and profit, the relative weights of the three elements in British and Japanese manufacturing sales in 1985 were:

	Material	Wages	Overheads and profit
Britain	58.1%	18.3%	23.6%
Japan	65.9%	13.1%	21.0%

The well-known fact that the labour share in total value added is greater in Britain than in Japan is also revealed by the above formulation.

4 The three customer companies

1 The information on JJ Electric is based on several visits to various parts of the company, company brochures and annual reports to the Japanese Ministry of Finance (*Yuka shoken hokokusho*). Interviews were with:

Acting departmental manager, PCB division, Site S, 22 October 1986.

Materials manager, Second OA division, Site B, 30 October 1986 and 20 October 1987.

Production control manager, Telecommunication terminals division, Site A, 19 November 1987.

General manager, MD, technical director, materials manager, Site C, 27 November 1987.

Materials manager, Site C, 7 April 1989.

Central procurement manager, Tokyo HQ, 14 April 1989.

Four other Japanese electronics companies were also interviewed.

2 This diversified product stragegy is in stark contrast to a recent trend among British and other European manufacturers to rationalise their operations, concentrating on what they call their 'core' business. For example, in the steel industry, Nippon Steel's strategy to have 50 per cent of its total sales in non-steel products and services by 1995 is in sharp contrast to British Steel's 'leaner and fitter' strategy of labour displacing automation within steel only.

3 By contrast, some British customer companies claim continuous trading with a supplier by virtue of it being on the computerised list of approved suppliers which they can tap into intermittently when required. See the analysis of GB Electronics and British suppliers in chapter 5.

4 See chapter 11 for more details on ranking hierarchy as an incentive scheme for suppliers.

5 The information on GB Electronics was gathered mainly through interviews with three managers, all in procurement: the Director of Procurement, 13 January 1987; a purchasing executive at Site X on 3 February 1987 and 15

November 1989; and a purchasing executive at Site Y on 21 July 1987 and 7 February 1989. The historical information is based on a Monopolies and Mergers Commission report. Interview visits were also made to four other UK customer companies in the electronics industry.

6 See Shimada (1987) for a similar point concerning US purchasing managers.

7 See chapter 11 for more details on how GB Electronics attempts to circumvent this problem of information asymmetry.

8 The information on Toshiba Consumer Products (UK) Ltd is based on 4 visits, on 1 July 1986, 14 August 1987, 10 November 1989 and 14 May 1991. Interviews were with the Managing Director (British), two Assistant Managing Directors (both Japanese), and purchasing managers, Mr Peter Bayliss and Mr John Moss. I would like to thank Mr Moss in particular for giving me generously of his time at each of my four visits. Three of TCP (UK) Ltd's suppliers were interviewed. A visit was also paid to the parent factory in Japan, at Fukaya, on 28 October 1987; interviewees were the factory manager and the materials manager. Lastly, four other Japanese electronics factories in the UK were visited.

9 The basic contract at Fukaya was said to have been signed with all suppliers long before the Fair Trade Commission started enforcing the 1963 Anti-Monopoly Law on sub-contracting. Although large suppliers tend to read the basic contract and demand that certain clauses be changed before signing, the Fukaya manager reckoned that small and medium-sized suppliers probably do not read the content of the contract carefully enough, trusting that a company of JBT Corporation's size and reputation would not harm them.

10 Fukaya's purchasing department consists of thirty-seven employees, who may be divided into two groups. One is a small group of HQ-recruited university graduates on job rotation who belong to the so-called mobile tribe (*tenkinzoku*) occupying the higher echelon of the department. The other is a locally hired group of high-school graduates who are either clerical staff or buyers doing the same job dealing with the same customers for as long as ten years. The mobile tribe moves from site to site every three to five years, but the stability of locally hired personnel is very high.

11 Unfortunately, because of bankruptcy, it is not possible to verify this story from K Plastics' viewpoint.

5 The analysis of supplier companies

1 As an indication, in 1984 there were 32,959 establishments forming 11,817 enterprises in the Japanese electrical and electronic engineering sector, and 8919 establishments forming 8069 enterprises in the same sector in Britain. Sources are MITI's *Kogyo Tokei Hyo* and British Census of Production.

2 The questionnaire responses by the supplier indicate that a higher degree of transactional dependence is associated with the supplier's customers giving out smooth orders (Q.1(iv)). The suppliers who replied that their customers gave continuous, stable orders had an average of 44.4 per cent dependence, which compares with the average of 23.6 per cent dependence by the suppliers who said that their customers changed their orders as it suited them. The t-test is significant at the 5 per cent level.

3 In the Japanese sample, eight strongly agreed, nine agreed and one said 'hard

to say'; in the British sample, fifteen strongly agreed and three agreed. The British–Japanese difference is not significant.

4 The British–Japanese difference is significant at the 1 per cent level according to the chi-square test.

5 A similar trend towards longer contracts was noted by Helper (1989a) for the US automotive industry.

6 The situation of a supplier as a sole source for a whole range of part numbers of a component type (e.g. PCBs, plastic parts) must be distinguished from that in which a customer has several suppliers for a component type but each being a single source for a part number. A supplier is a true monopolist in the former case, but not in the latter,.

7 See IBM manual for its buyers, *Doing business with our suppliers: A guide for IBM management*, instructing them to separate professional from personal relationships, and to pay promptly for everything they get. The manual states: 'Paying for everything means just that. We don't want favors, gifts or special arrangements, nor do we allow individual IBMers to accept them, because we want to be free of any obligations that might interfere with our ability to deal with all suppliers on the basis of their merits alone.'

8 Those in agreement were 10 in Britain and 13 in Japan to Q.4M, and 8 in Britain and 14 in Japan to Q.4N. The difference in British and Japanese mean scores was significant for Q.4N only, at 5 per cent level; the means are 2.1 for Japan and 2.8 for Britain.

9 For Q.41, 'In order to do business with a customer on the basis of mutual trust, you need some fairly deep personal acquaintance', the mean scores were 1.8 for Japan and 2.4 for Britain. For Q.4K, 'The customer company's reputation is normally sufficient to come to trust it as a trading partner', the mean scores were 2.9 in Japan and 2.3 in Britain. The t-test indicates that the differences are both significant at the 5 per cent level.

10 By contrast, an ACR practice is found at Motorola Suppliers Institute in the USA, which charges suppliers who attend courses on quality management and design for manufacturability. This follows the conventional human capital theory prescription that trainees (suppliers) bear the cost of training in general skills.

11 Sample suppliers were asked to indicate which of the following statements they agreed with more: (A) 'We would not have achieved our current technological capability had it not been for our customers' assistance' and (B) 'We have achieved our current technological capability on our own without customers' help' (Q.1(v)). the A:B ratios were 3:7 in the British PCB sector, 1:9 in the Japanese PCB sector, 2:6 in the British EA sector, but 7:1 in the Japanese EA sector. The sectoral difference (4:16 in PCB, 9:7 in electronic assembly) was significant at the 5 per cent level using the chi-square test, but the inter-country difference was not.

7 The legal framework

1 A 'parental' firm (*oya jigyosha*) is a customer firm to be distinguished from a parent company (*oya gaisha*) having shareholding stakes in its subsidiaries. As discussed in chapter 3, the parent-child metaphor pervades in the Japanese discourse on sub-contracting.

2 According to an interview with the section head of the Sub-contracting Section, the FTC, 15 October 1987.

8 Banks and financial links

1 Much of the discussion in this section is based on Aoki (1989), Berglof (1990), Corbett (1987), Dore (1987) chapter 6, and Okumura (1984).
2 A well-documented case of bank intervention is Toyo Kogyo which manufactures Mazda cars. See Pascale and Rohlen (1983); also Okumura (1984, p. 127).
3 These programmes obligate the trade association, JPCA, to devise a five-year plan, within which a detailed plan is set out annually. JPCA also conducted a survey of PCB manufacturers, final equipment manufacturers, and process machinery and raw material suppliers in order to put forward a medium- to long-term 'vision' of where the PCB industry would be heading. The survey resulted in the compiling of a 500-page report (JPCA, 1987b) which encourages and accustoms member firms to think long-term.

9 Employment system links

1 See Dore (1973) for the features of market-oriented and organisation-oriented employment relations.
2 See chapter 11 for more details on how the incentive structure for cooperation and competition created by the suppliers' association affects performance.
3 'Why?' is a natural question for most British businessmen, suspicious of cartelisation attempts at the mention of *kyoryokukai*. Reasons appear to be multiple. First, the patron company exercises a considerable degree of control by being present at most association meetings and workshops. Second, while members compete in a publicised ranking according to quality and delivery performance, prices are considered confidential and subject to bilateral negotiations only.
4 In 1982 and 1985, Denki Roren surveyed its members working for SMEs, 45 per cent of whom replied that the major reason for working long hours was 'there is no choice in order to maintain trust relations with customers by observing delivery deadlines'; the next most popular category was 'difficult to live without overtime earnings'. See Denki Roren 1985.

10 Entrepreneurship and the dynamics of small firm creation

1 Refer to Sengenberger et al. (1990) for more detailed statistics and discussion on the increasing significance of small firms over time in Britain and Japan.
2 Similarly, at Hitachi in 1955, 62.2 per cent of all sub-contracting companies were owned and managed by ex-Hitachi employees (Yamamoto 1987, p. 138).
3 The effect on contractual relationships of large-scale innovation associated with the Schumpeterian approach to entrepreneurship is not discussed in this book, as the present study can cast little light on this topic.
4 Kiyonari's survey overstated the extent of hive-offs because his sample was taken in urban areas only, and also concentrated on very small firms.

Moreover, his survey was conducted in 1969, when it was considerably easier to start up a business. It has become more difficult in the 1980s due to higher set-up costs, in terms of a larger sum of initial capital and more advanced technical expertise required (Inagami 1989, pp. 96–8), as is evident from the following trends in the Japanese manufacturing sector (Management and Coordination Agency *Jigyosho Tokei Chosa* (Establishment Survey)):

	% start-up	% closure
1966–9	6.0	2.5
1969–72	5.6	3.2
1972–5	4.3	3.4
1975–8	3.4	2.3
1978–81	3.7	2.5
1981–6	3.1	3.0

5 There is similar evidence in Britain that those who leave to set up their own businesses tend to come from smaller firms (SBRT 1989).

11 Implications of ACR–OCR patterns for competitiveness

1 The sectoral difference is significant at the 1 per cent level using the chi-square test.
2 The mean scores were 2.7 for Britain and 3.5 for Japan. The difference is significant at the 1 per cent level according to t-test.
3 In the British sample, five responded that it was quite acceptable, ten not quite acceptable but would continue dealing with the customer, and three unacceptable and would never deal with the customer. The corresponding responses in the Japanese sample were 0:12:6. The difference is significant at the 5 per cent level according to the chi-square test. The hypothetical situation was encountered 'quite often' by 7, 'occasionally from some; rarely from others' by 8 and 'hardly ever from any' by 3 in Britain; while the Japanese responses were 2:8:8. The inter-country difference is significant at 10 per cent level. Customers rarely behave as in the hypothetical situation because: 'customers are trustworthy' (Britain, three; Japan, eight); 'we have the power to prevent it from happening' (Britain two; Japan, two); 'a combination of trust and sanctions' (Britain, six; Japan, six). The British–Japanese difference is not significant.
4 These targets for electronic assembly sub-contractors appear severe compared to those faced by automotive parts suppliers. For example, Ikeda (1988) cites the case of Mazda requesting 10 per cent reduction per six months in 1988. In order to cope with the strong yen, Toyota is said to have demanded 4–5 per cent cost reduction for the 1986 financial year (see Aichi Keizai Jiho *Aichi Economic Journal*), no.159, October 1988, p. 46).
5 No data are available on British PCB prices for the 1970s and early 1980s.
6 These figures are based on companies' reports to the Japanese Ministry of Finance; computed averages are taken from Mitsubishi Research Institute *Kigyo Keiei no Bunseki* (The Analysis of Enterprise Management) various years.
7 See also Helper (1989b) who applies the exit-voice model to analyse the US automobile industry.

Bibliography

Akerlof, George A. (1982) 'Labour contracts as partial gift exchange' *Quarterly Journal of Economics* 97 pp. 542–6.

Alchian, A. A. and H. Demsetz (1972) 'Production, information costs and economic organisation' *American Economic Review* 62(5) pp. 777–95.

All Japan Subcontractors Promotion Association (1987) *Gaichu shitauke torihiki keiyakusho no mikata tsukurikata* (How to interpret and write basic contracts for sub-contract trading) Tokyo: Toho.

Aoki, Masahiko (ed.) (1984) *The Economic Analysis of the Japanese Firm* Amsterdam: North Holland.

(1988) *Information, Incentives, and Bargaining in the Japanese Economy* New York: Cambridge University Press.

(1989) 'The nature of the Japanese firm as a nexus of employment and financial contracts: an overview' *Journal of the Japanese and International Economics* 3 pp. 345–66.

Aoki, M., B. Gustaffson and O. E. Williamson (eds.) (1990) *The Firm as a Nexus of Treaties* London: Sage.

Arrow, Kenneth J. (1974) *The Limits of Organisation* New York: W. W. Norton.

(1975) 'Gifts and exchanges' in Phelps (ed.).

Arrow, K. J. (1962) 'The economic implications of learning by doing' *Review of Economic Studies* 29(80) pp. 155–73.

Arthur D. Little Ltd (1986) *The Japanese Experience in Wales* Cardiff: Winvest.

Asanuma, Banri (1984) 'Nihon ni okeru buhin torihiki no kozo: jidosha sangyo no jirei' (Contractual Framework for Parts Supply in the Japanese Automobile Industry) *Keizai Ronso* 133(3), pp. 137–58.

(1985) 'The organisation of parts purchases in the Japanese automative industry' *Japanese Economic Studies* Summer, pp. 32–53.

(1989) 'Manufacturer–Supplier Relationships in Japan and the Concept of Relation-Specific Skill' *Journal of the Japanese and International Economies* 3 pp. 1–30.

Axelrod, Robert (1984) *Evolution of Cooperation* New York: Basic Books.

Baldamus, W. (1961) *Efficiency and Effort: An Analysis of Industrial Administration* London: Tavistock Publications.

Barber, Bernard (1983) *The Logic and Limits of Trust* New Jersey: Rutgers University Press.

Berglof, Erik (1990) 'Capital structure as a mechanism of control: a comparison of financial systems' in M. Aoki et al. (eds.).

257

Bibliography

Binks, Martin (1991) 'Small businesses and their banks in the year 2000' in Curran and Blackburn (eds.).

Blau, Peter M. (1974) *Exchange and Power in Social Life* New York: John Wiley & Sons.

Blois, K. J. (1972) 'Vertical quasi-integration' *Journal of Industrial Economics* 20(3) pp. 253–72.

Broadbridge, Seymour (1966) *Industrial Dualism in Japan: A Problem of Economic Growth and Structural Change* London: Frank Cass & Co.

Buckley, P. J. and M. Casson (1988) 'A theory of cooperation in international business' in Contractor and Lorange (eds.).

Caves, Richard E. and Masu Uekusa (1976) *Industrial Organisation in Japan* Washington DC: The Brookings Institution.

Central Office of Information (1988) *Prompt Payment Please!* London: HMSO.

Chandler, Alfred D. (1977) *The Visible Hand: The Managerial Revolution in American Business* Cambridge, Mass: Belknap Press of Harvard University Press.

Clark, Kim B., Robert H. Hayes and Christopher Lorenz (eds.) (1985) *The Uneasy Alliance: Managing the Productivity Technology Dilemma* Boston, Mass.: Harvard Business School Press.

Clark, Kim B., W. B. Chew and T. Fujimoto (1987) *Product Development in the World Auto Industry: Strategy, Organisation and Performance* Paper presented at the Brookings Microeconomics Conference, December 3–4.

Coase, Ronald (1937) 'The Nature of the Firm' *Economica* 4(16) pp. 386–405.

CBI (Confederation of British Industry) (1983) *Working for Customers* London: CBI.

(1985) *Managing Change: the Organisation of Work* London: CBI.

(1989) *Subcontracting in British Business: A CBI Survey* London: CBI.

(1991) *Late Payment of Trade Debts: A Survey of Small and Medium-Sized Businesses* London: Cork Gully & CBI.

Contractor, Farok J. and Peter Lorange (1988) *Cooperative Strategies in International Business* Lexington, Mass: D. C. Heath & Co.

Corbett, J. (1987) 'International perspectives on financing: evidence from Japan' *Oxford Review of Economic Policy* 3(4) pp. 30–55.

Curran, James and R. A. Blackburn (eds.) (1991) *Paths of Enterprise: The Future of Small Firms* London: Routledge.

Curson, Chris (ed.) (1986) *Flexible Patterns of Work* London: Institute of Personnel Management.

Cusumano, Michael A. (1985) *The Japanese Automobile Industry* Cambridge Mass.: Harvard University Press.

De Alessi, Louis (1983) 'Property rights, transaction costs, and x-efficiency: an essay in economic theory' *American Economic Review* 73(1) pp. 64–81.

Denki Roren (Federation of Electrical Machinery Workers Union, Japan) (1985) *Chuken, chusho kigyo rodo kumiaiin ankeeto* (Questionnaire survey of union members in SMEs) Tokyo: Denki Roren.

(1986) *Jukkakoku denki rodosha no ishiki chosa kekka hokoku* (Survey of electrical workers' attitudes in ten countries) Tokyo: Denki Roren.

Dertouzos, M. L., R. K. Lester, and R. M. Solow (1989) *Made In America: Regaining the Productive Edge* Cambridge, Mass: MIT Press.

Dietrich, M. (1991) 'Firms markets and transaction cost economics' *Scottish Journal of Political Economy* 38(1) pp. 41–57.

Dore, Ronald (1973) *British Factory–Japanese Factory* Berkeley: University of California Press.

(1983) 'Goodwill and the Spirit of Market Capitalism' *The British Journal of Sociology* 34(3) pp. 459–82.

(1985a) 'The Confucian recipe for industrial success' *Government and Opposition* 20(2) pp. 198–217.

(1985b) 'Financial structure and the long-term view' *Policy Studies* 6(1) July pp. 10–29.

(1986) *Flexible Rigidities: Industrial Policy and Structural Adjustment in the Japanese Economy 1970–80* London: The Athlone Press.

(1987) *Taking Japan Seriously* London: The Athlone Press.

Dore, Ronald, J. Bounine-Cabale and K. Tapiola (1989) *Japan at Work* Paris: OECD.

Dore, Ronald P. and Mari Sako (1989) *How the Japanese Learn to Work* London: Routledge.

Dugger, William M. (1983) 'The transaction cost analysis of Oliver E. Williamson: a new synthesis?' *Journal of Economic Issues* 17(1) pp. 95–114.

Durkheim, E. (1947) *The Division of Labour in Society* Glencoe, Ill.: Free Press.

EPA (Economic Planning Agency, Japan) (1990) *Keizai Hakusho* (Economic White Paper) Tokyo: Okurasho.

Eccles, Robert (1981) 'The quasi-firm in the construction industry' *Journal of Economic Behaviour and Organisation* 2 pp. 335–57.

Eccles, R. G. and Crane, D. B. (1988) *Doing Deals: Investment Banks at Work* Boston: Harvard Business School Press.

Eisenstadt, S. N. and L. Roniger (1984) *Patrons, Clients and Friends: Interpersonal Relations and the Structure of Trust in Society* Cambridge: Cambridge University Press.

Elster, Jon (1989) *The Cement of Society: A Study of Social Order* New York: Cambridge University Press.

Etzioni, Amitai (1987) 'Entrepreneurship, adaptation and legitimation' *Journal of Economic Behaviour and Organisation* 8 pp. 175–89.

(1988) *The Moral Dimension: Towards A New Economics* New York: The Free Press.

FTC (1986) *Dokusen Kinshi Hakusho* (Anti-Monopoly White Paper) Tokyo: Okurasho.

Foster, George (1969) *Applied Anthropology* Boston: Little, Brown and Co.

Fox, Alan (1973) *Beyond Contract: Work, Power and Trust Relations* London: Faber & Faber.

(1985) *Man Mismanagement* London: Hutchinson & Co.

Francis, A. et al. (eds.) (1983) *Power, Efficiency and Institution* London: Heinemann.

Frantz, Roger S. (1988) *X-efficiency: Theory, Evidence and Applications* Boston: Kluwer Academic Publishers.

Friedman, Andrew L. (1977) *Industry and Labour* London: Macmillan.

Friedman, David (1988) *The Misunderstood Miracle: Industrial Development and Political Change in Japan* Ithaca & London: Cornell University Press.

Gambetta, Diego (ed.) (1988) *Trust: Making and Breaking Cooperative Relations* Oxford: Basil Blackwell.

Bibliography

Gerlach, Michael (1989) *Alliances and the Social Organisation of Japanese Business* Berkeley: University of California Press.

Gordon, Andrew (1985) *The Evolution of Labour Relations in Japan: Heavy Industry, 1853–1955* Cambridge, Mass.: Harvard University Press.

Gordon, Robert W. (1985) 'Macaulay, Macneil and the discovery of solidarity and power in contract law' *Wisconsin Law Review* 3 pp. 565–79.

Granovetter, Mark S. (1973) 'The strength of weak ties' *American Journal of Sociology* 78(6) pp. 1360–80.

(1985) 'Economic action and social structure: the problem of embeddedness *American Journal of Sociology* 91(3) pp. 481–510.

(1990) *Enterprise, Development and the Emergence of Firms*, Discussion Paper FSI 90–2, WZB, Berlin.

Hakim, C. (1989) 'New recruits to self-employment in the 1980s' *Employment Gazette* June pp. 286–97.

Haley, John O. (1978) 'The myth of the reluctant litigant' *The Journal of Japanese Studies* 4(2) pp. 359–90.

(1982) 'Sheathing the sword of justice in Japan: an essay on law without sanctions' *The Journal of Japanese Studies* 8(2) pp. 265–81.

Helper, Susan (1987) *Supplier Relations and Technical Change: Theory and Application to the US Automobile Industry* Ph.D. thesis, Harvard University.

(1989a) *Strategy and Irreversibility in Supplier Relations: The Case of the US Automobile Industry* presented at U. C. intercampus Group in Economic History Conference, Santa Cruz, California, May 1988.

(1989b) *Supplier Relations at a Crossroads: Results of Survey Research in the US Automobile Industry* Working Paper no. 89–26, Boston University School of Management.

(1990) 'Comparative supplier relations in the US and Japanese auto industries: an exit/voice approach' *Business and Economic History* Second Series 19 pp. 153–62.

Hirschman, Albert O. (1970) *Exit, Voice and Loyalty: Responses to Decline in Firms, Organisations and States* Cambridge, Mass.: Harvard University Press.

(1984) 'Against parsimony: three easy ways of complicating some categories of economic discourse' *American Economic Review Papers and Proceedings* 74(2) pp. 89–96.

Hirst, Paul, and Jonathan Zeitlin (eds.) (1989) *Reversing Industrial Decline? Industrial Structure and Policy in Britain and Her Competitors* Oxford: Berg.

Hodgson, Geoffrey M. (1988) *Economics and Institutions* Cambridge: Polity Press.

Ikeda, Masayoshi (1979) 'The subcontracting system in the Japanese electronic industry' *Engineering Industries of Japan* No. 19 pp. 43–71.

(1986) 'Eikoku no sabu assenburi shitauke kigyo no jittai' (The state of sub-assembly sub-contractors in the UK) *Shoko Kinyu* 36(2) pp. 3–18.

(1987) 'Evolution of the Japanese Subcontracting System' *Trade Scope* July pp. 2–6.

(1988) 'Series: JIT enters a new phase in the Japanese auto industry (II) – an approach to Japan's subcontracting system' *In Site* February pp. 3–21.

Imai, K. and H. Itami (1984) 'Interpenetration of organization and market: Japan's firm and market in comparison with the US' *International Journal of Industrial Organization* 2 pp. 285–310.

260

Imai, K., H. Itami and K. Koike (1985) *Naibu Soshiki no Keizaigaku* (The Economic Theory of Internal Organisations) Tokyo: Koyo Keisai Shimposha.

Inagami, Takeshi (1988) *Japanese Workplace Industrial Relations* Japanese Industrial Relations Series No. 14, Tokyo: Japan Institute of Labour.

(1989) *Tenkanki no Rodo Sekai* (The World of Work in Transition) Tokyo: Yushindo.

JETRO (1989) *State of Operations of Japanese Affiliates (Manufacturing) in Europe – Second Survey Report on Management* London: JETRO.

JIL (Japan Institute of Labour) (1989) *Japanese Working Life Profile: Statistical Aspects* Tokyo: JIL.

JPCA (Japan Printed Circuit Association) (1987a) *Purinto Haisenban Kogyo no Genjo* (The Current State of the Printed Circuit Board Industry) Tokyo: JPCA.

(1987b) *Purinto Kairo Kogyo no Chu-choki Tenbo: Chosa Hokoku sho* (Medium to Long-term Prospects of the PCB Industry: A Survey Report) Tokyo: JPCA.

Jarillo, J. C. (1988) 'On strategic networks' *Strategic Management Journal* 9 pp. 31–41.

Johanson, J. and L.-G. Matsson (1987) 'Interorganisational relations in industrial systems: a network approach compared with the transaction-cost approach' *International Studies in Management and Organization* 17(1) pp. 34–48.

Kahneman, Daniel, Jack L. Knetshch and Richard Thaler (1986) 'Fairness as a constraint on profit seeking: entitlements in the market' *American Economic Review* 76(4) pp. 728–41.

Kawasaki, S. and J. MacMillan (1987) 'The design of contracts: evidence from Japanese subcontracting' *Journal of the Japanese and International Economies* 1 pp. 327–49.

Kawashima, Takeyoshi (1967) *Nihonjin no hoishiki* (Legal Consciousness of the Japanese) Tokyo: Iwanami shoten.

Kiyonari, Tadeo (1970) *Nihon Chusho Kigyo no Kozo Hendo* (Structural Transformation of Japanese SMEs) Shin hyoron.

(1980) *Chusho Kigyo Tokuhon* (Introduction to Small and Medium-sized Enterprises) Tokyo: Toyo keizai shinpo sha.

(1985) *Chusho Kigyo* (Small and Medium-sized Enterprises) Tokyo: Nihon Keizai shinbun sha.

Klein, B., R. A. Crawford, and A. A. Alchian (1978) 'Vertical integration, appropriable rents, and the competitive contracting process' *Journal of Law and Economics* 21(2) pp. 297–326.

Koike, Kazuo (1981) *Chusho Kigyo no Jukuren* (Skills in Small and Medium Enterprises) Dobunkan.

Kreps, David M. (1990) 'Corporate Culture and Economic Theory' in James E. Alt and K. A. Schepsle (eds.) *Perspectives in Positive Political Economy* Cambridge: Cambridge University Press.

Latham, Gary and Edwin Locke (1979) 'Goal setting – a motivational technique that works' *Organisational Dynamics* Autumn pp. 68–80.

Lazear, E. and S. Rosen (1981) 'Rank order tournament as optimal labour contracts' *Journal of Political Economy* 89 pp. 814–64.

Bibliography

Lazerson, Mark (1988) 'Organisational growth of small firms: an outcome of markets and hierarchies?' *American Sociological Review* 53 pp. 330–42.

Leibenstein, Harvey (1966) 'Allocative efficiency vs X-efficiency' *American Economic Review* 56 pp. 392–415.

(1976) *Beyond Economic Man: A New Foundation in Microeconomics* Cambridge, Mass.: Harvard University Press.

(1984) 'The Japanese management system: an X-efficiency-Game theory analysis' in Aoki (ed.).

(1987a) *Inside the Firm: The Inefficiencies of Hierarchy* Cambridge, Mass.: Harvard University Press.

(1987b) 'Entrepreneurship, entrepreneurial training, and X-efficiency theory' *Journal of Economic Behaviour and Organisation* 8 pp. 191–205.

(1987c) 'X-efficiency theory' *The New Palgrave: A Dictionary of Economics* London: Macmillan pp. 934–5.

Lodge, George C. and E. F. Vogel (eds.) (1987) *Ideology and National Competitiveness* Boston: Harvard Business School Press.

Lorenz, E. H. (1988) 'Neither friends nor strangers: informal networks of subcontracting in French industry' in Gambetta (ed.).

(1989) 'The search for flexibility: subcontracting networks in French and British engineering' in Hirst and Zeitlin (eds.).

Lundvall, Bengt-Ake (1988) 'Innovation as an interactive process: from user–producer interaction to the national system of innovation' in G. Dosi et al. *Technical Change and Economic Theory* London and New York: Pinter.

Macaulay, Stewart (1963) 'Non-contractual relations in business: a preliminary study' *American Sociological Review* 28(2) pp. 55–67.

McKean, Roland (1975) 'Economics of trust, altruism and corporate responsibility' in E. S. Phelps (ed.).

McMillan, John (1990) 'Managing suppliers: incentive systems in Japanese and U.S. industry' *California Management Review* 32(4) pp. 38–55.

Macmillan, K. and D. Farmer (1979) 'Redefining the boundaries of the firm' *Journal of Industrial Economics* 27(3) pp. 277–85.

Macneil, Ian R. (1983) 'Values in contract: internal and external' *Northwestern University Law Review* 78(2) pp. 341–418.

(1985) 'Relational contract: what we do and do not know' *Wisconsin Law Review* pp. 483–525.

Malcolmson, J. M. (1984) 'Work incentives, hierarchy and internal labor markets' *Journal of Political Economy* 92(3) pp. 486–507.

Manpower Limited (1985) *Flexible Manning in Business* Slough: Manpower Limited.

March, James G. and H. A. Simon (1958) *Organisations* New York: John Wiley & Sons.

Marginson, Paul, P. K. Edwards, R. Martin, J. Purcell and K. Sisson (1988) *Beyond the Workplace* Oxford: Basil Blackwell.

Marglin, Stephen A. (1974) 'What do bosses do? The origins and functions of hierarchy in capitalist production' *Review of Radical Political Economics* 6(2) pp. 60–112.

Marsh, Robert M. (1988) *The Japanese Negotiator: Subtlety and Strategy Beyond Western Logic* Tokyo: Kodansha International.

Bibliography

Masten, Scott E. (1984) 'The organisation of production: evidence from the aerospace industry' *Journal of Law and Economics* 27 pp. 403–18.

Mauss, Marcel (1966) *The Gift* London and Henley: Routledge and Kegan Paul.

Miles, R. E. and C. C. Snow (1986) 'Organisations: new concepts for new forms' *California Management Review* 28(3) pp. 62–73.

Mill, J. S. (1891) *Principles of Political Economy* London: Longmans.

Minato, Tetsuo (1987) 'Ryotaisenkan ni okeru nihongata shitauke seisan shisutemu no hensei katei' (Historical background of the Japanese inter-firm production system: 1920–1945) *Aoyama Kokusai Seikei Ronshu* 7 pp. 87–118.

   (1988) 'Shitauke torihiki ni okeru "shinrai" zai no keisei katei' (The formation of 'trust' as an asset in sub-contracting) *Shoko Kinyu* 10 pp. 7–19.

MIRI (Mitsubishi Research Institute, Inc.) (1987) *The Relationship between Japanese Auto and Parts Makers* Tokyo: MIRI.

Mito, Seiichi (1977) *VA VE ni yoru kosuto daun nyumon* (Introduction to Reducing Costs Through VA. VE) Tokyo: Chuo keizai sha.

Monteverde, Kirk, and David Teece (1982) 'Appropriable rents and quasi-vertical integration' *Journal of Law and Economics* 25 pp. 321–8.

Nakamura, Hideichiro (1985) *Chosen suru Chusho Kigyo* (Small and Medium-sized Enterprises in Challenge) Tokyo: Iwanami shoten.

Nakamura, Sei (1983) *Chusho kigyo to daikigyo: nihon no sangyo hatten to jun suichokutogo* (SMEs and Large Firms: Japanese Industrial Development and Quasi-Vertical Integration) Tokyo: Toyo keizai shinposha.

Nakamura, Takafusa (1981) *The Postwar Japanese Economy: Its Development and Structure* Tokyo: University of Tokyo Press.

NAO (National Audit Office) (1988) *Department of Employment/ Training Commission: Assistance to Small Firms* London: HMSO.

NEDO (National Economic Development Office) (1983) *The Printed Circuit Board Industry* London: NEDO.

Niehans, Jung (1987) 'Transaction costs' *The New Palgrave: A Dictionary of Economics* London: Macmillan pp. 676–9.

Nishiguchi, Toshihiro (1987) *Strategic Dualism: An Alternative to Industrial Societies* D. Phil. thesis, University of Oxford.

OECD (1986) 'Self-employment in OECD countries' *Employment Outlook* Paris: OECD, pp. 43–65.

Odagiri, Hiroyuki (1992) *Growth through Competition, Competition through Growth* Oxford: Clarendon Press.

Odagiri, H. and T. Yamashita (1987) 'Price mark-ups, market structure, and business fluctuation in Japanese manufacturing industries' *Journal of Industrial Economics* 15(3) pp. 317–31.

Odagiri, H. and T. Hase (1989) 'Are mergers and acquisitions going to be popular in Japan too?' *International Journal of Industrial Organisation* 7 pp. 49–72.

Ohta, Yoichi (1985) *Intercompany Relationship in Japanese Manufacturing Industries* Unpublished M.Litt. thesis, The University of Oxford.

Okimoto, Daniel I. (1986) 'Regime characteristics of Japanese industrial policy' in Hugh Patrick (ed.) *Japan's High Technology Industries* Seattle: University of Washington Press.

   (1989) *Between MITI and the Market* Stanford: Stanford University Press.

Bibliography

Okumura, Hiroshi (1984) *Hojin Shihon Shugi* (Corporate Capitalism) Tokyo: Ochanomizu shobo.

(1987) *Shin Nihon no Rokudai Kigyo Shudan* (Six Largest Corporate Groupings in Japan) Tokyo: Daiyamondo sha.

Okun, Arthur M. (1981) *Prices and Quantities: A Macroeconomic Analysis* Oxford: Basil Blackwell.

Oliver, Nick and Barry Wilkinson (1988) *The Japanisation of British Industry* Oxford: Blackwell.

Ouchi, William G. (1981) *Theory Z: How American Business Can Meet the Japanese Challenge* Reading Mass.: Addison-Wesley.

Parsons, Talcott (1932) 'Economics and sociology: Marshall in relation to the thought of his time' *Quarterly Journal of Economics* XLVI(2) pp. 316–47.

(1951) *The Social System* London: Routledge & Kegan Paul.

Pascale, R. and T. Rohlen (1983) 'The Mazda turnaround' *Journal of Japanese Studies* 9(2) pp. 219–63.

Phelps, Edmund S. (ed.) (1975) *Altruism, Morality and Economic Theory* New York: Russell Sage Foundation.

Piore, M. J., and C. F. Sabel (1984) *The Second Industrial Divide* New York: Basic Books.

Powell, Walter W. (1985) *Getting into Print* Chicago: University of Chicago Press.

(1990) 'Neither market nor hierarchy: network forms of organisation' in Staw, B. M. and L. L. Cummings (eds.) *Research in Organisational Behaviour* Vol. 12 JAI Press, pp. 295–336.

Prais, Sig (1981) *Productivity and Industrial Structure* Cambridge: Cambridge University Press.

(1989) *Productivity, Education and Training* London: NIESR.

Pyke, F. et al. (eds.) (1990) *Industrial Districts and Inter-firm Co-operation in Italy* Geneva: IILS.

Rainnie, A. F. (1984) 'Combined and uneven development in the clothing industry' *Capital and Class* 22 pp. 141–56.

Rajan, Amin and R. Pearson (1986) *UK Occupation and Employment Trends to 1990* Brighton: IMS.

Ramseyer, J. and N. Nakazato (1989) 'The rational litigant: settlement amounts and verdict rates in Japan' *Journal of Legal Studies* 18 pp. 263–90.

Rhys, Garel (1988) 'Motor Vehicles' in P. Johnson (ed.) *The Structure of British Industry* Second edition, London: Unwin Hyman.

Richardson, G. B. (1972) 'The Organisation of Industry' *Economic Journal* 82(327) pp. 883–96.

Ricketts, Martin (1987) *The Economics of Business Enterprise* Brighton: Wheatsheaf Books.

Ronen, Joshua (1987) 'Comments on the papers by Etzioni and Leibenstein' *Journal of Economic Behaviour and Organisation* 8 pp. 207–12.

Sabel, Charles and Jonathan Zeitlin (1985) 'Historical alternatives to mass production: politics, markets and technology in nineteenth-century industrialisation' *Past and Present* 108 pp. 133–76.

Sabel, Charles (1990) *Studied Trust: Building New Forms of Cooperation in a Volatile Economy*, T. E. P. Conference 24–27 June 1990, mimeo MIT.

Sakai, Kuniyasu and H. Sekiyama (1985) *Bunsha* Tokyo: Taiyo Industry Co. Ltd. Kisshokai.

Bibliography

Sakai, K. (1986) ' *"Dozo" "Domo"* ': *Footsteps of a Japanese company, 300 years on* Tokyo: Taiyo Industry Co. Ltd. Kisshokai (translated from the 1983 Japanese original titled *Karakurishi no Massho*).

Sato, Yoshio (ed.) (1980) *Teiseichoki ni okeru Gaichu Shitauke Kanri* (The management of purchasing and sub-contracting during recession) Tokyo: Chuo keizaisha.

Sengenberger, W. et al. (1990) *The Re-emergence of Small Enterprises* Geneva: IILS.

Scherer, F. M. (1980) *Industrial Market Structure and Economic Performance* Chicago: Rank McNally College.

Shimada, Katsumi (1987) 'Boeki masatsu to torihiki kanko' (Trade frictions and trading custom and practice) *Kyotogakuen University Review* 16(2) pp. 24–76.

Shoya, Kuniyuki (1988) 'Nihon sangyo no shitauke kankei ni okeru fukosei torihiki' (Unfair practices in sub-contracting relations in Japanese industry) *Shakaigaku Ronshu* (Momoyama Gakuin Daigaku) 21(2) pp. 175–219.

Simon, Herbert A. (1957) *Administrative Behaviour* Second edition New York: MacMillan.

(1978) 'Rationality as process and as product of thought' *American Economic Review* 68 pp. 1–16.

SBRT (Small Business Research Trust) (1985a) *Defence Sector Procurement* London: SBRT.

(1985b) *Quarterly Survey of Small Business in Britain* 1(3).

(1989) *Quarterly Survey of Small Business in Britain* 5(1).

SMEA (Small and Medium Enterprise Agency, Japan) (various years) *Chusho kigyo Hakusho* (White Paper on Small and Medium Enterprises) Tokyo: Okurasho.

Smith, Adam (1930) *The Wealth of Nations* Fifth edition. Edwin Cannan ed. London: Methuen & Co. (first published 1776).

Smith, Robert J. (1983) *Japanese Society: Tradition, Self and the Social Order* Cambridge: Cambridge University Press.

Smitka, Michael (1989) *Competitive Ties: Subcontracting in the Japanese Automotive Industry* Ph.D. Dissertation, Yale University.

Stinchcombe, Arthur L. and Carol A. Heimer (1985) *Organisation Theory and Project Management: Administering Uncertainty in Norwegian Offshore Oil* Oslo: Norwegian University Press.

Subcontracting Research Association (Shitauke kigyo kenkyukai) (1986) *Kokusaika no naka no Shitauke Kigyo* (Sub-contracting Firms in Internationalization) Tokyo: Tsusho sangyo chosa kai.

Taira, Koji (1970) *Economic Development and the Labour Market in Japan* New York: Columbia University Press.

Telser, Lester G. (1987) *A Theory of Efficient Cooperation and Competition* Cambridge: Cambridge University Press.

Trevor, Malcolm (1988) *Toshiba's New British Company* London: Policy Studies Institute.

Trevor, Malcolm and Ian Christie (1988) *Manufacturers and Suppliers in Britain and Japan* London: Policy Studies Institute.

Tse, K. K. (1985) *Marks & Spencer: Anatomy of Britain's Most Efficiently Managed Company* Oxford: Pergamon Press.

Bibliography

Upham, Frank K. (1987) *Law and Social Change in Postwar Japan* Cambridge, Mass.: Harvard University Press.

Vogel, Ezra F. (1987) 'Japan: adaptive communitarianism' in Lodge and Vogel (eds.).

von Hippel, Eric (1987) 'Cooperation between rivals: informal know-how trading' *Research Policy* 16 pp. 291–302.

Wachter, M. L. and O. E. Williamson (1978) 'Obligational markets and the mechanics of inflation' *The Bell Journal of Economics* 9(2) pp. 549–71.

Watanabe, Toshimitsu (1987) 'Sengo saikenki no chusho kigyo seisaku' (SME policy in the postwar reconstruction period) *Chusho Kigyo Kiho* (Quarterly Journal of Small Business) No. 4 pp. 1–10.

Watanabe, Yukio (1983–4) 'Shitauke kigyo no kyoso to sonritsu keitai' (Competition and structure of sub-contracting enterprises) *Mita Gakkai Zasshi* 76(2), 76(5), 77(3).

Wellman, Barry (1983) 'Network analysis: some basic principles' in Randall Collins (ed.) *Sociological Theory 1983* San Francisco: Jossey-Bass.

Whittaker, D. H. (1990) *Managing Innovation: A Study of British and Japanese Factories* Cambridge: Cambridge University Press.

Wiener, M. (1981) *English Culture and the Decline of the Industrial Spirit* Cambridge: Cambridge University Press.

Wilkinson, Frank (ed.) (1981) *The Dynamics of Labour Market Segmentation* New York: Academic Press.

Williams, K., J. Williams, and D. Thomas (1983) *Why Are the British Bad at Manufacturing?* London: Routledge & Kegan Paul.

Williamson, Oliver E. (1975) *Markets and Hierarchies: Analysis and Antitrust Implications* New York: The Free Press.

(1979) 'Transaction-cost economics: the governance of contractual relations' *Journal of Law and Economics* 22(2) pp. 3–61.

(1985) *The Economic Institutions of Capitalism* New York: The Free Press.

(1986) *Economic Organisation: Firms, Markets and Policy Control* Brighton: Wheatsheaf Books.

Williamson, O. E. and W. G. Ouchi (1983) 'Markets and hierarchies programme of research: origins, implications, prospects' in Francis et al. (eds.).

Wintrobe, Ronald and Albert Breton (1986) 'Organisational structure and productivity' *American Economic Review* 76 pp. 530–38.

Womack, James P. et al. (1990) *The Machine that Changed the World* New York: Rowson Associates.

Yamamoto, Kiyoshi (1987) 'Chusho kigyo mondai ni kansuru ichikousatsu – shitauke tanka kettei hoshiki o chuchin to shite (Some thoughts on the SME problem: the mode of sub-contract price determination) *Shakai Kagaku Kenkyu* 39(2) pp. 121–80.

Yamamura, K. and Y. Yasuba (eds.) (1987) *The Political Economy of Japan* Volume I Stanford: Stanford University Press.

Yoshino, Michael Y. and Thomas B. Lifson (1986) *The Invisible Link: Japan's Sogo Shosha and the Organisation of Trade* Cambridge, Mass.: The MIT Press.

Index

Index

Index

in ACR-OCR, 222–4
see organisational efficiency
transactional dependence
  at GB Electronics, 84–5
  at JJ Electric, 70–1
  at TCP, 96–7
  in ACR–OCR, 11
  of suppliers, 107–9
trust, 1–2
  and demand growth, 155
  and sanctions, 227
  and trade credit, 174–5
  as social norm, 41
  conditions for creating, 43–7, 244–5
  definition of, 37–9
  economics, of, 40–2
  evidence on, 122–5, 131–2

unions, 204, 211
Upham, J., 161

VA (value analysis), 231–2
VE (value engineering), *see* VA
vertical disintegration
  in electronics industry, 188
  see buyer–supplier relations
von Hippel, E., 44

Williamson, O. E., 15, 24, 146, 147, 155
Womack, J., 23, 231
work hours, 202

X-efficiency, 22, 31–3
  see also organisational efficiency

Yoshino, M. Y., 23, 27

zaibatsu, 180
Zeitlin, J., 216